Consuming Fictions

Consuming Fictions

The Booker Prize and Fiction in Britain Today

RICHARD TODD

BLOOMSBURY

First published in Great Britain 1996

Copyright © 1996 by Richard Todd

The moral right of the author
has been asserted

Bloomsbury Publishing Plc,
2 Soho Square, London W1V 6HB

A CIP catalogue record for this book
is available from the British Library

ISBN 0 7475 2822 5

Typeset by Hewer Text Composition Services, Edinburgh
Printed in England by Clays Ltd, St Ives plc

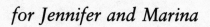

for Jennifer and Marina

CONTENTS

Acknowledgements

Parts of this book have previously appeared elsewhere. I am grateful to the following for permission to draw on material that has since been rethought, updated and substantially recast: Matei Calinescu and Douwe Fokkema, eds., *Exploring Postmodernism* (Amsterdam & Philadelphia: Benjamins, 1987); Theo D'haen and Hans Bertens, eds., *Postmodern Fiction in Europe and the Americas I* (Amsterdam: Rodopi & Antwerp: Restant, 1988); Theo D'haen, Rainer Grübel and Helmut Lethen, eds., *Convention and Innovation in European and American Literature* (Amsterdam & Philadelphia: Benjamins, 1989); and Theo D'haen and Hans Bertens, eds., *Liminal Postmodernisms: The Postmodern, the (Post-)Colonial, and the (Post-)Feminist* (Amsterdam & Atlanta, GA: Rodopi, 1994), for sections of Chapters 1, 5, and 6; Lois Parkinson Zamora and Wendy B. Faris, eds., *Magical Realism: Theory, History, Community* (Durham, NC: Duke UP, 1995) for a version of Chapter 7; Hans Bertens, Theo D'haen, *et al.*, eds., *Post-war Literatures in English: A Lexicon of Contemporary Authors* (Houten, NL: Bohn Stafleu Van Loghum & Groningen: Martinus Nijhoff, 1988ff.) for some of the material in Chapter 8; Theo D'haen and C. C. Barfoot, eds., *Colonial, Post-Colonial, 'New' and Ethnic Literatures in English* (Amsterdam & Atlanta, GA: Rodopi, 1992) for a version of Chapter 9.

For supplying and allowing me to quote information that is not (or not reliably) available in printed sources, I thank Steve Bohme of Book Marketing Ltd, Peter Harland of Bookwatch Ltd, Philip Flamank of the Publishers Association, John Mitchinson, former

Marketing Director of Waterstone's Booksellers, and Robert
Topping of the Deansgate, Manchester branch of Waterstone's.
Karen Tomlinson, Merchandise Controller of Dillons, kindly
answered queries by letter. Gail Lynch and Koukla MacLehose
provided much useful information on publicity and marketing,
and on literary prizes elsewhere in Europe, respectively. I also
thank Michael Sissons of The Peters, Fraser & Dunlop Group
Ltd and Nicki Kennedy of the Intercontinental Literary Agency
associated with that Group. The British Council in Amsterdam
has shown kindness over a long period, and I am also grateful to
Kate Bostock, Literature Director at the British Council's London
office. Book Trust allowed me access to their Wandsworth
archives; for this, specific thanks to Christine Shaw and Sandra
Vince. The Society of Authors answered various queries, and
Martyn Goff discussed the Booker Prize with me.

Grateful acknowledgement is made to the following sources:
Random House UK Ltd, Jonathan Cape and Chatto & Windus
and the authors listed below for quotations from the work of
Fred D'Aguiar, Martin Amis, Paul Bailey, Julian Barnes, A. S.
Byatt, Angela Carter, Alasdair Gray, Alan Hollinghurst, Timothy
Mo, Mordecai Richler, Iain Sinclair and Marina Warner; Hamish
Hamilton and the authors listed below for quotations from the
work of Peter Ackroyd and Barry Unsworth; Macmillan and
Little, Brown and the author listed below for quotations from
the work of Iain Banks; Viking and the authors listed below for
quotations from the work of Pat Barker and Salman Rushdie;
Canongate and the author listed below for quotations from the
work of Alasdair Gray; Secker & Warburg and the authors
listed below for quotations from the work of J. M. Coetzee,
A. L. Kennedy and Irvine Welsh; Faber & Faber Ltd and the
author listed below for quotations from the work of Peter Carey;
Sinclair-Stevenson and the author listed below for quotations
from the work of Lawrence Norfolk; William Heinemann and
the author listed below for quotations from the work of Graham
Swift; Bloomsbury Publishing Plc and the authors listed below for
quotations from the work of Alasdair Gray and Caryl Phillips.

I am deeply grateful to the British Academy, whose award of a Small Personal Research Grant in 1994 significantly facilitated the final stages of research. I was able to make optimal use of that Grant thanks to an Honorary Research Fellowship conferred on me by my much-loved *alma mater* University College London for the 1994–95 year, and I wish to express particular thanks to John Sutherland for his support and generosity. Both the Board of Regents and Faculty of Arts at the Vrije Universiteit Amsterdam generously granted me, and co-subsidized, the study leave that enabled me to spend the 1994–95 year in Britain.

Many colleagues and friends in Amsterdam have been supportive: I'd like to thank especially Theo Bögels, Daniel Carroll, Charles Forceville, Christien Franken, Elrud Ibsch and Rod Lyall, and to remember the late August Fry. Further thanks are due to the following, from Britain, The Netherlands, Belgium and the USA, and to many more: Margaret Bartley, Elleke Boehmer, Graa Boomsma, Steve Boswell, Malcolm Bradbury, Jonathan Burnham, A. S. Byatt, Elizabeth Dipple, Douwe Fokkema, the late Jim Gindin, David Godwin, Peter van Gorsel, Luc Herman, Jeremy Maule, John Peereboom, Janice Price, Nicole Slagter, Miriam van Staden, Peter Straus, Jenny Uglow and Lies Wesseling. I am entirely responsible for whatever shortcomings remain. I'd like to thank Simone Lemstra and Jack Horton for countless acts of lavishly generous hospitality.

I am most grateful to Liz Calder, who expressed her interest in this book from the moment our paths crossed, and subsequently commissioned it; to Maggie Traugott and Carmen Callil for commenting on earlier versions; to Bill Swainson and Mary Tomlinson for helping me to see what was trying to emerge from the typescript they copy-edited. The sharp eye of Katherine Manville was indispensable at proof-reading stage. Vicki Robinson kindly prepared the index.

I've drawn strength from the ways in which both dedicatees have helped me keep things in perspective. But it is to their mother and my partner, Winnie Kooy, that I owe the deepest debt of gratitude, one that would take a very long lifetime indeed to repay.

Richard Todd, January 1996

Introduction

Why, in the last quarter of a century that has seen an exponential growth in the means and speed of communication, do people continue to buy, read and enjoy new literary novels? What forces guide their choice of such reading matter? How are such novels brought to public attention? What is distinctive about the fiction of the last fifteen years? This book is an attempt to throw light on these questions.

My assumption is that the unforeseeable changes that have taken place since the mid to late 1970s in Britain in the cultural atmosphere within which such fiction is now written, as well as in its publication for and consumption by the general reader, have led to a need for a guide to those changes. Such a guide should both offer direction through the dense thicket of the fiction itself, and illuminate the various preoccupations of that fiction.

The book is divided into three parts. The first begins with an attempt to account for the phenomenal international success of A. S. Byatt's *Possession: A Romance* (1990), which won Britain's 1990 Booker Prize. Although Byatt herself is English, and *Possession* is discussed as a quintessentially English achievement, the Booker Prize is open to virtually all fiction in English except that written by US citizens. *Possession* has seen success and recognition not only in Britain's traditional export markets such as Australia, New Zealand, Canada and South Africa, but to a remarkable extent in Europe and even the United States (where interest in British, let alone English, fiction is intermittent and unpredictable). While casting about for a suitably representative exemplar I thought of several other English titles that have achieved a high international profile, and would lend themselves to discussion along these lines. Strong contenders included Martin Amis's *London Fields*, Kazuo Ishiguro's *The Remains of the Day*, Julian Barnes's best-selling *A History of the World in 10½ Chapters* (all of which appeared in Britain in 1989) or Jeanette Winterson's *Written on the Body* (1992). All four were warmly received in the United States, bringing their authors to public attention and in certain cases academic notice there for the first time.

In the end I decided on *Possession* because I felt that it appealed to the largest number of reading constituencies. Subsequent chapters in Part I present more systematically a wider background against which to try to account for phenomena like the success of *Possession*. Topics covered include the increasing profile given to literary prizes through press and TV coverage in Britain, and concomitant changes, many of them formidably entrepreneurial, in Britain's book trade in so far as these concern the production and consumption of fiction. These changes have been brought about by a number of interrelated developments in the publication and marketing of serious literary fiction and the promotion of such fiction by the book trade. I touch more lightly on aspects such as the attention paid to new writing, most recently by the British Council and, since the early 1980s, by the magazine *Granta*.

The second part of the book, while discussing a selection of themes that have preoccupied novelists in the past two decades, also explores literary fiction's existence as a consumer product. Its underlying assumption is that those whose task it is to promote books to the reading consumer are making unprecedented efforts to exploit particular niches, angles or selling points. All the fiction discussed in the second section answers in a variety of ways to some such heading as 'margin and privilege'. By this I mean that the novels I discuss show an awareness of their place in an atmosphere of constantly changing literary trends. To give a wider context to that discussion, I have supplied a third section.

Here individual case studies are presented as *performances*: they may be seen as representing attempts to define (or redefine) their existence as consumer products.

I have introduced the contentious terms 'serious literary fiction' and 'the general reader', so I had better explain what I mean by them. By 'serious literary fiction' I mean self-consciously literary novels intended to appeal to 'the general reader': that is, a reasonably sophisticated, largely but not exclusively professional readership with an interest in, but not unlimited time for, the leisured consumption of full-length fiction.

Most readers still wish, and will continue to wish, to hold a book physically in their hands – or indeed to curl up with one, often on holiday – however attractive they may find scrolling through the increasingly rapid and sophisticated retrieval facilities of interactive multimedia packages in offices and libraries. These readers are increasingly affected by the various interrelated ways in which serious literary fiction is promoted and discussed when making their own choices from bookstore or library.

One might say that a process of 'canon-formation', guided but not dictated by consumer forces, in ways that have not been seen before, has come into being over the past fifteen years or so. I use 'canon' here specifically as a piece of shorthand for what has been termed 'the glacially changing core' of consensus about certain novels that is surrounded by 'the rapidly changing periphery' of debate about others.[1] My book has grown out of a period of reading and writing equivalent to the period it describes, one in which Western consumerism, the place of goods (including fiction as a purchasable, consumable commodity), has begun to be formulated as a subject worth attention, perhaps for the first time.[2]

The results of a survey carried out by Book Marketing Ltd

[1] See Wendell V. Harris, 'Canonicity', *Publications of the Modern Language Association of America* 106/1 (January 1991), p. 113.
[2] In their Introduction to *Consumption and the World of Goods* (London & New York: Routledge, 1993), pp. 1–15, John Brewer and Roy Porter provide a fascinating overview of the historiography of Western consumerism.

between 1989 and 1993 were intended to sharpen the profile of the reader of serious literary fiction in Britain.[3] In using 'Britain' in this book, I refer to England, Scotland and Wales unless otherwise stated. This is the geographical area covered by Book Marketing Ltd's data. But there seems no reason not to believe that the results shed as much light as we are likely to get at the moment on the profile of the readers and buyers of serious literary fiction produced since about 1980 in Britain as a whole.

The survey shows that book purchases remained steady or even increased slightly over the period despite a growth in sales of videos and computer games. (But it can always be argued that even though sales have increased, books are being bought by fewer people, as some believe.) In 1989 56 per cent of all respondents taking part in the survey had read a book (of whatever kind) for pleasure or interest during the previous four weeks; by 1993 that percentage had increased to 66 per cent. In each year between 10 per cent and 15 per cent fewer readers had used a book for purposes of reference or information during the previous four weeks. However, between 1989 and 1993 the percentages buying or reading twentieth-century fiction (or both) during the year prior to that in which the survey was conducted showed no discernible trend, fluctuating to within 2 to 3 points of 15 per cent. During the same period the proportion buying twentieth-century fiction not as a gift but for self-consumption hovered within 1 point of 5 per cent.[4] These findings confirm a sense that the development of hi-tech forms of leisure activity during the period 1989 to 1993 has so far had little or no effect on the buying and reading habits of the general reader. In each of

[3]For the data in the following paragraphs I am obliged to Steve Bohme of Book Marketing Ltd.
[4]John Mitchinson, former Marketing Director of Waterstone's Booksellers, estimated (conversation with the author, 18 January 1995) that 15–20 per cent of Waterstone's overall market nationwide is in literary fiction, with *contemporary* (rather than twentieth-century) literary fiction accounting for perhaps 5–6 per cent of Waterstone's overall market in hardback, and 8–10 per cent in paperback.

the years 1989 through 1993 the sample size was plus or minus 1,800 people; 1,792 were questioned in 1993.

Of whom does the constituency of buyers and readers of twentieth-century fiction in Britain itself consist? The figures for 1993 suggest that a majority of readers and an even larger majority of buyers live in the South of England.[5] Of the 1993 sample of 1,792, the number emerging nationwide as 'readers' was 261 and the number of 'buyers' was 82. On a national basis three times as many people read as bought twentieth-century fiction, but in regional terms there are strong variations: in the South the figures were 56 per cent and 69 per cent respectively, in the Midlands and Wales they were 17 per cent and 11 per cent respectively, and in the North, including Scotland, they were 27 per cent and 20 per cent respectively. The total sample breakdown reveals that of the 1,792 people surveyed, 39 per cent came from the South, 26 per cent from the Midlands and Wales and 36 per cent from the North including Scotland. Slightly more women (52 per cent) than men (48 per cent) were questioned: it is not surprising to learn that almost twice as many women as men buy novels nationwide, and that women also make up the majority of readers of twentieth-century fiction (61 per cent to 39 per cent of men).[6] When sample sizes are levelled out, the number of readers averages around 20 per cent to 25 per cent in all the age-groups above 35 (with a slightly decreased exception in the 55–64 age group); in 1993 all groups above 35 read more than did those in the 15–24 and 25–34 age-groups, for which the figures level out at about 17 per cent. Although there are

[5] Larger-scale data compiled over the longer term, such as those owned by Bookwatch Ltd, suggest that London and the South-East region account for a third of book sales in the United Kingdom, including Northern Ireland, but Bookwatch Ltd does not research attitudinal aspects of its database, which is why the data supplied by Book Marketing Ltd are preferred here.

[6] John Mitchinson believes that three times as many women as men are readers of contemporary literary fiction, and that if anything, the proportion is increasing. Buyers of contemporary fiction in Britain are divided along gender-specific lines as perhaps never before, a point worth considering if one attempts to break down sales of Angela Carter and Jeanette Winterson, as opposed to sales of Martin Amis and Iain Banks.

proportionately slightly fewer buyers in the 25–34 age group than in the 15–24 and 35–54 age groups, it is in the 55–64 and 65+ age-groups that the proportion of buyers decreases quite markedly. The levelled-out range is between 25–30 per cent in the 35–54 age groups compared with 10 per cent among the over-65s. The higher proportion of buyers in the 15–24 age group presumably includes the nation's student population.

Book Marketing Ltd's 1993 sample consisted of 66 per cent who had left school at 16 or younger and a further 14 per cent who had left at 17 or 18. Of the remaining 20 per cent, 12 per cent had experienced some form of higher education and another 8 per cent were still studying. These findings would seem to tally with a national socio-economic breakdown of 30 per cent DEs (semi-skilled and unskilled manual workers, those dependent on income support), 27 per cent C2s (skilled manual workers and dependants), 25 per cent C1s ('white-collar', non-manual, workers and dependants) and 18 per cent ABs (the professional and business sector, with or without private means). If one levels out these four classified socio-economic groups one finds, not surprisingly, that the AB group accounts for more than 55 per cent of twentieth-century fiction's readers and nearly 67 per cent of its buyers. The C1 group accounts for 26 per cent of readers and 29 per cent of buyers, and (perhaps most surprisingly) the C2 group for 13 per cent of readers and just under 14 per cent of buyers respectively. In this sense only the DE group is an exception in that just under 17 per cent read and only just under 7 per cent buy twentieth-century fiction: in other words, to every section of Britain's population, save the semi- or unskilled (DE) manual worker and/or her or his dependants, the twentieth-century novel is *at least* as much a purchasable commodity as it is a means of literary communication. The 'reader-buyer' discrepancy – and thus the degree of commodification of twentieth-century fiction in Britain – increases directly the higher up the socio-economic scale one goes. The pattern of buying books as gifts suggests that the book trade has withstood the recent recession remarkably well.

Two-thirds of the 1,792 people sampled in 1993 (66 per cent to 34 per cent) were without children. That proportion was exactly reflected in the number of twentieth-century fiction readers, and slightly exceeded (70 per cent to 30 per cent) among the buyers of that fiction. Of the readers sampled, 7 per cent had bought no twentieth-century fiction during the previous twelve months, 15 per cent had bought between 1 and 5 novels, 22 per cent between 6 and 15, and a remarkable 56 per cent (still, it will be borne in mind, of those considering themselves readers rather than buyers) had bought more than 16 novels. In contrast, 6 per cent of the twentieth-century fiction buyers described themselves as 'light' buyers (1 to 5 novels per year), 13 per cent as 'medium' buyers (6 to 15) and 81 per cent as 'heavy' (over 16 novels per year).[7]

Serious literary fiction tends to exclude best-selling genre-fiction categories such as crime or science fiction but may make use of some of the conventions of these genres. It also includes novels that have become part of the global academic discussion of the phenomenon of literary 'postmodernism'. I've not attempted to add to the enormous body of secondary work on that very disparate and self-regarding phenomenon, one that has recently too frequently been propagated beyond a level of real usefulness by academia itself. I have, however, naturally taken account throughout of constructs of literary postmodernism that I regard as genuinely serviceable. But most significant of all, for my purposes, is the fact of Booker-eligibility, and there can be no doubt that from about 1980 onwards 'fiction in Britain' has come increasingly to include the work of novelists who are not solely British, but are citizens of the

[7]'Light', 'medium' and 'heavy' are of course relative terms here. Robert Topping, manager of the Deansgate, Manchester branch of Waterstone's, by general consent the most successful branch on the British mainland, suggests to me that he and his staff regard a 'heavy' book-buyer as someone who makes upwards of 40 purchases annually. A higher cut-off point for the 'heavy' book-buyer, if applied to Book Marketing Ltd's survey, would have been more revealing than the level actually chosen.

Commonwealth, as well as of countries such as the Republic of Ireland and present-day Pakistan and Bangladesh (which are not members of the Commonwealth) and South Africa (which in its post-apartheid condition has rejoined the Commonwealth it left in 1948).[8] Booker-eligibility and its implications are assessed more fully in the pages that follow. Suffice it to say here that the catchment area represented comprises one quarter of the world's population. In other words, 'the novel in Britain' (as distinct from 'the English novel') now includes fiction from Australia, New Zealand, Canada, South Africa, Nigeria, the Caribbean, and many other areas of the English-speaking world which is published in Britain. Contemporary Scottish and Irish literature, whether or not it asserts its non-Englishness, also falls into this category.

Somewhere between 4,500 and 7,000 new Booker-eligible fiction titles appeared annually in Britain during the 1980s alone,[9] the total rising throughout the decade from the lower figure to the higher. These figures can be given context by looking back over the present century. In 1939 the number of serious literary fiction titles appearing annually was roughly what it was in 1980, that is, approximately 5,000. But the 1980 figure resulted from a steady climb from the depths of the post-war paper shortage in the late 1940s, when the number of serious literary fiction titles appearing annually had dropped to a quarter of the 1939 total. By the mid 1960s that figure had doubled to half what it would become in 1980. In other words, if the 1980s ushered in a period of rich choice for the consumer of fiction, such choice was by no means unprecedented. On the contrary, it represented recovery to a position of parity with the situation that had been disrupted by the 1939–45 war.

[8]I also include Nigeria, despite this country's two-year suspension from the Commonwealth following the hanging of a group of human rights activists, including the playwright Ken Saro-Wiwa, in November 1995.
[9]In certain years in the 1980s, these figures have not differed substantially from those in the US, a country with between four and five times the total population of the UK.

A quick calculation will reveal that a study of British literary fiction published in the last twenty years is faced with a potential corpus of more than 100,000 titles. Of course, only a minority of these would be considered as serious literary fiction as construed above, but even if one were to apply the stricter criteria whereby upwards of 100 titles annually are submitted by publishers according to the varying rules for consideration by the Booker judges, one would still need to take account of something approaching 2,500 titles. I have set about constructing my own much smaller corpus in the belief that it is better to say more about fewer than the other way round. All the novels discussed (and many of those mentioned) in the pages that follow are novels by which I have myself been in various ways consumed – intrigued, excited and even enthralled.

My intention in this book is to place serious literary fiction in Britain over the past two decades in its cultural context. Several extremely original and level-headed studies of twentieth-century fiction within various kinds of broader context have appeared since the late 1960s – indeed, I particularly wish to acknowledge Malcolm Bradbury, Bernard Bergonzi and John Sutherland, to name but three, whose work has helped me define the space for my own. Even the controversial polemics of D. J. Taylor (I am thinking of his substantial study *After the War* [1993] rather than *A Vain Conceit* [1989]) argue a socio-political background, albeit one that not all will recognize.

My own view of the cultural context within which serious literary fiction in Britain has prospered during the 1980s and 1990s is likewise one that not all my readers may share. Despite a certain reluctance – often on the part of academics themselves – to accept the real extent to which contemporary literary canon-formation is subject to powerful, rapidly changing market forces affecting and influencing the consumer, I believe that the academic reader of contemporary serious literary fiction must reflect on the impact of such forces on the general reader. These include the development of the Booker Prize *and its shortlist*; how other literary prizes have reacted to the Booker; how both agents and publishers have responded to the commercial possibilities of the serious literary blockbuster that can achieve both 'fastseller' as well as 'bestseller' status (this includes the controversial issue of authors' advances); how the serious literary fiction title and/or author can enter the canon through a (sometimes fortuitous) combination of skilful commercial promotion, publicity and review coverage in the various media (including radio and TV), and even be taken up into academic discussion; how booksellers co-operate with novelists to promote contemporary fiction; how adaptation for film and/or TV can affect a given title. What follows is my attempt to explain how this conviction has been arrived at in the assumption that consumerism now actively strives, as never before, to be part of Britain's cultural life. It has been suggested (not wholly frivolously) that the late twentieth-century prize and media consumer culture does not differ substantially from aristocratic patronage in the age of Shakespeare. All I can say is that, if indeed prizes have replaced patronage, it seems absurd to make the claims I do for the fiction for which such prizes are offered without acknowledging the need for some fuller understanding of the culture that has spawned the growth of those prizes, enhanced their power, and – I genuinely believe – enriched our literature.

The conviction of a polymath such as George Steiner that it is only through assaults on freedom of expression within a given culture that there can be genuine and radical and first-rate artistic achievement cannot naïvely be conscripted in discussion of the topic in hand. Although Steiner is dismissive of the vast majority of fiction produced in Britain today (in spite of, or perhaps because of, the fact that he served as a Booker judge in 1972), the Thatcher years and after did usher in a number of disturbing retrenchments in civil liberties in Britain, ranging from anti-Union legislation through a tightening of the qualifications for immigration to the passing of the 1994 Criminal Justice Law. It is also, I think, significant that the most spectacular literary success of the Thatcher decade in Britain, Salman Rushdie, ended that decade as a prisoner of conscience guarded by the British security services. Rushdie's work will be discussed in the last chapter of this book, but he is now widely perceived as perhaps Britain's only global writer, a figure to stand beside Havel or Kundera, Vargos Llosa or García Márquez. The Rushdie case is part of a global tension that quickly boiled over into a conflict between a relatively liberal secular literary culture and a fundamentalist theocracy.

It is in the nature of things that there should have been little sustained commentary on the work of the younger writers discussed in this book: I have made modest use of reviews while bearing in mind the constraints of time, space and divination or foresight with which the reviewer, writing to deadline, is faced. It is in any case the rarer, longer, more thoughtful review rather than the 'blurb-bite' the literary equivalent of a 'sound-bite' – that is of most use. It is in keeping with 'the American future' of fiction in Britain that John Sutherland first brought to notice nearly twenty years ago that paperback reprints frequently carry several pages of endorsements. Iain Banks's *The Wasp Factory* (1984) and Alasdair Gray's *Poor Things* (1992) actually incorporate 'blurb-bites' into the fictional text. I have also drawn on published interviews and profiles, while attempting to take sufficient account of the disparity between teller and tale.

A word, in conclusion, on sales and my use of sales figures. During the period in which I have been working on this book, it has become evident that among the many changes that have occurred in the past decade, not the least is the frankness with which sales figures are divulged in Britain by agents and publishers on behalf of authors and promulgated in the British press. Nevertheless, this aspect of my book has been the most difficult to research, and for a number of reasons. In the late 1970s it would have been virtually impossible to gain the permission of a British publisher or agent to publish details of hardback sales; even now, while those possessing such information and prepared to discuss hardback sales frankly may no longer be in a minority, figures are still customarily given in confidence. Indeed, the figures made available by publishers to organizations such as Bookwatch Ltd and the Publishers Association are actually sold as copyright, and to quote them without permission would leave one liable to legal action.

I make this point with some hesitation because two remarkably candid *Bookseller* articles about the impact on week-by-week hardback sales of a Booker Prize win – the first by Liz Calder (then at Jonathan Cape) on Salman Rushdie's *Midnight's Children* (1981) in 1982, and the second by Ion Trewin (then at Hodder & Stoughton) on Thomas Keneally's *Schindler's Ark* (1982) in 1983 – do give a fascinating glimpse of the turning point in Booker's influence on sales. In order to assess the effect of Booker shortlisting and success on sales in the last quarter of each year over the past decade or so, I have been given permission to use the copyright data tracked by Bookwatch Ltd during this period, although I am asked to make clear that these data are not always complete. Although electronic information retrieval such as that based on EPOS (electronic point of sale) is growing increasingly sophisticated – it has now reached a level of accuracy higher than in many other areas of the retail trade as a whole – its very existence is still subject to human failings. It is generally accepted that the Booker Prize exercises a more substantial effect on sales patterns than any other kind of award, even though those given for children's books do without any shadow of doubt influence adult book-buying, as does the NCR Book Award for Non-Fiction: each of these awards, however, falls outside the scope of this book. The commercial impact of the Booker Prize and its effect on the formation of the literary canon is more complex; indeed, it is this very complexity as much as any other single factor that has contributed to the Booker's high profile.

Where no other source is available in the public domain, I have honoured the confidence in which I have been given hardback sales figures, a confidence based on the understanding that sales, particularly hardback sales, are a matter of concern to no one other than author, agent and publisher. This protocol differs markedly from the situation in the United States, which has long operated with far greater candour and a completely different understanding of professionalism. The upshot has been that British reticence has been increasingly harder to maintain, as accurate figures in the public domain in the United States allow extrapolation back into Britain. Extrapolation, however, is not necessarily the same as reliability, and a number of influential people in the British book trade would maintain that accurate and objective assessment of hardback sales figures that does not break confidences is paradoxically more than ever impossible in the present climate in Britain.

What has become steadily impossible as the 1980s have progressed is concealment of the extent of British paperback sales. In 1979 Alex Hamilton initiated what has become a book-trade institution in his annual survey of Britain's top hundred paperback fastsellers, compiled each January for the preceding year. It is now issued not just in the *Guardian*, where it originated, but reprinted in the *Bookseller* and the *Writers' & Artists' Yearbook*. Only towards the end of the 1980s, however, was Hamilton able to feel assured that the figures he was passing on were reliable to within 5 per cent either way. Hamilton's surveys cover *fastsellers*, not necessarily bestsellers; that is, a title may make it to his annual list of 100 whether issued in paperback in the January or the September of the year in question. Only in exceptional cases does Hamilton include a title published in the previous year, usually where not to do so might give a seriously distorted impression of a given year's yield. The figures relate to total paperback sales, home and export, for that calendar year for titles published and/or distributed in Britain (regardless of authorial citizenship). They reveal that, in virtually every year since 1979, with the exception of the recession that hit the book trade at the beginning of the 1990s (that is, characteristically late), over 100 titles per year managed at least 100,000 sales. At the top end of the scale, a paperback fastseller could notch up over 1,000,000 copies in one calendar year in Britain; often the first 10 titles on the list would have sold more copies than all the others put together.

A significant change that has taken place since the 1970s, and should be mentioned here, is the increased proportion of 'B format' paperbacks. Formerly associated, in the early 1970s, with specialist publishers such as Paladin, followed by Picador later in that decade, the B format (196 × 129mm/7$\frac{3}{4}$″ × 5$\frac{1}{8}$″) is now preferred over the A format (180 × 110mm/7 × 4$\frac{3}{8}$″) still frequently used by, say, Penguin Books, for serious literary fiction in paperback. The B format has contrived to enhance the consumer profile of serious literary fiction through means of presentation alone. The larger C format (233 × 153mm/9$\frac{1}{4}$″ × 6″) is now appearing (often for paperback originals) and may well reinforce this process in the next few years as novels published in Britain come increasingly to resemble some of their counterparts elsewhere in Western Europe.

At the present time, Bookwatch Ltd compiles a weekly bestseller list on the basis of EPOS data recorded by bookshops contributing to the *Sunday Times* Bestsellers List scheme; this, printed in Bookwatch Ltd's weekly copyright publication *Books in the Media*, is in turn distributed to media such as the *Bookseller* and the Sunday broadsheets. Bookwatch Ltd's list falls into five categories: hardback fiction, hardback non-fiction, paperback fiction, paperback non-fiction (25 titles in each group) and books for children in the 6–11 age-group (20 titles). About 700 retail outlets in the UK are consulted but not all are consistently reflected in the weekly list, often (as suggested above) for reasons to do with human interaction with database technology. Paperback fiction accounts for 50 per cent by volume and value of the paperback market; an appreciably lower percentage of the hardback market is represented by hardback fiction. Hardback non-fiction is the biggest single item in the entire book market at 25 per cent by volume and 50 per cent to 60 per cent by value. Weekly sales in all categories will be higher in the Christmas run-up than at any other time in the year.[10] No figures are given but they can be guessed at: if one assumes, not unreasonably, that annual hardback sales of the latest Jeffrey Archer or Catherine Cookson title are likely to be around 50,000 to 60,000 (as opposed to annual paperback sales around 1,000,000),[11] and if one further bears in mind the seasonal fluctuation as indicated above, one could soon gain a rough idea of current weekly sales of most if not all of the hardback fiction titles in Bookwatch Ltd's top 25 titles.

Comparison between the number of weeks in which Jung Chang's autobiography *Wild Swans* topped the 1993 and 1994 Bookwatch Ltd lists thus finds confirmation in Hamilton's most recent charts at the time of writing. From these one could learn that in 1993 this title 'made more money than any paperback had ever done in one year in Britain'.[12] All that can be noted as far as bestsellers from the past are concerned are Hamilton's concessions of 'spectacular' posthumous success for writers such as D.H. Lawrence and George Orwell (whose works are often used as 'set texts'), alongside the longer-term assured successes of 'Bibles, classic authors [such as Shakespeare and Chaucer], cookbooks, dictionaries and other reference books', for which figures of 'over 20 million copies' appear founded. Among novelists, 'Agatha Christie, Alistair MacLean, Mickey Spillane, Ed McBain and Catherine Cookson prompt claims between 50

[10]I owe these data to a discussion with Peter Harland of Bookwatch Ltd.
[11]Archer tends to do well in the US whereas Cookson does not, although she is to be found in European bookstores.
[12]Alex Hamilton, 'Top Hundred Chart of 1993 Paperback Fastsellers', reprinted in the *Writers' and Artists' Yearbook 1995* (London: A. & C. Black, 1995), p. 257. *Wild Swans*, which won the 1993 NRC Book Award for Non-Fiction, was actually in second place in terms of sales (behind Michael Crichton's *Jurassic Park*) in 1993, with home and export sales totalling just under 950,000. But the title grossed over £7.5m, nearly half as much again as Crichton's. In 1994, home and export sales of *Wild Swans* were still in excess of 685,000, with the title grossing just under a further £5.5m. According to Alex Hamilton's 1994 fastseller list (*Guardian*, 10 January 1995), this title '[had] been among the top sellers for 80 consecutive weeks'. We may conservatively estimate that the weekly sales of *Wild Swans* continued into the opening months of 1995 at still well over 10,000.

million and 300 million copies', with Barbara Cartland's 100
million sales apparently spread over 400 titles (Hamilton, 'Top
Hundred Chart of 1993 Paperback Fastsellers', *op. cit.*). Not
surprisingly, it is writers such as these, enjoying success spread
over the longer term, with a combination of blockbusting success
or steady though spectacular sales, who are the principal financial
beneficiaries of library use: Public Lending Right (PLR) in British
libraries now stands at 2p per book issued (with a ceiling per
PLR-registered author of £6,000 in any one year),[13] a sum
unlikely to affect significantly all but the bestselling writers[14].

The hardback figures that have gradually passed into the public
domain suggest that since the early to mid 1980s, sales in Britain
and overseas of more than 10,000 for a serious literary novel
would be regarded as evidence of sound commercial success,
and anything above 20,000 would be outstanding although by
no means unique. Perhaps only 20 or 30 writers of serious literary
fiction are fortunate enough to reach these heights regularly at the
present time; by the end of the 1980s, fewer still had extended
their steady success into the United States. Those who principally
come to mind are Anthony Burgess, Margaret Drabble, John
Fowles, William Golding and Graham Greene, all of whom
were then still alive; since then Burgess, Golding and Greene
have died.[15] In recent years, the yield of small print-runs of
serious literary fiction in Britain has reached a level of efficiency
such that hardback sales as low as 2,000 or 3,000 can – in

[13]Source: *Writers' and Artists' Yearbook 1996* (London: A. & C. Black, 1996),
p. 529. The year in question runs from July to June, and PLR payments are
made the following February.
[14]*Bookseller*, 7 January 1994, p. 6. The fullest extant treatment of the
entire popular fiction phenomenon remains John Sutherland's authoritative
Bestsellers (London: Routledge & Kegan Paul, 1981). It could be argued –
although I would be reluctant to do so in the space available – that the
socio-economic and age-groups most likely to *read* Cookson and Cartland
in Britain are least likely to be *buyers* of fiction, and thus more likely to
boost such writers' PLR dividends still further.
[15]See, for example, Michiko Kakutani, 'British Writers Embrace the Offbeat',
NYT Magazine, 5 July 1990, pp. C11, C15.

commercial terms – responsibly justify paperback publication:[16] in other words, finding a given title in paperback is no longer by any means a guarantee (as it once was) that exceptionally high hardback sales have been the cause of that paperback issue. The broader picture in Britain and Europe suggests in a conservative estimate that at any one time between 150 and 200 hardback titles from perhaps 65 to 70 novelists (relatively few of whom publish fiction annually, most appearing with a new title every few years) are commercially supporting the fiction lists of London's major literary publishers. Increasingly, those fiction lists in their totality have come to include popular titles. This fact alone justifies the view of today's fiction-publishing industry in Britain as subsidized by the lottery of bestsellerdom. A single blockbusting title of the kind known as a 'loss leader', an article offered *below* cost in the hope that customers attracted by it will buy other (profitable) goods, whether such a title is 'literary' or not, can underwrite a great deal of commercial speculation.

Towards the end of 1994 the loss-leader issue broke loose controversially. Martin Amis sidelined his British agent Pat Kavanagh when Jonathan Cape (now an imprint of Random House UK Ltd) declined to pay an advance of at least £480,000 for his new novel *The Information* and a collection of short stories. Early in 1995 Amis's American agent Andrew Wylie also failed to secure a deal with Random House, and HarperCollins took the title for a sum variously reported as only slightly in excess of the amount asked for to as high as £505,000. The controversy centred not so much round the sum itself as on the assumption that on past form – Amis's most successful novel to date, *London Fields*, cannot have netted Amis much more than one half of this amount – Amis would be most unlikely to earn back an advance of this

---

[16] Although it could equally well be argued that efficiency here is a euphemism for a desperation for the product that has been generated by the demands of vertical publishing, a point touched on in Chapter 3 below.

size.[17] Kavanagh informed Amis that she could no longer act for him.

The eve-of-publication promotion, including an excerpt from *The Information* in the *Observer* and a South Bank Show interview with Melvyn Bragg (both on Sunday, 19 March 1995), led to strong sales initially, though by July 1995 some bookstores were reporting that they were returning as many as half the copies they had originally ordered. At the time of the collapse of the Net Book Agreement (NBA) and in part as a result of Amis's failure to be shortlisted for the 1995 Booker Prize, *The Information* was being offered at a minimal price by Waterstone's, providing customers bought the 1995 Booker shortlist in its entirety. This is a fascinating case, in which *The Information*, promoted as a best-seller by a publisher anxious to establish its literary credentials,

---

[17]The advance a publisher pays to an author is set against the royalties it is anticipated the book will earn. Thus an advance of £50,000 for a novel with a recommended retail price of £14.99, with a typical royalty escalator, and assuming that high discount provisions do not apply (i.e. that home market royalties are paid at full value), might be earned back over a period of 12 to 18 months as follows:

	Price	unit sales	royalty (as a percentage of cover price)	escalator	£	£
Advance						(50,000)
Hardback						
Home	£14.99	2,500	10 per cent	(to 2,500 copies)	3,747	
	£14.99	2,500	12.5 per cent	(to 5,000 copies)	4,684	
	£14.99	2,500	15 per cent	(thereafter)	5,621	
Export	£14.99	2,500	5.5 per cent		2,061	
sub-total		10,000				16,113
Balance due to author/(Unearned advance)						(33,887)
Paperback						
Home	£6.99	25,000	7.5 per cent	(to 25,000 copies)	13,106	
	£6.99	25,000	8.5 per cent	(thereafter)	14,854	
Export	£6.99	10,000	6 per cent	(to 25,000 copies)	4,194	
			7 per cent	(thereafter)		
sub-total		60,000				32,154
Balance due to author/(Unearned advance)						(1,733)

NB These figures take no account of subsidiary rights sales (e.g. foreign editions, radio adaptation, serial, etc.).

actually became a loss leader. A fair estimate suggests that by the end of 1995 it had earned out not much more than 10 per cent of the advance. As we shall see, Amis, vilified as a misogynist on the publication of *London Fields* (1989) and as an anti-Semite on the publication of *Time's Arrow* (1991), seems fated to court hostile publicity, often but not always drawn along gender fault-lines.[18]

In the same year it emerged that Timothy Mo, three times shortlisted for the Booker Prize (with *Sour Sweet* [1982], *An Insular Possession* [1986] and *The Redundancy of Courage* [1991]), had been so dissatisfied with Vintage/Chatto & Windus's offer for his latest manuscript *Brownout on Breadfruit Boulevard* (1995) that he had decided to publish the novel himself under his Paddleless imprint. This novel begins with a now famous scene of coprophilia, and anal sex figures in both title and narrative. The imprint's name was thus widely seen as a joke, albeit in dubious taste.

The Booker is often reputed to *enhance* hardback sales by between 40,000 and 80,000 for the winner and to guarantee extra hardback sales in four or more likely five figures for the other shortlisted titles. This may have been true for a while in the mid 1980s, but as we have seen, hardback sales figures quoted in the British press, in particular in recent years, should be treated with considerable caution: sales figures 'talked up' in the press tend not to be contested by the hardback publishers involved. Being shortlisted for the Booker generally enhances hardback sales by around 5,000 copies.

Until the collapse of the NBA it was not unknown to find shortlisted titles remaindered a couple of years later, but of course that would have been *after* selling many more copies at full price than would otherwise have been the case. According to the *Bookseller*, the most successful Booker winner to date,

[18]See the report in the *Independent*, 12 January 1995; Nicolette Jones, 'The Selling of Martin Amis', *Bookseller*, 20 January 1995, pp. 10–11; Robert McCrum, 'Lunatics and Suits', *Guardian Weekend*, 4 March 1995, pp. 22–27, esp. p. 24, and Mark Lawson, 'Molars, money and martyrdom', *Independent*, 14 March 1995, p. 15.

the relatively low-priced 1993 title, Roddy Doyle's *Paddy Clarke Ha Ha Ha*, had achieved hardback sales of 72,000 when the award was announced, and a further 135,000 copies were sold between then and the end of 1993, a total for 1993 of 207,000.[19] Booker's own press release, dated 5 September 1994, states without attribution that Doyle's hardback sales through the summer of 1994 had reached 320,000; on 6 September 1994 the *Guardian* felt able to revise the hardback figures upwards still further to 360,000, and to claim that since its paperback publication in June 1994 the novel had sold an extra 340,000 in that form. Alex Hamilton's fastseller figures, published in the same newspaper on 10 January 1995, indicate that over the *entire* year 1994 the paperback sales of *Paddy Clarke Ha Ha Ha* were just over 355,000, with the title grossing over £2.1m in paperback. All this suggests a gross revenue for Doyle's title exceeding £6m by the end of 1994, and rising fast. Doyle's publisher, Secker & Warburg, has not to my knowledge contested the extraordinarily high hardback figures; indications are, however, that they may represent overestimates in the region of 25 per cent to as much as 35 per cent or even 40 per cent (whereas the paperback figures may be reliable to within 5 per cent or so, as has been argued already).

At the other end of the spectrum, we have the assertion by many leading booksellers in October 1994 that that year's Booker winner, James Kelman's *How Late It Was, How Late*, had been a catastrophic flop. The term 'flop' is relative: Kelman's title is probably guaranteed an extra 7,500 to 10,000 in hardback sales through having won the Booker; even at this level, however, it will have proved the least commercially successful Booker winner since before 1980.

---

[19] *Bookseller*, 24/31 December 1993, p. 27. The EPOS figures tracked within the UK by Bookwatch Ltd between the beginning of November 1993 and the beginning of January 1994 are considerably lower. Because the *Bookseller* figures almost certainly include overseas sales, along with sales recorded by other means than EPOS, the truth is evidently somewhere in between, as we shall see in more detail in Chapter 3.

The next three chapters elaborate on the points raised here and set the stage for a discussion of a selection of fiction produced and consumed in Britain since about 1980. I begin with an account of the celebrated success of A. S. Byatt's *Possession*, broadening the picture out into a discussion of the development of Britain's prize culture during the past fifteen years and the ways in which both the book trade and the consumer have responded to what this development represents.

I

THE
CULTURAL
BACKGROUND

1

A. S. Byatt's Possession: *An International Literary Success*

On the evening of Tuesday 16 October 1990, at the customarily extravagant Guildhall ceremony marking the award of that year's Booker Prize, a slightly bemused A. S. Byatt was seen live by millions of TV viewers receiving the winner's £20,000 cheque from Sir Michael Caine, Chairman of Booker plc. It was an exciting moment, because the finish had been a close one. Two quite different kinds of writers and novels, John McGahern with *Amongst Women* and Brian Moore with *Lies of Silence*, had also been strongly tipped in the days immediately prior to the award.

Like the other five contenders, both the 54-year-old Byatt and her novel *Possession: A Romance* had been subjected to scrutiny and speculation over the six weeks since the shortlist had been announced in the first week of September. The privacy of the six writers brought to public notice always becomes difficult to guard, but Byatt's case offered an unusually wide range of interest. *Possession*, in one of the many senses of that title, involves for at least one of its characters the 'daemonic' power exercised by her ancestors: 'I don't quite like it [. . .] I feel they have taken me over.'[1] Doubtless Byatt felt the same way about her own life and book; however, as the reading public was to learn, she proved by experience and temperament as well equipped as any of her fellow shortlisted colleagues to handle the intrusions involved. A *Daily Telegraph* feature dated 3 November 1990 reported Byatt

[1]A. S. Byatt, *Possession: A Romance* (London: Chatto & Windus, 1990), p. 505. Page-references in the text are to this edition.

as having selected for a public reading a passage late in *Possession*
that includes the words 'Burn what they [posterity] should not
see' (p. 442). Supporting a debating motion that novelists made
better biographers than biographers, she wrote that there was
something 'ghoulish and daemonic about the way biographers
[. . .] live only through the dead'.

The reading public, if it didn't know already, quickly came to
realize that the manly initials concealed a writer who was in fact a
woman, significantly one who was regarded among professional
initiates as a late twentieth-century English intellectual with a
dense and voraciously allusive style that had elicited comparisons
with George Eliot. Like that of Eliot, A. S. Byatt's male-sounding
name was a *nom de plume*; unlike Eliot's, the *nom de plume* was
that of her former spouse. Byatt had in fact been producing fiction
since the 1960s. Her novels had done respectably in commercial
terms, and had attracted a small but discerning following. Byatt
had long been active in London's media world, reviewing, as
well as broadcasting for the BBC, on a regular basis. In 1983
she had given up a prestigious academic post at University
College London to devote herself, once the immediate demands
of motherhood had begun to recede, full-time to writing. Her
previous novels consisted of *Shadow of a Sun* (1964), *The Game*
(1967), *The Virgin in the Garden* (1978) and *Still Life* (1985).
By the autumn of 1990 she was prepared to discuss a personal
tragedy that had occurred in the summer of 1972, when the
eldest of her four children (her only son, Charles, to whom
The Virgin in the Garden is posthumously dedicated) had been
killed in a road accident just after his eleventh birthday.

In addition to writing novels, Byatt had achieved during the
1960s and 1970s (it would be further revealed) a high reputation
in the academic world for scholarly studies of Wordsworth and
Coleridge (1970), and of Iris Murdoch (Byatt's monograph, the
first full-length work on this writer, had been published in 1965
when less than a third of her subject's *oeuvre* had appeared).
She had also made a name, one powerfully enhanced by several
of the short stories in *Sugar*, for a rare talent – the sensitive,

intelligent but not precious description of the visual arts. There were stories of sibling rivalry – many interviewers were to note that Byatt had specified that she wanted to discuss her own work, not that of her younger sister Margaret Drabble, who had preceded her into print and into public recognition. Analogies with the Brontë sisters were dragged up, examined and for the most part discarded. In the weeks between being shortlisted for and winning the 1990 Booker Prize, Byatt won the *Irish Times*/Aer Lingus Award, then worth IR£25,000. She subsequently made it to the Whitbread Award shortlist in the 'Best Novel' category, provoking speculation (unfulfilled, as it turned out) that the first 'Grand Slam' of an unprecedentedly entrepreneurial decade might occur the following January.[2] (In the event, whatever a Grand Slam may now be, it has not yet taken place.) Byatt is, however, one of the handful of Booker winners for whom nothing has been the same since.

In terms of the prize novel's overall sales, including those in the United States, *Possession* has now been superseded only by the 1993 Booker winner Roddy Doyle's *Paddy Clark Ha Ha Ha* and (whether or not we include the media 'tie-in' phenomenon, that is, the spin-off resulting, usually, from a film adaptation) the 1982 winner Thomas Keneally's *Schindler's Ark*. The belated commercial success of the total Byatt *oeuvre* is striking, although by no means unprecedented. Vintage, the paperback imprint of the Random House Group, which had acquired Byatt's hardback publisher, Chatto & Windus, in 1987, reissued almost all of Byatt's backlist fiction, as well as a collection of essays called *Passions of the Mind*, in 1993, and a substantially augmented version of the 1965 Murdoch study in 1994. The only title not included was *Sugar and Other Stories*, to which Penguin still held the rights. Today, six years later, all these books remain in print, and post-*Possession* sales of the earlier fiction titles have in every case exceeded ten times the original hardback

[2]See the *Observer Review*, 21 October 1990, p. 58.

sales.[3] The subsequent novellas or long short stories collected in *Angels and Insects* (1992), *The Matisse Stories* (1993) and *The Djinn in the Nightingale's Eye* (1994), now all available in Vintage paperback, have certainly been positively affected by the success of *Possession*. *The Djinn in the Nightingale's Eye* actually contains two of the Grimm-like fairy tales from *Possession*, isolated from their surrounding narrative. In the case of *Angels and Insects*, success has extended into the medium of film: the US rights to the first of that collection's two stories, 'Morpho Eugenia', were quickly sold, and the film was launched at Cannes in 1995. The paperback tie-in of *Angels and Insects* in turn aroused fresh interest in the filming of *Possession* itself.

How high were *Possession*'s sales? The quotation of hardback sales figures in Britain is, as has already been pointed out, a tricky business, as the following data – all of them in the public domain – confirm. Figures supplied by publishers are frequently distorted by the British press: thus on 18 October 1990, *The Times* attributed to Vintage's Frances Coady the assertion that the Booker win had led to the exhaustion of the 29,000 Chatto stock and the immediate prospect of a 50,000 reprint of the hardback; and along with this assertion the prognosis that the 70,000 paperback sales that could have been envisaged were now likely to exceed 150,000. On 5 November 1990 *Time* magazine declared that 60,000 hardback copies of *Possession* had been sold in Britain since March, a figure also quoted by Terry Trucco in the *Wall Street Journal* of 7/8 December 1990. On the other hand, W. H. Smith, reflecting the caution customarily exercised by bodies such as Bookwatch Ltd, announced towards the end of 1990 that its 450 stores (this, admittedly, was before the incorporation of Waterstone's) had together sold just 1,496 copies; more surprisingly still, in the seven months after

[3]This claim is based on confidential information obtained in conversation with Michael Sissons of The Peters, Fraser & Dunlop Group Ltd, who is Byatt's literary agent. The '*Possession* effect' has operated in Australia and the United States too, though perhaps less spectacularly.

publication and just prior to winning the Booker Prize, those stores appeared to have sold only 82 copies of *Possession*. If the 1,496 copies sold during 1990 were to be extrapolated on the basis of W. H. Smith's then 16 per cent share in the market, it was reasoned, a total hardback sales figure of 9,000 might be inferred; W. H. Smith was prepared, however, to concede that in this respect its share of the market might not be typical, and that 20,000 copies might have been sold. This information is presented not so much in any attempt to get at the 'truth' as to underline how impossible it is to reach any meaningful consensus on sales of hardback fiction in the present climate in Britain short of quoting confidential royalty figures, which I have undertaken not to do. One may reasonably estimate, however, that the 'true' figure lay between the extremes represented here, and nearer the higher figure.

The situation in Britain contrasts with that in the United States, where more reliable information suggests that in the four or five months after winning the Booker Prize, the Random House hardback of *Possession* had sold between 91,500 and 100,000 copies in at least ten printings, at one stage selling between 7,500 and 10,000 copies per week.[4] In Australia, traditionally the best market for fiction from Britain, the hardback sales were proportionally lower, between a third and a half of the US figures, but the Vintage paperback sales were to exceed the hardback sales by a factor of over twenty.

By December 1995, *Possession* had been translated into sixteen languages, including Japanese, Korean and Russian; Portuguese translation rights had also been sold in Brazil. *Angels and Insects, The Matisse Stories* and *The Djinn in the Nightingale's Eye* were available in eight, ten and six languages respectively; their success, though deserved, cannot be attributed to any other cause than the greater success of *Possession*.

[4]See Mervyn Rothstein, 'Best Seller Breaks Rule on Crossing the Atlantic', *NYT*, 31 January 1991, pp. C17, C22; and Mira Stout, 'What Possessed A. S. Byatt?', *NYT Magazine*, 26 May 1991, pp. 13–15, 24–25.

Possession made a strong impact in translation in Europe. In Germany, for example, between August 1992 and late 1994 sales had reached figures comparable with the highest claims made for hardback sales in Britain during 1990.[5] The translations into Danish and French all received acclaim in their own right. *Possession*'s apparent failure in The Netherlands and Flanders should not be assumed, for, although the translation performed comparatively poorly there, there is a strong tradition of reading fiction in English in the original – as there is in the Scandinavian countries, which makes the success of the Danish translation perhaps the most striking of all.

For the first incontrovertible information concerning sales of *Possession* in Britain and its export market it was necessary to await not just the paperback publication in Britain by Vintage in February 1991 (at a price 40 per cent above the average 1991 paperback), but the appearance in January 1993 of Alex Hamilton's annual survey. Hamilton's 'Top Hundred Chart of 1991 Paperback Fastsellers' reveals that *Possession* came 26th with over 250,000 sales (home and export) and grossed over £1.75m.[6]

There was clearly something in *Possession* that appealed to a quite astonishing variety of readers' tastes in the British Isles, mainland Europe, the 'Commonwealth' market and – unusually – the United States. Was Byatt's particular success in English in The Netherlands at least partly attributable to her well-attested passion for, and finely judged writing on, Vincent

[5]For foreign rights information, I am indebted to Nicki Kennedy of the Intercontinental Literary Agency associated with The Peters, Fraser & Dunlop Group Ltd. I have refrained from quoting the German translation figures I was given; suffice it to say that the Vintage paperback sales in Australia exceeded them: a figure was given to me in confidence by John Cody of Random House Australia Pty Ltd. The population of Australia is a quarter to a fifth of that in the re-unified Germany, and the German translation will of course have sold in Austria and Switzerland as well.
[6]See the *Writers' and Artists' Yearbook 1993* (London: A. & C. Black, 1993), pp. 241–47. In proportional terms, the Vintage paperback sales in Australia were comparable.

van Gogh? Or to the Amsterdam setting of the unflinchingly autobiographical story 'Sugar' that documents the death of the writer's father? Or to the possibility, mooted by the openly indeterminate ending of the twentieth-century part of *Possession*, that the academic Roland Michell will settle there as he pursues 'a modern way' of ensuring that his relationship with his colleague and lover Maud Bailey will last (*Possession*, p. 507)? Or to the Browningesque Randolph Henry Ash's creation of the ill-fated dramatic monologue *Swammerdam*, recounting the voice of an historical seventeenth-century Dutch microscopist?

There are indeed compelling grounds for seeing *Possession* as the kind of English novel likely to exert a strong appeal throughout the European mainland, where there is widespread popular and academic interest in those novels with which *Possession* showed affinities. One influential Anglophile American reviewer, Christopher Lehmann-Haupt, was not just to draw the commonplace comparison with John Fowles's *The French Lieutenant's Woman* (1969), a comparison bred of a superficial similarity in iconoclastic treatments of Victorian sexuality,[7] but much more significantly to advance Charles Palliser's *The Quincunx* (1990). Palliser is a US citizen with UK resident status who has spent by far the greater part of his life in the UK and Europe. *The Quincunx*, a complex literary pastiche of aristocratic inheritance, suspense and detection, which Lehmann-Haupt had recently also reviewed enthusiastically, sold extremely well in both the USA and Canada. *The Quincunx* also topped bestseller lists in The Netherlands and Belgium, and attracted considerable academic interest in Spain, France, Germany and Italy, all countries in which the study of literature

---

[7]This topic has been analysed by Michael Mason in two studies, *The Making of Victorian Sexuality* and *The Making of Victorian Sexual Attitudes* (Oxford: Clarendon, 1994). The research presented in these books seems explicitly to contest the Fowlesian view of nineteenth-century sexuality, and implicitly to condemn the kind of contemporary novelist who would hide behind an authorial mask to present misinformation on the topic.

in English remains strikingly centred on the UK and Ireland.[8] This pattern was matched by *Possession*, and for the kinds of reasons suggested by Lehmann-Haupt. A potent element in *Possession*, not mentioned by Lehmann-Haupt, but one that has become steadily more prominent as the 1990s have progressed, is the strong feminist interest in myths and fairy-tale promoted not just by Byatt but by writers such as Angela Carter and Marina Warner as well. Today it is Carter's short-story collection, *The Bloody Chamber*, which appeared as long ago as 1979, that is generally seen as having, in advance of its time, bred this fascination of the 1990s.[9]

Pan-European though this last-mentioned interest may be, the fact remains that *Possession* is a very English book. Although the nature of its Englishness would assure it of a warm reception in those parts of Europe mentioned above, contemporary British – let alone English – fiction is assured of nothing if not an unpredictable and in immediate commercial terms volatile reception in the United States. The executive editor of Byatt's American publisher (by then Random House), Susan Kamil, is quoted as saying: 'It wasn't just that the book was well reviewed. It was celebrated. And the celebration of the book, the tone of the reviews, pulled the buyers into the bookstores.'[10] It was striking how rival American publishers actually praised Random House's

[8]There is a considerable body of evidence, much of it deriving from activities and publications of the recently established ESSE [The European Society for the Study of English], to demonstrate a strong academic interest in English fiction in Spain and the Canary Islands and in Irish fiction in Flemish-speaking Belgium, to take two specific cases.

[9]This point is made by several of the contributors to Lorna Sage, ed., *Flesh and the Mirror: Essays on the Art of Angela Carter* (London: Virago, 1994), and by Sage herself in *Angela Carter, Writers and their Work* (Plymouth: Northcote House in association with the British Council, 1994).

[10]This quotation is derived from Mervyn Rothstein, from whom the other American information in this paragraph is abstracted (*NYT*, 31 January 1991, pp. C17 and C22). Michael Sissons, in discussion, has confirmed this celebratory sense that *Possession* was not just widely bought in Britain, too, but has been read and enjoyed, and that it can be seen to have benefited from an unusually strong word-of-mouth promotion among its readers.

aggressive commercial commitment to *Possession* – it is hard to imagine a similar response having been voiced in Britain at that time. An extremely strong selling point appears to have been Byatt's choice of cover illustration: this depicts a fine reproduction of the pre-Raphaelite Edward Burne-Jones's *The Beguiling of Merlin*. Byatt herself had expressed her enthusiasm for Chatto's cover-design, especially 'the way the illustration is reversed on the back, because you've got the two couples on the cover looking forwards and backwards and the whole book between them'. She has related this aspect of the cover to the persistent ventriloquy in *Possession* itself ('I like the fact that Merlin's face is actually Dante's face, which means that you've got this recession [. . .] of people being people being people. It's based on Giotto's Dante, it has to be').[11]

The Reception of English Fiction in the USA

The enthusiastic response to *Possession* from the general reader in the United States contrasts strikingly with a narrower academic attitude in the US to contemporary English fiction. Insofar as such fiction is academically discussed at all in the US, the prevailing orthodoxy still seems to derive from the dismissive line taken by Rubin Rabinovitz (*The Reaction Against Experiment in the English Novel: 1950–1960* [1967]) and Frederick R. Karl (*A Reader's Guide to the Contemporary English Novel* [1959, 1963]). That orthodoxy needs little further description than that given in Rabinovitz's title. More sympathetic commentators such as James Gindin (*Postwar British Fiction: New Accents and Attitudes* [1962]) or William Van O'Connor (*The New University Wits and the End of Modernism* [1963]) tended to focus on the 'post-war' nature of English fiction, the 'angry' generation and little-Englandism even when sufficient occasion

[11]Quoted in Richard Todd, 'Interview with A. S. Byatt', *NSES* [*Netherlands Society for English Studies*] *Bulletin* [now *ESSENSES*] 1/1 [April 1991], pp. 43–44. A truncated version in Dutch of this interview first appeared in the *NRC Handelsblad*, 17 October 1990, p. 6.

later arose to look at younger writers.[12] Thus even for a
much younger commentator and a much more recent study
– Michael Gorra, *The English Novel at Mid-Century* (1990)
– it is the immediate pre- and post-war generation, in fact the
late modernist period, that remains apparently central to North
American institutional concerns.

Clearly there are exceptions to this orthodoxy in the United
States, but closer examination usually shows that other agendas
are paramount. One such agenda is literary postmodernism
in an international context. It informs the excellent work of
Brian McHale, *Postmodernist Fiction* (1987) and the Linda
Hutcheon of *A Poetics of Postmodernism* (1988). True, Alison
Lee, a former graduate student of Hutcheon's, restricts herself
to contemporary English fiction (*Realism and Power* [1990]),
but her more selective approach limits her to not much more
than half-a-dozen writers, including the Scot Alasdair Gray, and
in all cases but that of John Fowles the discussion is restricted
to one main text. Lee's book is further symptomatic of the
way most academic discussion about literary postmodernism,
whether national or international, restricts itself to literature
by men, and in most cases by white men. This view actually
flies in the face of repeated claims, not just by thoughtful
English writers of feminist sympathies such as Byatt, but by
American novelists such as the 1993 Nobel Prize winner Toni
Morrison – whom it has been convenient to conscript into
feminist and/or African-American agendas – that they, too,
are mainstream postmodernists. A point to be made about
all three academic authorities of the postmodern cited here is

[12]Most of these data may be abstracted from Malcolm Bradbury and David
Palmer, eds., *The Contemporary English Novel* (London: Arnold, 1979), pp.
9–10, etc., which incidentally contains a strongly polemical opening chapter
by Byatt, reprinted in *Passions of the Mind*. I should myself want to argue an
even stronger distinction than do Bradbury and Palmer between Rabinovitz
and Karl on the one hand, and James Gindin on the other, excluding Gindin
from many of their strictures. Gindin continued to admire, as well as research
in and teach, the less than fashionable British fiction produced into the 1970s,
1980s and 1990s by the post-war generation until his own death in 1994.

that none is professionally attached to the United States itself. McHale, an American by upbringing, lives and works in Israel, and Hutcheon and Lee are both Canadian.

Another 'displaced' North American commentator who in a maverick, individual but impressive way has pressed strong and admirable claims for contemporary English fiction should be mentioned here. Elizabeth Dipple has published *Iris Murdoch: Work for the Spirit* (1982) and *The Unresolvable Plot* (1988). The latter book includes markedly idiosyncratic analyses of Graham Greene and Iris Murdoch. Lest it be pointed out that the younger of these writers was born in 1919, a generous concluding assessment entitled 'Roads not taken' expresses Dipple's admiration for Martin Amis, Julian Barnes and Angela Carter, among others.[13] Yet even this degree of admiration does not seem to show much awareness of the cultural pluralism of 1980s and 1990s Englishness, and one must regretfully conclude that even the most sympathetic academic North American perceptions of the field show unusual caution in the face of what is new and exciting in Britain.

With this kind of backing from North American academe, it is all the more necessary for any serious literary novelist now working and publishing in Britain to achieve recognition in the United States at the consumer level, primarily through media and market intervention. Projection into the American cultural consciousness can occur through fortuitous circumstances, and it might be argued that things have always been like this, and in Britain and elsewhere as well. But the situation in the United States is particularly worrying because it shows the widening gulf between even mainstream academic writing about the kinds of novel with which this book is concerned and more general interests of those who buy, read and enjoy those novels.

Projection into the American market seems to take one of three main forms, sometimes more than one in combination: either

---

[13]Dipple (private communication) does not, however, share my enthusiasm for *Possession*.

(firstly) through an Americanization of the way in which a given novel is published, or (secondly) through media tie-in, or (thirdly) through a substantial notice in a highbrow literary journal such as *The New York Review of Books* or even, and more dramatically, favourable notice in the *New York Times*, the nearest United States equivalent to a national newspaper in the British sense.

The first of these routes, 'the American future of British fiction', was discussed by John Sutherland nearly two decades ago,[14] and although his data pertain to the 1960s and 1970s, many of the names he mentions are still current and his general conclusions still for the most part valid and relevant. In addition to genre-fiction bestsellers, a phenomenon Sutherland has separately considered,[15] writers mentioned in the context of Americanization in Sutherland's *Fiction and the Fiction Industry* are Anthony Burgess, Muriel Spark, Margaret Drabble, and Graham Greene (then according to Sutherland 'the doyen of English international novelists' [p. 60]); with the deaths of Burgess and Greene this aspect of the picture has shifted somewhat. Sutherland goes on to mention other international writers not necessarily British by nationality who are or were resident in Britain in the mid 1970s: the reputations of some of these (Dan Jacobson, Ruth Prawer Jhabvala, Mordecai Richler and Brian Moore) have stood the test of time better than those of others. To their ranks can now be added – as a result of 1980s success – names such as Alasdair Gray, Vikram Seth and D. M. Thomas. As the *New York Times* regular reviewer of British fiction Michiko Kakutani put it in an interesting comparison that appeared in the *NYT Magazine* several months before Byatt's transatlantic success:

> While the generation of American writers that gave us such expansive social novels as *Gravity's Rainbow*, *Mr Sammler's Planet*, *Armies of the Night* and *The Confessions of Nat*

[14]John Sutherland, *Fiction and the Fiction Industry* (London: Athlone Press, 1978), pp. 46–62.
[15]John Sutherland, *Bestsellers* (London: Routledge & Kegan Paul, 1981).

Turner has been succeeded by a group of writers that focuses on the creation of small-scale stories about families and relationships (one thinks of writers from Jane Smiley to David Leavitt, Richard Ford to Sue Miller), a new generation of British writers has begun to produce ambitious novels that employ a hodge-podge of styles and postmodernist pyrotechnics to tackle the daunting themes of history, time, politics, social change and art.[16]

Kakutani's analysis may not stand over-close scrutiny, and the replacement of apocalypticism by regional parochialism by mainstream American novelists may by now be something of a commonplace, but it has this merit: it is typical of the kind of source on which the general reader in the United States has increasingly to depend for information about new fiction from Britain. Kakutani does at least update the transatlantic view by suggesting that in the 1980s the influence of Jonathan Swift and Laurence Sterne came to challenge that of Jane Austen, Arnold Bennett and Evelyn Waugh (I feel more sympathy towards this characterization of the new rather than that of the old). Kakutani makes it clear that, by 1990, the British novelists being noticed in American highbrow circles included Martin Amis, Julian Barnes and William Boyd, writers whose sense of tradition was more international than hitherto. Although Kakutani omits to point out that some of them entered into print more than twenty years ago, other 'younger' British writers now 'embrac[ing] the offbeat' include – for Kakutani – Peter Ackroyd, Kazuo Ishiguro, Ian McEwan, Graham Swift and Jeanette Winterson. Belated though the American breakthrough of some of these writers may have been, Kakutani's main point is that all of those on this list were born after 1945:

They were children during that period of expectancy, when it was hoped that a brave new world would emerge from

[16]Michiko Kakutani, 'Britain's Writers Embrace the Offbeat', *NYT Magazine*, 5 July 1990, pp. C11, C15.

the ashes of war, they grew up with the disappointment
of those hopes, and they matured as writers under the
Conservative Government of Margaret Thatcher in a Britain
increasingly exposed to influences from America and the rest
of the world.

Naïve though this may be, it is nonetheless to be preferred to the
attitude, such as it is, of American academe. Interestingly, six of
the eight 'younger' writers listed by Kakutani are white males.
   One of the examples of Americanization provided by John
Sutherland in 1981 is Thomas Keneally, whose *Schindler's Ark*
has subsequently afforded the most spectacular instance of media
tie-in, partly because the film in question allowed a second bite
at the cherry for a single novel. To mention *Schindler's Ark*
is to cheat a bit, since Keneally has retained his Australian
identity and indeed spends more time in Australia than many
other compatriot writers; but one could almost as well point
to John Fowles, whose *French Lieutenant's Woman* achieved
remarkable popular *and* academic recognition on both sides of
the Atlantic during the 1970s and 1980s, spurred by Harold
Pinter's stylish screenplay for the 1981 film, which then boosted
further sales of the book and other Fowles titles such as *The
Magus* (1965 etc.) and *Daniel Martin* (1977).[17] With Keneally
the process of media tie-in was more complex.
   The book now generally known as *Schindler's List* in fact
first appeared in Britain in 1982 as *Schindler's Ark* from
Hodder & Stoughton, when it won that year's Booker Prize.[18]
Controversy raged as to whether a documentary fiction based
on real events was the same as a 'straight' historical novel, and
whether either or both were eligible for the Booker rules as they

[17]The original publishing history of the first of these books is uncharacteristic
of many British novels. *The Magus* first appeared in the United States (Boston,
MA: Little, Brown, 1965) and a year later in Britain (London: Cape, 1966).
Just over a decade later it was controversially reissued in a 'revised version'
(London: Cape, 1977; Boston, MA: Little, Brown, 1978).
[18]As a Booker winner it is discussed more fully in Chapter 3 below.

then stood. Booker allowed Keneally's title, as an instance of the intermediate category that has come to be dubbed 'faction', but in the United States the book was published and marketed by Simon & Schuster as non-fiction, under the title *Schindler's List*, with 'significant differences, not least in the final chapter before the epilogue'.[19] The differences had apparently arisen in the first instance through the mutual reluctance of Hodder's Ion Trewin and Simon & Schuster's Patricia Solomon to embark on 'joint editing with one typesetting', Trewin feeling that so European a subject would be coloured by American usage and spelling, and Solomon, presumably, guessing that British usage and spelling would inhibit sales in the US. It was the American imprint that Steven Spielberg encountered a decade later. Keneally is no Fowles, and the book would likely have been noticed by the academy (if at all) under the rubric of popular culture rather than international postmodernism. There is evidence that Keneally's hardback sales by 1989 (thus *before* his discovery by Spielberg) were by far the highest of any Booker Prize winner to date, and the paperback sales at the second (or third) throw, as media tie-in, moved during 1994 into the same kind of league in both Britain and the US that might be expected of Fowles's title.[20]

The third, perhaps most fortuitous, route by which a serious literary novel or novelist working in England may be projected into the American and indeed international literary consciousness is

[19]See Ion Trewin, 'Handling a High-Flying Winner', *Bookseller*, 5 March 1983, p. 816.

[20]Source: Len England, comp., *Book Trade Year Book 1989* (London: Publishers Association, 1989), Table § 7.15 ('Hardback Sales of Booker Prizewinners [UK and Commonwealth] to end 1988'). This publication is available only to its membership, and so the sales figures it gives, supplied by Bookwatch Ltd, cannot legitimately be regarded as 'in the public domain'. Keneally's sales between 1981 and 1988 are more than double the next Booker-winning title – Keri Hulme's *The Bone People* (1985) – over the same period. The hardback version of Salman Rushdie's *Midnight's Children* (1981) is the least commercially successful of these titles, at about one sixth of the Keneally total. This information is in striking contrast to press figures given elsewhere in the present book, where the sales figures for the Keneally tie-in are also discussed (see, for instance, Chapter 3 below).

exemplified by the effect of two major review articles by Frank
Kermode. One, ostensibly a review of Julian Barnes's *Flaubert's
Parrot* (1984) but praising its two predecessors as well, is to be
found in the *New York Review of Books*; another in the *London
Review of Books* contrived by means of an account of *Sacred
Country* (1992) to bring Rose Tremain to wider attention.[21]
Likewise, and interestingly extending the terms of reference
of the English novel, a substantial *NYRB* review by Gabriele
Annan of Kazuo Ishiguro's *The Remains of the Day* appeared
shortly after that novel had won the 1989 Booker Prize, and
was constructed around all three Ishiguro titles to date, one
of which was even announced at the review's head as out
of print.[22] Such pieces quickly helped secure reputations for
these writers that might otherwise have taken a considerable
time to transcend the bounds of a national culture. Similar but
not identical literary-journalistic coverage of *Possession* seems
to represent the moment of Byatt's American breakthrough. It
does not seem necessary, although it is obviously helpful, to have
one's work endorsed by a reviewer with name-recognition on
both sides of the Atlantic. Rather, it seems to be the effect of
the review as sales pitch that can be just as powerful. Timing
plays its part, too: in Byatt's case there had been immediate
prior transatlantic press coverage of both the *Irish Times*-Aer
Lingus and the Booker successes, followed up within days
by enthusiastic reviews in both the *New York Times Book
Review* and the *New York Times* itself.[23] The effects of these

[21]In French translation, as *Le Royaume interdit*, Tremain's novel won the
1994 *Prix Femina Etranger*. Previous winners of this prize include J. M.
Coetzee, Ian McEwan and David Malouf.

[22]Frank Kermode, 'Obsessed with Obsession', *NYRB*, 25 April 1985, pp.
15–16; collected in Frank Kermode, *The Uses of Error* (Cambridge, MA:
Harvard UP, 1991), pp. 362–68; Kermode, 'Wannabee', *LRB*, 8 October
1992, p. 14; Gabriele Annan, 'On the High Wire', *NYRB*, 7 December
1989, pp. 3–4.

[23]Jay Parini, 'Unearthing the Secret Lover', *NYTBR*, 21 October 1990, § 7,
pp. 9, 11; Christopher Lehmann-Haupt, 'When There Was Such a Thing
as Romantic Love', *NYT*, 25 October 1990, p. C24. The *Irish Times*-Aer
Lingus may well have played a significant role in itself in the US.

reviews are worth considering as a whole, and contrasting with each other.

Possession and Consumerism

The first of these reviews, Jay Parini's, is less perceptive and accurate, but it does argue some kind of relationship between Byatt's novels and the characters it could be said to stereotype. Such coverage might well arouse the interest of the Anglophile American reader looking for something new. Thus Sir George Bailey 'seems to have walked right out of the pages of P. G. Wodehouse into a novel by David Lodge' (he – Bailey – is part of a portrayal of 'consummate wit and parodic skill'); and Parini goes on to claim that '[a]s *Possession* progresses, it seems less and less like the usual satire about academia and more like something by Jorge Luis Borges'. Leonora Stern is 'a heavyset lesbian from the United States'; James Blackadder 'a Dickensian figure'; and Mortimer Cropper is 'devilishly caricatured by Ms Byatt as a cross between Leon Edel and Liberace'.

What is the effect of claims such as these? If the descriptions of Stern and Blackadder are uncomfortably off-target, others stand up to more scrutiny. 'Wodehouse' can be decoded as stereotypical philistine and reactionary Englishness, but the reader would not, without further help, gain any sense of Sir George's financial canniness if the Lodge reference were not there to suggest that he has been transplanted into a setting in which the forces of philistinism and reaction are going to surrender (although not without a struggle) to what they exist to oppose. 'Lodge', again, can be decoded as the David Lodge of *Small World* (1984), a global campus novel that quickly gained a strong cult following in United States academia. Still, 'Lodge', in this sense, is what Parini's readers may be assumed to have understood by 'the usual satire about academia' in its English manifestation. These terms would connote a mixture of intelligent, informed but detached coverage of literary theory (what might once have been termed 'a novel of ideas'), coupled with that particular form of comedy that in its graceful symmetries and withheld denouements might be termed 'Shakespearian'. To suggest that this kind of writing can be transformed, by an English writer, into the alternative fictional worlds of Borges is to prepare the reader of Parini's review for its conclusion, that *Possession* 'opens every narrative device of English fiction to inspection without, for a moment, ceasing to delight'.

There is a sleight of hand here in the use of the word 'English' of which it is as well to be aware.[24] The implicit claim is that a warmly received English novel of the 1990s *can* be identified with a literary tradition that it is still possible to term 'English'. 'English' can be used 'globally', both to encompass the review-reader's no doubt fascinated suspicion as to what the precise nature of 'a cross between Leon Edel and Liberace' might be, and to conscript the most Anglophile Latin-American magical realist: Jorge Luis Borges. Parini's review, in other words, for all its allusive and at times off-the-wall cultural shorthand, is about as good a piece of advertising copy for *Possession* as could be imagined: it cannot have failed not only to arouse but also to challenge the general reader in the United States. To stress the appeal to consumerism – if you want to know what is hot in English fiction in the fall of 1990, and in passing to gain insight into what is apparently a plethora of both inherent treasures *and* 'every narrative device of English fiction' now on offer, you need only acquire and read *Possession* – to speak of the novel as a commodity in this way is neither to patronize the American reader nor to denigrate *Possession* or its writer: this is, increasingly, how the literary product is marketed and consumed. In a world in which there is quite simply too much to read, and intense peer pressure to keep up with what there is, the reader

---

[24]There is, of course, an historical literature on this definitional point. One of the best recent analyses is Linda Colley, *Britons: Forging the Nation, 1707–1837* (1992; London: Pimlico, 1994). See also Tom Nairn, *The Break-Up of Britain: Crisis and Representation* (1977; 2nd, expanded, edn London: New Left Books, 1981).

(particularly the reader of a literature from overseas) needs a guaranteed return on her or his investment. Parini's review can be seen, like many of its kind, as a favourable review that is at the same time a skilfully pitched consumer guide.

It was a few days after Jay Parini's *NYTBR* piece that Christopher Lehmann-Haupt's very much more committed review appeared in the *New York Times* itself. Given the tight word limits within which Lehmann-Haupt evidently had to work, a strikingly high proportion of his 1,800-word review is given over to plot summary and direct quotation, the latter accounting for about 15 per cent of the total. The Palliser comparison noted above occurs in the context of Lehmann-Haupt's assertion of the pleasure to be had from literary detection. Lehmann-Haupt cites at considerably greater length than I can do here Maud Bailey's remarks on the theory that 'the classic detective story arose with the classic adultery novel' (*Possession*, p. 238). He characterizes *Possession* as illustrating this generic hybrid '[a]nd . . . a good deal more'. He identifies not simply religious faith and romantic love, but also the poignancy of their loss (and the possibility that only the novelist can redress that loss by showing us *what* we have lost). The suspicion that this is little more than nostalgia is deflected by Lehmann-Haupt's insistence that *Possession* 'is most of all about speech, language, the pleasure of reading, the singularity of reading [. . .] it makes one read and reflect on language and consider what it meant to another age'.

Although Lehmann-Haupt does not make the point explicitly himself, such a reading of *Possession* brings it into the company of 1980s texts of international literary postmodernism (male texts, it should be stressed) such as Umberto Eco's *The Name of the Rose*. Yet Lehmann-Haupt seems unwittingly to have been drawn into reading *Possession* as a realistic nineteenth-century novel in his assertion that 'one bridles at the liberty [Byatt] takes in describing at first hand certain scenes involving Ash and LaMotte that no one could plausibly have witnessed', and not as a postmodernist text involving ventriloquy as a privilege that begins with the authorial voice itself. But for all its omissions and flaws as well as its perceptiveness, Lehmann-Haupt's review contrived, I believe, to present Byatt's *Possession* to the American reading public as simultaneously an English and a European novel.

The Riches of *Possession*

What, then, did *Possession* offer the American and European reader that supports both the literary pedigrees cited by its reviewers, as well as Parini's further claim that this novel offers 'every narrative device of English fiction'? And more interestingly still, is it possible for a novel for which such claims can be made to avoid accusations that it is a customized literary blockbuster, a consumer product too knowing for its own good or too self-aware of its own riches? The first of these questions can be answered fairly straightforwardly by means of a discussion that offers an inventory of the major thematic and technical preoccupations of *Possession*. The second question, obviously, is harder to answer, and there will always be cynically dismissive, as well as naïvely receptive, readers. Yet in a larger sense, it is what lies behind this second question that motivates much of the discussion of the rest of the present book, and indeed drives it: *Possession* is a novel that has proved commercially attractive to today's publishers' promotional need for the generic consumer product – at the same time, if it can be marketed as the 'romance' announced by its subtitle, it is, as we shall see, an astonishingly successful hybrid.

Two points, one general and one specific, ought to be made straight away. The general point is that *Possession* is a compelling, addictive read, and the reader submits to it out of passion, along with something one might even term 'virtue'. *Possession* reminds us of what we have lost or teaches us what we wished we had known: the reader is explicitly reached out for in as many ways as there are riches to be savoured. It could certainly be argued, for instance, that the skilful pan-European combination of fairy-tale and myth, ranging from the Brothers Grimm to Melusina, exercised an appeal that differed in nature according to whether *Possession* was read in Northern or Southern Europe. At various stages Byatt is rumoured to have battled, both in London and New York, for the inclusion of what was initially believed – wrongly as it turns out – would weigh down what everyone recognized as a potential blockbuster with a bulk of unsaleable freight. That freight is the vast amount of ventriloquial pastiche that has survived in the book we have: what was feared might make the book most reader-repellent were the often substantial poetic extracts from the work of Randolph Henry Ash and Christabel LaMotte.[25] Indeed, there can be few bestselling novels that contain so much verse, and one can only wonder at what sort of book is read in Japanese or Korean translation. (Byatt herself, it might be added, has no quarrel with readers who wish to omit the poetry.)

In *Possession*, Byatt engages with the strength of mid-nineteenth-century English (or English-language) literary tradition in such a way that the nineteenth-century characters appear more vivid and colourful than their twentieth-century counterparts. Indeed, it could be claimed that the sole *raison d'être* of *Possession*'s twentieth-century counterparts is the very retrieval of the nineteenth-century originals that give them such colour as they have. Thus the present-day scholar Beatrice Nest is engaged, apparently endlessly, in editing the diaries of the nineteenth-century Ellen Ash. Appropriately, Nest counterpoints her taskmaster, Professor James Blackadder, in his long-term edition of the complete works of the polymath Randolph Henry Ash, famous husband to obscure wife. Yet Ellen Ash's work is now being conscripted to the interests of feminist scholarship, while the original twentieth-century justification of that work,

[25]Byatt's publisher Carmen Callil, who was strongly supportive of the verse, was apparently instrumental in solving the *impasse* at Chatto & Windus and later at Random House, Inc.

Nest's chaotically philological working method, has been pushed
to the margins of her profession, as indeed has Nest herself. There
is a revealing conversation between Nest and Maud Bailey that
conveys the width of the generational chasm between the two
methods and their practitioners:

> 'I expect you think I've very little to show for all these years
> of work on these papers. Twenty-five years to be precise,
> and sliding past at increasing speed. I've felt very conscious
> of that – that slowness – with the increasing interest shown
> by – your sort of scholar – people with ideas about Ellen
> Ash and her work. All I had was a sort of sympathy for
> the – helpmeet aspect of her – and to be truthful, Dr Bailey,
> a real admiration for him, for Randolph Ash. *They* said it
> would be better to – to do this task which presented itself
> so to speak and seemed appropriate to my – my sex – my
> capacities as they were thought to be, whatever they were. A
> good feminist in *those* days, Dr Bailey, would have insisted
> on being allowed to work on the Ask and Embla poems.'
> 'Being allowed?'
> 'Oh. I see. Yes. On *working* on the Ask and Embla poems.'
> She hesitated. Then: 'I don't think you can imagine, Miss
> Bailey, how it was then. We were dependent and excluded
> persons. In my early days – indeed until the late 1960s –
> women were *not permitted* to enter the main Senior Common
> Room at Prince Albert College [. . .] We thought it was bad
> being young [. . .] but it was worse when we grew older.
> There is an age at which, I profoundly believe, one becomes
> a *witch* [. . .]
> 'You will think I am mad. I am trying to excuse twenty-five
> years' delay – with – personalities – You would have produced
> an edition twenty years ago.' (*Possession*, pp. 220–21)

Characteristically, Blackadder's patriarchal counterclaim as one
of Nest's generation is two-pronged: it is that Nest's work will

never be completed (this may represent the flipside of his fear about his own work), and that although Ellen Ash is being privileged by feminist scholarship, the effort is wasted because the work is not just obscure (a neutral conception) but mediocre (a value judgement).

Another distinct set of cultural values is simultaneously being played out subtextually here. The inability to 'finish', or 'let go', that typifies the Anglo-Saxon and Celtic scholarship of (respectively) Nest and Blackadder, is counterpointed by the hard-nosed professionalism of the American scholars Leonora Stern and Mortimer Cropper. These are more than cultural stereotypes, however. Each stance is shown to be inadequate, though for different reasons: thus Cropper's wealth and complacency, as well as his almost libidinally driven conscription of his research project to his own identity and ancestry, must be taken together with his ostensible success – and all these aspects are thrown into contrast with the ineffectiveness, yet arguably greater integrity and moral attractiveness, of Nest and Blackadder. The younger generation of British scholars, Roland, Maud and Fergus Wolff, are profiled as somewhere in between these extremes but as moving towards the professionalism of Stern and Cropper, even though for much of *Possession* Roland, like all too many young academics in the 1980s and 1990s, is as professionally 'dependent and excluded' as Beatrice Nest's gender has made her. Ironically, this is something she fails to realize throughout the entire narrative.

There are additional nineteenth-century figures. Some seem to have no direct twentieth-century counterpart to retrieve their voices: thus Christabel LaMotte's house-companion and (we are to assume) lover Blanche Glover's diary only gains significance (a significance that may or may not, as it at first seems, exist) when Roland Michell perceives in it references to the principal 'story' of *Possession*, a story he is the first to begin to attempt to reconstruct. There is also the journal of Sabine de Kercoz, kept during LaMotte's visit to her Breton relatives. This journal is accidentally discovered by a French feminist scholar, Ariane le

Minier, for whom it cannot have the significance it must have
for both Roland Michell and Maud Bailey, who has by now
become co-partner in his quest. Even this potential significance is
both provisionally yet, at the same time, seemingly finally hidden
when the journal apparently fails – on their first encounter with
it – to tell Roland and Maud what they want to hear. What they
want to hear is what has happened to LaMotte, clearly in the
advanced stages of pregnancy, during her self-imposed exile in
Britanny. Has the child been born? Has it been stillborn? Can
the religious sorority among whom LaMotte has been confined
conceivably have acted duplicitously towards Sabine, and by
extension towards Roland and Maud, and – by further extension
– towards us as readers, intellectual consumers of the quest
undertaken by Roland and Maud? Lastly may be mentioned
here a piece of authorial omniscience, which is not Ellen Ash's
diary but a stream-of-consciousness, imagistic fragment of a
wedding-night sexual trauma: this, coming almost at the end of
Possession, casts its long shadow over the events that have been
revealed so far, and powerfully renders them with significance.
At the same time this, almost the last voice to be retrieved, is
the most difficult and painful:

The nightdress embroidered for these nights, white cambric,
all spattered with lovers' knots and forget-me-nots and roses,
white on white.

A thin white animal, herself, trembling.

A complex thing, the naked male, curly hairs and shining
wet, at once bovine and dolphin-like, its scent feral and
overwhelming.

A large hand, held out in kindness, not once, but many
times, slapped away, pushed away, slapped away.

A running creature, crouching and cowering in the corner
of the room, its teeth chattering, its veins clamped in spasms,
its breath shallow and fluttering. Herself.

A respite generously agreed, glasses of golden wine, a few
days of Edenic picnics, a laughing woman perched on a rock

in pale blue poplin skirts, a handsome man in his whiskers,
lifting her, quoting Petrarch.[26]

In the most resonant case, that of Maud Bailey, retrieval leads
to a kind of appropriation, as she is shown to be descended from
the progeny of the union, that is indeed finally discovered to have
arisen, between the principal lovers in the nineteenth-century
plot, that is, Randolph Henry Ash and Christabel LaMotte.
Maud's collaborative reconstruction of the nineteenth-century
plot becomes a disturbing reconstitution of her own past and
in turn of her own self. The curiously paradoxical effect
is that, emerging as the principal literary detective of the
twentieth-century narrative, Maud is simultaneously placed
in the limelight, and edged into the wings, of her own story.
The authorial voice withholds and proffers an omniscience
exceeding that of *all* the characters right up until the last page
of the novel.

A major purpose of this account of *Possession* has been to
show something of the powerful array of voices the narrative
sets up, an array wherein all the twentieth-century voices can
be said to owe their existence to their attempts to reconstruct
their various nineteenth-century counterparts. Some, such as
Blanche, are difficult to retrieve: the 'glove' that her last name
is prodigally used to play on echoes a figure that is repeated
at several points in the novel, leading indeed at one point to
Roland's frustration, in conversation with Maud, at its very
plethora of figurative possibilities:

'Do you never have the sense that our metaphors *eat up* our
world? I mean of course everything connects and connects –
all the time – and I suppose one studies – I study – literature
because all these connections seem both endlessly exciting

---

[26]*Possession*, p. 459. The word 'spattered', echoing 'scattered' but suggesting
– in a kind of unfulfilled prolepsis – the hymeneal loss of blood, enhances
the many animal words and images in this extract.

and then in some sense dangerously powerful – as though
we held a clue to the true nature of things? I mean, all those
gloves, a minute ago we were playing a professional game
of hooks and eyes – medieval gloves, giants' gloves, Blanche
Glover, Balzac's gloves, the sea-anemone's ovaries – and it
all reduced like boiling jam to – human sexuality. Just as
Leonora Stern makes the whole earth read as the female
body – and language – all language. And all vegetation is
pubic hair.'

Maud laughed, drily. Roland said,

'And then, really, what is it, what is this arcane power we
have, when we see that everything is human sexuality? It's
really *powerlessness*.'

'Impotence,' said Maud, leaning over, interested.

'I was avoiding that word, because that precisely *isn't the
point*. We are so knowing. And all we've found out, is primitive sympathetic magic. Infantile polymorphous perversity.
Everything relates to *us* and so we're imprisoned in ourselves
– we can't see *things*.' (*Possession*, pp. 253–54)

As 'knowing' as it undoubtedly is, *Possession* nevertheless
examines itself pitilessly on its own knowingness. Among the
elements that offer powerlessness in the face of overwhelming
figurative significance is the ventriloquy of the novel at all its
many levels. Voices are read and heard by other voices, which
are in turn read and heard by yet other voices. Motifs such
as Christabel's Dog Tray and the dog in her fairy-tale 'The
Glass Coffin' are both, but in chillingly different ways, dumb,
inarticulate, in a text that throbs with knowing articulacy.

As might be guessed, the interplay of voices works across
the generations. Beatrice Nest's fear of being thought, in her
professional life, a witch the older she grows echoes or is echoed
– knowingly yet unknowingly – by Christabel in her message to
the dying Ash: '. . . *here I sit, an old witch in a turret, writing
my verses*' (*Possession*, p. 500). Lady Bailey discusses Maud
with Roland:

'She's a beautiful girl, Dr Bailey. Stand-offish or shy, maybe both. What my mother used to call a chilly mortal. She was a Yorkshirewoman, my mother. Not County. Not a lady.'
(*Possession*, p. 144)

On their Yorkshire 'honeymoon' Christabel denies to Ash his assertion that she is 'the life of things':

'Oh no. I am a chilly mortal, as Mrs Cammish said yesterday morning, when I put on my shawl. It is you who are the life of things. You stand there and draw them into you. You turn your gaze on the dull and the insipid to make them shine.'
(*Possession*, p. 285)

All one can say is that Christabel's insight is given more passionate intensity – that is, it is used by the narrator to allow us to find out *more* about the intellectually and spiritually virtuous voraciousness of Ash – than is Lady Bailey's. The latter's insight can only be expressed in terms of social hierarchy coupled with a dim sense of the potential numinousness of Maud (a quality Maud and the moderns all try, in various ways, to reject or – as with Fergus Wolff – manipulate).

Probably the most unnerving literal echo occurs at the strongest of these transgenerational pivots. At one point in *Possession*, Roland's embittered girlfriend Val remarks, prior to the final break-up of their sterile relationship: 'I'm a superfluous person.' (*Possession*, p. 218) This sense of superfluousness is grounded in Val's belief that she is being excluded not just from the scholarly discovery Roland and Maud have made, but from a developing affair between the two. Later it will become evident that the ending of the relationship between Roland and Val enables Val to *liberate* herself into a relationship with Euan McIntyre, a solicitor in the office at which Val works. It is Euan who will give legal advice on the copyright of unsent letters (another aspect, incidentally, of the concept of 'possession'). Some pages later, Maud (unaware, of course, unlike *Possession*'s readers, of Val's remark) rereads the suicide note of Blanche Glover, LaMotte's companion in the house they have shared in Putney. Blanche's journal earlier intimates that she has been rescued by LaMotte from a life of endless governessing posts, and that the two women have been relieved and even elated to have been able to set up house together. In the correspondence between LaMotte and Ash, it has become evident that Blanche is beginning to behave almost pathologically, intercepting and even destroying several of Ash's letters to LaMotte. The final paragraph of Blanche's suicide note includes the words: 'It has indeed been borne in upon me that *here* I am a superfluous creature. *There* I shall know and be known' (*Possession*, p. 309).

What has apparently proved fatal to Blanche will prove enabling to Val. Yet the apparent absoluteness of the contrast may also conceal a parallel between the two cases, linked as they are by the striking echo in the word 'superfluous'. Blanche has no choice but to leave this life for what she believes to be a spirit world 'on the other side'. This will (in Blanche's mind) enable her construction as an existential human being who has faith in a hereafter in which her 'capacities – great and here unwanted and unused' can be employed 'for love and for creative Work' (*Possession*, p. 309). Val is transformed and fulfilled, as she could never be with Roland, by her relationship with Euan. Whether or not Blanche's beliefs are shared by her twentieth-century reader, her very recovery into the twentieth-century plot of *Possession* gives her a voice and a role 'on the other side' that she despairingly, in the nineteenth-century plot, believed herself not to be capable of having.

Byatt's nineteenth-century pastiche makes use of painstakingly uncompromising reconstructions of voices recognizable as those of Robert Browning, Emily Dickinson, and (possibly) Christina Rossetti. Yet Ash and LaMotte are, as writers, themselves also pasticheurs or ventriloquists: thus the polymath Ash is a skilled practitioner of the Browningesque monologue, whereas LaMotte not only recalls Dickinson but raids and appropriates fairy-tale tellers such as Grimm. Byatt has not underrated the complexity

of what she set out to achieve; Christabel is, as Byatt put it in
a conversation I conducted with her in October 1990:

> . . . trying to break their narrative structure because she keeps
> pointing out that the story requires that she ends it in this
> way but actually she thinks it should end in that way. That
> applies to her fate as well as to her story-telling.[27]

One of the most interesting voices, because one could argue that
it encapsulates the entire *modus operandi* of *Possession*, is the
voice of a child apparently communicated with in a seance: that
child may be dead, or never have existed. The seance plays an
important role in serving as a figure by means of which given
characters 'speak through' other characters. Ash's attempt to
disrupt the seance (referred to as his 'Gaza exploit') can be
read as a patriarchal attempt to suppress what these hitherto
unheard voices are attempting to communicate. The effect is far
from being a crude manipulation of gender politics, however, for
the reader never ascertains whether the seance is 'genuine'.

It is the retrieval and reconstruction of the nineteenth-century
plot, then, that form the subject of the twentieth-century plot.
The nineteenth-century plot hinges on the discovery that Ash and
LaMotte have indeed had a brief but intense love affair, that this
affair has been brought to a close under circumstances that are
never made entirely clear, and that LaMotte has conceived and
borne a daughter, Maia. The deliberately thrilling denouement
involves the discovery of LaMotte's apparently unread last letter
to Ash, which has been buried along with his remains. LaMotte's
letter (unread and unheard by Ash, equivocally suppressed by
his widow) is 'heard' for the first time by the twentieth-century
scholars in a carefully staged gathering while all are stranded
in a country hotel as the hurricane of October 1987, a real,
historically attested event, rages outside.

The fictional letter reveals the existence of the daughter

[27]For details, see n. 11 above.

to both the twentieth-century characters and the reader of
Possession. Yet this appropriation is at once itself undercut by a
further authorial denouement involving readerly complicity with
the nineteenth-century narrative, so that readerly omniscience
includes the discovery that the nineteenth-century characters
were in every sense more 'real' than their twentieth-century
rescuers. Ash passes on an oral message destined for LaMotte,
but it is forgotten and never reaches its destination: we come
to know this as readers; neither Ash nor any of the other
nineteenth-century characters can ever have known its fate;
and that fate is by definition epistemologically withheld from
Possession's twentieth-century characters.

2

Literary Prizes and the Media

At about the beginning of the 1980s, Britain's literary culture in respect of the novel began to undergo a series of rapid and fascinating changes. Prior to this time – in other words during the immediate post-war period until well into the 1970s – Britain's serious literary novelists were likely to achieve notice through either (a) the production of one title that captured the public imagination, or (b) a steady output that contrived to reach a faithful, and usually increasing, readership. Among the best-known examples of the former are the successes of William Golding and John Fowles. Golding's *Lord of the Flies* first appeared in 1954; by the 1960s it had become a 'set text' both in Britain and overseas. By the 1980s Fowles's *The French Lieutenant's Woman* (1969) had taken its place in academe as Britain's best-known postmodernist novel. Both books were subsequently filmed, Fowles's novel more recently and famously as we have seen, than Golding's (although it was Peter Brook who wrote the screenplay for *Lord of the Flies*). Well-known examples of the latter category of steady output include the achievements of Graham Greene from the 1940s onwards, and Doris Lessing, Iris Murdoch and Muriel Spark from the 1950s onwards.

There were prizes to be won by the serious literary novelist, to be sure, but their significance was not noticed by the majority of the reading public, nor were they promoted as being of interest to consumers of contemporary fiction, whether borrowers or buyers. These awards still exist. They include the James Tait Black Memorial Prizes (these were established in 1918 and are awarded annually, one for fiction and one for biography), the

Geoffrey Faber Memorial Prize (then a relative newcomer that was established in 1965 and awarded in alternate years for verse and prose fiction), the Hawthornden Prize (established in 1919 and awarded for 'the best work of imaginative literature published during the preceding year by a British author'), and – most significantly – the Somerset Maugham Awards (first made in 1947 and intended to encourage writers under 35 to travel). None is specifically for the novel.

The prestige that went with winning any of these prizes in the 1960s was confined to the literary world. The sums of prize-money were certainly appreciated by the winners, but they were not substantial by today's standards (it would have been impossible to turn to writing full-time on the proceeds unless one were already of independent means), and the awards themselves had no really discernible effect on an author's sales.

The British literary establishment (as was often lamented) had no equivalent of France's Prix Goncourt, established in 1903, whose (symbolic) financial value is a nugatory 50 francs or Italy's Premio Strega, whose monetary value is 1m lire (about £400). However, to win the Goncourt or the Strega was and is to be assured of massive sales. The total readership for a winning novel is of a size rarely if ever achieved in Britain. For example, Jean Rouaud's first novel, *Les Champs d'honneur*, was a highly regarded recent winner. Published on 1 September 1990, it had sold several thousand copies; after the prize was awarded in November it went on to sell a further 1m copies on the basis of the prestige of the prize and favourable reviews.

For British writers, as for their colleagues worldwide, there always remained the phantom of Nobel Prize recognition. Whatever else might be said about it, the Nobel Prize remains the most financially lucrative award in the entire world. Its 1994 value has been placed variously at between £650,000 and £900,000. Although Nobel laureates from Britain and Ireland in the first half of the twentieth century included Rudyard Kipling in 1907, W. B. Yeats in 1923, John Galsworthy in 1932 and T. S. Eliot in 1948, the only Britons to have won the Nobel Prize for Literature in the second half of the century, as the 1970s came to an end, were the philosopher Bertrand Russell in 1950 and the historiographer Winston Churchill in 1953. Of the entire list, only Kipling and Galsworthy could be counted as novelists. Their number was swelled by the Irish-born French-speaking exile Samuel Beckett in 1969. In 1983 William Golding became to date the only post-war British novelist to be awarded the Nobel Prize. His achievement, however, was marred by an apparent breaking of ranks from within the Swedish Academy, with a sour press as the result. There has been a very recent spate of English-language (though not British) Nobel laureates: Nadine Gordimer in 1991, Derek Walcott in 1992, Toni Morrison in 1993 and Seamus Heaney in 1995.

By the 1990s Britain's prize culture had changed dramatically. Any of the writers mentioned or discussed in this book is in theory eligible for between forty and fifty literary awards, only a minority of which are not made annually. Of these awards, at least half-a-dozen now available to novelists published in Britain exceed (sometimes considerably) £10,000. Winning one of these more significant prizes not only brings the novelists a cash windfall: it can exercise spectacular effects on sales figures. On several occasions, as we have seen with A. S. Byatt's *Possession* and will see in subsequent instances, a big win has catapulted hitherto less well-known or even unknown writers to fame, enabling them to devote their careers to writing full-time. This, coupled with shrewd business sense on the part of a publisher and/or an agent, can empower writers to achieve a global profile that would otherwise have been out of their reach.

One could make out a case in terms of success of this kind for at least ten or fifteen, and probably more, writers of serious literary fiction working today and published in the first instance in London since 1980. It is probably true to say that not since before 1914 have so many serious literary novelists been able to make a living from writing fiction in Britain. Of Arnold

Bennett, for example, Frank Kermode observed well over ten years ago:

> It may not seem credible, but I calculate that [his] income in 1913, expressed in terms of our money in 1982, amounted to something over £800,000.[1]

The presence in the modernist literary canon of writers such as James Joyce and Virginia Woolf (both 1882–1941) may blind many of their academic readers to the fact that each sold relatively poorly in their lifetimes.[2] In the 1920s Woolf, for example, could not have begun to envisage the kind of sales she achieved posthumously more than half a century later (prior to coming – briefly – out of copyright, Woolf was published by Penguin in arrangement with The Hogarth Press). An indication of Woolf's current sales is given by the effect of the 1992 filming of *Orlando* (1928). In March 1993 Virago issued an offset of the 1990 Vintage edition of the novel, having bought the rights to a film tie-in cover from Penguin; in 1993 alone Virago's sales of *Orlando* (that is, sales excluding the Vintage and Penguin editions of the novel) totalled 15,000 and by September 1994 had exceeded 17,000 – this in addition to continuing steady Penguin and Vintage paperback sales.[3] These figures exceed the original world sales of *Orlando* in the four-and-a-half

[1]Frank Kermode, *The Art of Telling: Essays on Fiction* (Cambridge MA: Harvard UP, 1983), p. 10. This figure, if accepted, would have to be revised upwards to something in the region of £1.5m by 1996.

[2]John Sutherland, *Fiction and the Fiction Industry* (London: Athlone Press, 1978), cites Leonard Woolf on his wife's income from fiction between 1920 and 1924: £106/5/10, £10/10/8, £33/13/–, £40/0/5, £70 exactly (Sutherland, p. 110). The pound of this period had the purchasing power of between £30 and £50 today; thus in the best of these years Woolf's income from fiction was equivalent to a few thousand pounds in today's terms, the leanest equivalent to a few hundred. Woolf was fortunate to have private means, unlike many of her 1990s sisters.

[3]These figures were kindly supplied by Lennie Goodings and Sarah White of Virago.

years between November 1928 (the date of its appearance) and February 1933.[4]

Today's serious literary novelists in Britain, however, unlike those of sixty to seventy years ago, are alive to commercial possibilities that for most of the twentieth century have been available only to writers deliberately aiming at the best-selling, genre-fiction end of the market such as crime or science fiction. The media consequences for this new constituency have been varied and lucrative. A TV serialization or the sale of film rights have been frequent occurrences; once again, in shrewd hands these can generate vast amounts of extra income, fame and far wider prestige than was the case a generation ago. I am not arguing that external events have only recently begun to assist sales; I am drawing attention to the fact that such sales are no longer exclusively the preserve of the genre-fiction writer. Agatha Christie's carefully scripted and notorious 'disappearance' in 1926 boosted her sales considerably, beginning with *The Murder of Roger Ackroyd*, which had appeared earlier that year. A fictional instance, quite possibly inspired by the Christie case, occurs soon afterwards in the work of Dorothy L. Sayers. Sayers' *alter ego*, the detective writer Harriet Vane, having been acquitted of murdering her fiancé thanks to the persistent genius of the sleuthing aristocrat Lord Peter Wimsey, finds herself 'a very much richer woman than she had ever dreamed of becoming' as a result of increased sales of all her

---

[4]Virginia Woolf, *Orlando* (London: Vintage, 1992), p. xv. The figures are quoted as 14,950. The case of Woolf is particularly piquant because from 1 January 1996 a pan-European copyright period of seventy years *post mortem* replaced the half-century that had been mandatory in Britain since 1911. Woolf is among a number of writers who have gone back into copyright until the early twenty-first century as British titles, while copyright in the UK, come or remain out of copyright in the US, where the fifty-year rule will still apply. See Hugh Jones, 'Life Plus Seventy', *Bookseller* (1 April 1994), pp. 20–21. The seventy-year rule will be grist to the mill of the James Joyce Estate, which has been fighting the consequences of the fifty-year copyright rule in a variety of ingenious ways since the early 1990s. Britain's Department of Trade and Industry (DTI) accepted the EU ruling as a *fait accompli* after a minimum of consultation.

titles and – interestingly – transatlantic coverage arising from intense press curiosity about the case.[5]

The element of good fortune that can attend the early stages of a career should not be underestimated, although in mentioning it one is in no way trying to belittle individual achievement. The celebrated 'two-horse races' between William Golding's *Rites of Passage* and Anthony Burgess's *Earthly Powers* in 1980, and D. M. Thomas's *The White Hotel* and Salman Rushdie's *Midnight's Children* in 1981 impressed the Booker Prize on the public imagination. The serious literary novelists of the 1980s and 1990s tend to have a much higher media profile than their peers of a generation ago.

There are other kinds of good fortune too: 'mediagenic' writers glide through doors that now open to just the gentlest of pushes.[6] Much depends – more than ever before – on the efforts of literary agents, and on the editorial and sales and marketing expertise of a given publishing house in appealing to the reading public as consumers of the product on offer. A publisher may decide to make a particularly strong push for a given author with a later title following a debut that does not quite live up to expectations: thus Jonathan Cape decided to promote Martin Amis's *Other People* (1980) after initial lack of real commercial success with *The Rachel Papers* (1973) and the two novels succeeding it. The gamble paid off: the entire Amis *oeuvre* to date was reprinted by Penguin, and by the end of the 1980s Amis had become – in Britain at least – the most notorious serious literary novelist of his generation.

A 1994 promotional initiative from W. H. Smith, 'Something to Shout About', caters for 'the sort of [novel] that is often published in a void'. Its aim, in collaboration with the publishers concerned, was to price selected £14.99 hardback titles (the

[5]Dorothy L. Sayers, *Have His Carcase* (1932; rpt. London: Coronet, 1989), p. 9.
[6]This point was made to me by Peter Straus, then publisher at Hamish Hamilton, now literary publisher at Macmillan/Picador, in conversation in October 1989.

generally accepted 1994 retail price) at £9.99 in order to benefit:

> . . . an excellent first novel, that might receive good reviews, but has little chance of turning them into sales. Or perhaps the second novel (often harder to sell than a first novel), or even the excellent new novel from an established author whose sales need that extra lift or push.[7]

This and the next chapter both examine more closely some of the changes that have occurred since the late 1970s, and accept (while attempting to analyse them in some detail) that they are in many ways interlinked. The aim is to portray the cultural atmosphere in which serious literary fiction is produced and consumed, or more specifically arouses passion on the part of those responsible for producing it and is enjoyed by those who are persuaded to purchase it, as the twenty-first century approaches.

The Booker Prize: History and Adjudication

The Booker Prize is the best-known of the awards whose prominence during the 1980s is associated in the public mind with the entrepreneurship that characterized the Thatcher decade. Indeed, a major aim of this chapter is to try to show *how* the general reader now makes significant use of the Booker Prize as a consumer guide to serious literary fiction.

Some readers may be surprised to learn that the Booker was initiated as long ago as 1968 and first awarded the following year.[8] Booker's model, as has always been admitted, was the Prix Goncourt, yet at £5,000 Booker's prize money was very

---

[7]Michael Neil, 'Something to Shout About at £9.99', *Bookseller*, 22 April 1994, p. 28. This W. H. Smith initiative follows a first, 'Fresh Talent', launched in 1990, and its successor 'Thumping Good Read'.

[8]In what follows I am indebted to material supplied by Book Trust (in particular to Christine Shaw and Sandra Vince, both of whom have allowed me access to material in Book Trust's archives), and to Martyn Goff's Introduction to his edited collection *Prize Writing* (London: Hodder & Stoughton/Sceptre, 1989), as well as to a subsequent conversation with Martyn Goff.

much higher. It was also high by the standards of the time in Britain; however, although the value of the award has since risen, it could just about be said to have kept pace with inflation during the past quarter-century. The prize-money was increased to £10,000 in 1978, rising further to £15,000 in 1984 and to £20,000 in 1989.

The monetary value of the Booker is worth considering at the outset, since it contrasts so strikingly with the minuscule amount awarded to Goncourt or Strega winners. Only the Booker and the Whitbread Prizes really have any significant impact on fiction sales, despite the immense amounts of prize money now on offer (as we will see below). Supposing high sales were the sole aim of the Booker, as they appear to be with the Goncourt or the Strega, would lowering the prize money contribute to this aim? The corollary of this speculation is the conclusion that the Goncourt and Strega juries do not necessarily set out to judge 'the best novel of the year', whatever that may be, but are more or less bound by tradition to select a serious literary novel that is not a formidably difficult read (in the case of the Strega, after intense lobbying by publishers). By those criteria, it might be said that a Booker winner such as James Kelman's *How Late It Was, How Late* could never have achieved success; other Booker winners, it might be argued, have lacked the *élan* that might have been expected in their Goncourt or Strega counterparts.

Although it is administered by Book Trust, with Colman Getty PR handling press aspects since 1994, the Booker Prize itself is financially backed by Booker plc, an international conglomerate specializing in three major sectors: poultry and plant-breeding (including farming and forestry), a range of aspects of the food processing industry (including fish and convenience foods) and food wholesaling and catering (in which sector of the UK food market it now has the largest share). The nature of Booker's culinary interests has been a source of quiet amusement to the foodies who populate the book industry, and arouses mildly ribald comment in the press coverage of the gastronomic aspect of the award ceremony.

Book Trust is an independent charity funded by Britain's Arts Council that aims to promote books and reading. Among the other prizes Book Trust sponsors, the most relevant for present purposes are the *Mail on Sunday*/ John Llewellyn Rhys Prize ('for the best work of literature . . . by a writer under 35') and the David Higham Prize ('for a first novel or book of short stories'). Book Trust's portfolio was expanded in 1994 by an interesting acquisition that failed to get off the ground: the Uni Prize ('for the best novel written by a woman') was to have been sponsored by the Mitsubishi Pencil Company at £30,000 until Mitsubishi withdrew after adverse press coverage in the late summer of 1994. The award was revived as the Orange Prize for Fiction in January 1996. The Booker Prize itself (still worth £20,000) is awarded 'for the best full-length novel'. The implications of this formula (What is 'best'? How short is 'full-length'? Does eligibility extend to 'faction' or documentary fiction – Thomas Keneally or even Pat Barker? Or to fiction in verse – Craig Raine or even Vikram Seth?) have proved complex.

The administrator of the Booker Prize has, from its inception, been Martyn Goff, who has carved out a unique position in Britain's literary world as a bookseller of independent means dedicated to bringing serious or 'quality' literary fiction to the attention of an increasingly large and variegated sector of the reading public. Goff has been the Booker Prize's one constant factor throughout the quarter-century of its existence: judges, appointed annually, have come and gone, and the constitution of the Booker Prize Management Committee has itself changed over the years.

The turnover of Booker plc in 1994 was £3.7bn and the group of companies employs 22,000 people worldwide.[9] It has moved into its present commanding position through earlier strengths in the sugar and engineering industry and, more relevantly for present purposes, through an interest – established in the 1960s – in buying the copyright of super-selling genre-fiction authors

[9]Source: 1995 Colman Getty PR press release.

such as Ian Fleming, Agatha Christie and Dennis Wheatley. It
may be inferred that the attraction of tax-shelter schemes was
particularly strong during the years of Harold Wilson's Labour
administration (1964–70), a time of unprecedentedly high
income tax for the wealthy (98 per cent in the top bracket).

We shall see that controversy has in many respects actually
been the making of the Booker Prize: among some thoughtful
and intelligent annual press comment there is always the fatuous
element, even (perhaps especially) in the highbrow literary press,
claiming that every Booker jury 'gets it wrong'. It is surely evident
that it is precisely by 'getting it wrong' that the Booker survives.[10]
Each year's Booker shortlist is to a greater or lesser extent by
definition a disappointment; in other words every year's selection
answers to what John Coldstream, writing in the *Daily Telegraph*
(6 September 1994), calls a 'something-for-everybody' list, a
'caricature', 'the essence of compromise'. Every decision, in
other words, must be more or less contentious. It's useful to
distinguish between the element of public good will amongst
the Booker-reading public and the business of serious literary
judgement. At the same time, I should state that I do not
endorse 'getting it wrong' as a particularly fine-tuned formula
for success: indeed, in some years more than others, Booker's
aims have seemed remarkably unfocused when contrasted with
the situation in other countries, as I try to show in passing in
this chapter.[11]

Roddy Doyle's 1993 success probably provides the best
example of a year in which these two elements – public good

---

[10]Mark Lawson makes a rather similar point in an elegant examination of
the arbitrariness of the adjudication process, 'Never mind the plot, enjoy
the argument', *Independent*, 6 September 1994. Lawson has the advantage
of having served as a Booker judge in 1992 (the year of the shortlisting
of Ian McEwan's remarkable *Black Dogs* and the joint award to Michael
Ondaatje and Barry Unsworth), and epigrammatically concludes that 'It's
the rows that keep [the Booker] going' (p. 12).

[11]Certain novelists who might normally have been expected to appear on a
Booker shortlist – John Fowles and Margaret Drabble among them – have
publicly declared that they do not wish their work to be put forward.

will and serious literary judgement – coincided, and others would include William Golding in 1980, Kingsley Amis in 1986, Peter Carey in 1988, Kazuo Ishiguro in 1989, A. S. Byatt in 1990 and Pat Barker in 1995. Conversely, no success will prevent a pronouncement such as that by Rabbi Julia Neuberger in 1994. As a Booker judge, Neuberger was 'implacably opposed' to that year's winner, James Kelman's *How Late It Was, How Late*, saying that she had felt 'outmanoeuvred' during the lengthy discussions prior to the judges' final decision. As Robert Winder, writing in the *Independent*, drily put it, '[f]or outmanoeuvred, read outvoted'.[12]

The Booker Prize rules have undergone a number of refinements over the years, responding to various kinds of changing reality, even sometimes themselves generating phenomena to which they have had to be adapted in order to create maximum commercial impact. There have been experiments with the number of shortlisted titles. In the early years 1969 through 1971 these amounted to six, but the identity of the winner was almost invariably leaked in advance. The size of the shortlist was then reduced so that by 1975 only two titles were shortlisted; it was once more raised the following year and the present set-up of six titles has prevailed since 1982, with a break in 1995 when only five novels were shortlisted. In 1974 the prize was shared, by Nadine Gordimer (*The Conservationist*) and Stanley Middleton (*Holiday*); this occurred again in 1992, when Michael Ondaatje (*The English Patient*) and Barry Unsworth (*Sacred Hunger*) shared the prize, and was all the more surprising as Martyn Goff had been quoted in the Autumn 1990 issue of *The Author* as saying:

> . . . dividing a prize does not halve but almost decimates the resulting impact and publicity. The [Management] Committee

---

[12]Robert Winder, 'Highly Literary and Deeply Vulgar', *Independent*, 13 October 1994, p. 18. The *Observer Review*'s 'Grapevine' column, 'How late it was and how cross it was', carried an 'inside account' of unusual acrimony (16 October 1994), p. 24.

were loth to make an absolute rule that henceforth the prize could never be divided, but left it to me to indicate annually in no uncertain terms that they hoped it would not again be split. And so far it has not been.

Goff's persuasive powers were evidently insufficient to the events of 1992 and his fears proved unduly pessimistic; in the event the co-winner who benefited more was Ondaatje, whose paperback sales had exceeded 140,000 by 1993. Unsworth had sold over 80,000.[13]

Since 1977 the judges have numbered five, including a Chair. Despite a popular perception of walkings-out, there have in fact been only two resignations in the history of the Booker Prize. In 1971 Malcolm Muggeridge resigned in highminded disgust at what he considered too much sexual candour in the novels under discussion; in a more bizarre spat twenty years later, in 1991, Nicholas Mosley (who, ironically, had as a novelist himself been on the first Booker shortlist in 1969) resigned in protest at the shortlist representing not a single novel of his choice, specifically Allan Massie's *The Sins of the Father* (1991). The Chair (in that case Jeremy Treglown) may in theory have had to give a casting vote as a result of the Mosley walk-out, but in principle such a vote is not felt to be in the Prize's interests, and Martyn Goff has only acknowledged it to have occurred once.[14] For practical reasons the judges are customarily resident

[13]Source: Alex Hamilton, in the 1995 *Writers' & Artists' Yearbook* (London: A. & C. Black, 1995), p. 260. Combined hardback sales of *The English Patient* and *Sacred Hunger*, as tracked by Bookwatch Ltd in the three months between sharing the award and January 1993, together exceeded by about 10 per cent the total hardback sales of Ben Okri's *The Famished Road* over the same period the previous year; they were, however, about two-thirds of those of A. S. Byatt's *Possession* over a similar period two years previously.

[14]This was in 1983; for details see Goff, *Prize Writing*, p. 16. Malise Ruthven, *A Satanic Affair* (1990; London: The Hogarth Press, 1991), p. 22, remarks that Salman Rushdie's 'disappointment at failing to win [the Booker] a second time with *Shame* was visible even to those who watched the presentation on television'. Rushdie's *Midnight's Children* was awarded the twenty-fifth anniversary 'Booker of Bookers' in December 1993.

in Britain; on a couple of occasions, however, visiting American academics (Samuel Hynes in 1981, Walton Litz in 1990) have acted as judges. In the early years judges from overseas included the writers Saul Bellow in 1971 and Mary McCarthy in 1973; desirable as this was, it has since proved impracticable as the deliberations have intensified.

Since much of the public reaction to a given year's shortlist and prize is directed at the judges, it is worth pausing briefly to make clear how they themselves are appointed. The Booker Prize Management Committee meets early each year primarily to discuss amending the rules (if necessary), and then to decide on a Chair for that year's proceedings. Booker's 1994 publicity leaflet names as its Management Committee the following: Sir Michael Caine, Chairman of Booker; his Booker colleagues Antony Haynes, Matthew Prichard, Anne Riddoch and Maggie van Reenen; the publishers Peter Straus and Ion Trewin, the librarian Alison Shute, the writer P. D. James, the bookseller Willie Anderson, with Martyn Goff as the Prize's Administrator. In the natural course of things there are resignations from the Management Committee from time to time, but how the resulting positions are subsequently filled remains not wholly clear. Martyn Goff is at pains to stress that the judges are chosen by the entire Management Committee, and not, as is sometimes maintained, by Goff himself.

It is customary for three possible Chairs to be nominated in order of preference, and it is apparently on the basis of the choice of Chair that the other judges are selected: that is, on grounds of compatibility or personal chemistry. A balance is sought through the presence of 'an academic, a critic or two, a writer or two and the man [*sic*] in the street'.[15] Each judge's honorarium is £3,000, with the Chair receiving an extra £500. Another few hundred pounds may be gained by a freelance account of that year's contest in the national press: each judge must presumably weigh up such perks against the task of reading about 120 books and

[15] Goff, *Prize Writing*, p. 18.

not necessarily supporting the shortlist or outcome. The 1995 list was a record: over 140 books were read. It is possible that the unprecedentedly high number of submissions in 1994 and 1995 led to the controversial change in the ruling for the 1996 award. According to this change, publishers may now submit a maximum of two titles instead of three; the number of previously shortlisted and winning authors has been drastically cut down; and the judges' 'calling in' prerogative has been extended. These changes, which have increased judges' influence at the expense of publishers', have understandably angered the latter, particularly those who have built up strong serious literary fiction lists.

Goff's laconic formulation is usually picked up annually by the literary press, yet there is no reason why London's literary life should be more or less incestuous than that of other cultural centres. In 1994, Iris Murdoch, who is married to that year's Chair John Bayley, properly withdrew *The Green Knight* (1993) from consideration; it had been shortlisted under the rule of automatic eligibility for previous winners. There were gleeful press reports of the surprisingly belated discovery of another of the 1994 judges, James Wood (at 29 surely the youngest to date), that a novel by his wife, Claire Messud's *When the World was Steady*, had also been submitted. In 1974 Elizabeth Jane Howard had been one of three judges in a year in which her then husband Kingsley Amis's *Ending Up* was considered seriously for the award. Suggestions that previous judges, shortlisted authors and winners should be excluded from further adjudicatory duty are pertinent, if not practical, when we realize that most years have seen at least one Booker judge whose work in other years has been, or would come to be, seriously considered for the Prize.

When I talked to Martyn Goff in November 1994, he made it clear that 'the man in the street' had now been dropped, largely because she or he was usually anyway a media celebrity in her or his own right – one thinks of Robin Ray in 1977, Libby Purves in 1983 or Joanna Lumley in 1985. Goff admitted that celebrity status can sometimes obscure the reviewing and academic credentials for which a more recent judge, such as Julia

Neuberger in 1994, has primarily been chosen. At the same time he made it clear that his own preference as to the make-up of an ideal team of Booker judges would exclude not just media celebrities but booksellers too, whom he felt might have too vested an interest in the outcome.

Goff's ideally matched team – personal chemistry allowing – would by now consist of a respected academic (not necessarily a literature specialist), a literary editor of a quality newspaper, a writer (preferably two) and a qualified reviewer. That this kind of team is a risky compromise is reflected in Goff's admission that literary editors and reviewers are increasingly subject to a conflict of loyalties between their own newspapers' interests and the protocol surrounding Booker secrecy. Although Booker judges are by common understanding supposed to refrain from any pre-award press announcements, or from comment on how other judges voted, it is clear that several such recent accounts have come close to breaking with that protocol. John Bayley's account of the 1994 proceedings arguably oversteps the mark.[16]

Despite Martyn Goff's defence of the make-up of the judging committee ('There has been none of Whitbread's doubtful employment of some non-reading celebrities for the last round': *The Author*, Autumn 1990), there remains the unpredictability of what John Sutherland has termed the 'Mary Wilson factor'.[17] By this I take Sutherland to mean that even though Goff's 'man in the street' may have been dropped, other judges may exercise an unpredictability in judgement that is unsuited to the Booker's terms of reference. In his defence Goff is probably right to stress the degree to which individual convictions are clearly altered in

[16]John Bayley, 'Diary', *LRB*, 10 November 1994, p. 33.
[17]John Sutherland, 'Exceptionally Wonderful Book', *LRB*, 6 October 1994, p. 15. Mary (now Lady) Wilson, wife of the then Labour Prime Minister Harold Wilson, was one of the judges in 1976, coincidentally the year of Wilson's unexpected resignation. Her choice was a calculated gamble, as she was actually the first 'general reader' to have taken part in the adjudication of the Booker Prize, then the eighth in its history. Mary Wilson's literary aspirations were at the time being parodied in *Private Eye*'s 'Mrs Wilson's Diary'.

discussion; a more cynical description of the process of personal chemistry would be that what the final decision comes down to is a form of horse-trading.

The 1984 team contained an interesting selection of maverick judges. The Chair, the historian Richard Cobb, was widely quoted as having claimed, apparently without remorse, that he had never read Proust or Joyce; and the Labour MP, Ted Rowlands, who had apparently been conscripted on to the panel 'to lower the brow', expressed his enthusiasm for what he called 'readability' and 'rather old-fashioned values', declaring himself deeply hostile to what he termed 'English middle-class novels about middle-aged hang-ups, sex and writers'.[18] The conundrum that the Booker has never really faced up to is that there is no real consensus as to what its terms of reference actually are. John Bayley's remarks as Chair ten years later were hard to read as other than pessimistic:

> Highbrow critics sometimes object that although the Booker is the most prestigious in the world of the English novel, all such prizes tend to commercialize art. I find this rubbish. On the contrary I think that fashion and pretension are the great enemies of all fine art today [. . .] In looking for good fiction I feel the Booker judges should make no distinction between different kinds of excellence in the genre. Personally I would be pleased to give the prize to a really good murder mystery or scientific fantasy or to a gripping tale about cooks or ikons, astronauts or tennis players – whatever had real and rare talent in its own line and is not merely modish junk, seeking to show off.[19]

[18]Quoted by Peter Kemp, 'Hobby-horsical' [review of LWT's Channel 4 coverage of the 1984 Booker-McCónnell Prize], *TLS*, 26 October 1984, p. 1216.

[19]John Bayley, excerpted from one of the 1994 Booker press releases distributed by Colman Getty PR. It is unclear whether by 'the English novel' Bayley means 'the novel in Britain' or 'the English-language novel', or whether he believes that the Booker's prestigiousness has now outstripped that of (say) the Pulitzer Awards.

On the other hand, there are many who feel that this is just the kind of statement that the general reader wants to hear. It does seem important to be able to distinguish reactionary philistinism from a judge's wish to protest at the promotion of a certain idea of what 'serious literary fiction' is (at the expense of 'real and rare talent in its own line'). Sutherland observes that '[n]o one would appoint Julia Neuberger, distinguished person though she is, to judge a high-diving competition' ('Exceptionally Wonderful Book'), but this argument can backfire since a literate diver or diving judge should surely have every right to judge the Booker. The Booker judges' judgements are clearly intended to be different in nature from their counterparts in the sporting world.

The Booker shortlist, however controversial, acts as a consumers' guide. Together with a further loose grouping of titles that have been touted by reviewers, promoted by bookstores as possible contenders, and publicized to a greater or lesser extent on the appearance of the actual shortlist and after the award of the prize, the entire constellation forms a kind of commercial 'canon' in the sense defined in the Introduction above as a dense mass of certainty surrounded by an ever-changing swirl of debate. How has this situation come about? And *does* it, thus described, really form an accurate assessment of public reaction to the promotion of fiction in Britain, an area of human endeavour somehow constantly seen as being in a state of crisis, yet buoyant nevertheless?

The Booker Prize: Rules and Mythology

At the time of the Booker's rise to fame during the early 1980s, the award was made every October, in a widely publicized TV ceremony, for a novel *bearing the publication date of that year*. This qualification, which applied to no other literary prize in Britain, was clearly intended to give the Booker Prize a topical edge that could not be matched by any of its competitors. In 1984 the Society of Authors noted with some disquiet that of the six titles shortlisted for that year's Booker Prize, three (at the time of their shortlisting in September) had still to be published. As a result the ruling was changed, so that from 1985 onwards, publishers now had to ensure that titles they wanted considered were published by 30 September. However, it was soon pointed out that this development would lead, as for a while it did, to the last three months of the year being moribund ones for the publication of significant new fiction.

In this way the Booker Prize came so dramatically to affect the economics of the book trade, ensuring the highest possible profile for the six shortlisted titles at the most auspicious time of year for book sales (the months September through December), that the rule was revised in the late 1980s. Any novel published between 1 October of the previous year and 30 September of the year in question is now eligible. A shrewd publisher can in effect bring about a 'double publication', by releasing a potential (but not all too well-known) winner early in the year, and capitalizing on press coverage in the event of its being shortlisted later the same year.[20]

By 1989 the rules relating to submission of titles had evolved to the point that any one publisher could nominate up to three novels for consideration, excluding titles from past winners. Until the rules changed again in 1996, each publisher was entitled to submit a list of a maximum further five titles, explicitly justifying its or their submission. In this sense, publishers too came to act as 'judges' in helping to influence the make-up of

[20]Recent data tracked by Bookwatch Ltd suggest a boost in the Booker winner's sales in the weeks immediately following the award, after which there is a slight decline before a further boost. This second boost can approach three times the October sales during and after the Christmas rush. That pattern was most marked with Roddy Doyle's *Paddy Clarke Ha Ha Ha* in 1993–94. Once a potential winner becomes a hot property in its own right, however, this caution can be dispensed with: thus Jonathan Cape brought out Salman Rushdie's *The Moor's Last Sigh* on 7 September 1995 with a massive promotional effort that obviated the need for 'double publication'.

the pile from which the unpublished 'long shortlist', and finally
the official shortlist, was chosen. An astute publisher might, for
instance, have included relatively unknown writers among the
three nominees, counting on the judges' prerogative to 'call in'
additional titles by the better-known novelists on a given year's
list, especially as after 1988 (when no extra titles were called
in) it was stipulated that the judges *must* call in between five
and fifteen of these listed (as opposed to nominated) titles. After
1996 the judges more than ever before reserve the right to call in
potential candidates that have not been nominated or listed.

Before the 1996 rule changes the situation was that by the
July or August of each year (the precise date depending on the
day in October or November for which the Guildhall, a clear
preference of Booker plc, has been reserved), a long list of
approximately twenty-five to thirty titles had been drawn up.
In the early days this used to be leaked but by the 1980s was
no longer released into the public domain. Each title on the long
list had to have majority support. All in all the total number of
titles from which both long and shortlist were drawn up could
amount to 120, although the 1994 figure was 130 and that for
1995 (as we have seen) over 140. Even under the new rules
the shortlisted titles continued to be announced in September
or early October, six weeks before the ceremony. The winner
is chosen from those six, and cannot (in principle at least) be
leaked because the judges are almost always in conclave right
up to the start of the presentation dinner.

In a perceptive memoir, David Lodge has pointed to two
aspects of the Booker Prize that do indeed, on the surface, seem
to mark the dramatic change that took place in its status at the
end of the 1970s and beginning of the 1980s.[21] The first was not
simply and nakedly to 'award' the prize – as had been the case
with the by today's standards obscure announcements of prizes
awarded in the late 1960s – but to *postpone* its announcement.
By delaying the judges' final decision until several weeks after

[21]David Lodge, 'Prized Winning', *The Author* (Spring 1990), p. 9.

the shortlist had been made public, Booker managed to create a potent brew of suspense and speculation. So much so that it has been taken up by Britain's betting industry, and it is now customary to find odds being offered on the six shortlisted titles from the time they have been made public. (The only odds-on favourite in Booker history, at 4/5 on, was Salman Rushdie's *The Moor's Last Sigh* in 1995, which failed to win.) It is the British propensity towards gambling that has led to talk of 'favourites' and 'runners-up' – in fact the contest does not officially recognize either term, but is clearly content to let each continue in currency. Lodge's second point is equally cogent, and that is that since 1981 Booker has collaborated with Britain's TV networks to ensure that the announcement of the award not only spawns suspense and speculation but is made live.

Early TV transmissions of the Booker award ceremony showed that the media had much to learn: in a celebrated exchange in 1983 ITV's Selina Scott enquired of that year's Chair, Fay Weldon, whether she had read the shortlisted books 'all the way through'. Much as Scott was mocked at the time, this was in the days when between 85 and 115 titles were submitted, and it's worth reflecting that the 1995 jury, at the start of the statutory six or seven months, must have had to contemplate a reading list of up to five books a week throughout that period. Later transmissions were handled more deftly by Melvyn Bragg (1984) and by Hermione Lee, who managed in a remarkable *coup* to track down the 1985 winner Keri Hulme for a live telephone interview from Salt Lake City, Utah, where she was lecturing. For a while London Weekend Television (LWT), as it then was, continued to transmit the proceedings on Channel Four, but coverage transferred to the BBC in 1988.

Until the BBC2 *Late Show* was axed in 1995, its presenter Sarah Dunant adroitly chaired studio discussions with both disaffected and enthusiastic experts asked to comment on the shortlisted titles while an on-site reporter (in the past few years this was Dunant's *Late Show* colleague Tracy McLeod) covered the lengthy gastronomic preface to the final announcement live from London's Guildhall. Dunant's recent studio guests have included A. S. Byatt, Germaine Greer and Tom Paulin. In 1994 the *Late Show*'s studio was actually set up within the dining area itself. This proved a success, and the Dunant-McLeod team was recalled for a Booker Prize special in 1995 (which some TV reviewers saw as having become a parody of itself), their guests being Bill Buford, Howard Jacobson and Michèle Roberts.

Lodge's argument can, I think, be enhanced. It should not be forgotten that the pre-1980s way of doing things does still continue. Thus on 12 May 1994, in an absence of any media razzmatazz, V. S. Naipaul presided over the Society of Authors' annual award ceremony at the Middle Temple Hall in London; this involved the distribution of as much as £89,000 worth of prize money divided over more than twenty separate awards. The Society of Authors' winners, as is customary, were known beforehand, and the evening's event was in that sense purely ceremonial, without any Booker suspense element; although no individual award approached Booker value, the total sums of money involved have become considerable. Lodge's argument also overlooks what we may term 'the Booker mythology'. Let us turn to some aspects of this briefly before pushing some of its implications further towards a more studied examination of the kind of award the Booker has become by the mid 1990s.

The aspect of the Booker Prize that has come under the most scrutiny during the past fifteen years or so is whether it is really awarded to 'the best full-length novel' of the year (in whatever way a board of judges may choose to assess that imponderable question), or whether there are other, hidden, agendas. Have there been years in which it has been awarded to a deserving novelist who had failed to win despite being shortlisted in a previous year, even though the novel that failed had arguably been 'better'?

The case has been put for the 1988 winner. Peter Carey's *Oscar and Lucinda* was seen by some as a consolation prize for what was even by Booker standards a controversial decision in 1985, when the award went to Keri Hulme for *The Bone*

People – a novel recently described, incorrectly, as 'the most commercially disastrous winner ever'[22] – despite the presence of Carey's *Illywhacker* on the list. It could be argued that the award to Pat Barker for *The Ghost Road* in 1995 (whether consciously or not) took account of the fact that the winning book was the culmination of a highly acclaimed trilogy.

Has the award ever been seen as a crowning achievement to a distinguished career? That case could have been made about the 1977 award, although it was clearly fitting that Philip Larkin's comments as Chair did not do so. Paul Scott, who was at the time dying of cancer, was presented with the award *in absentia* for *Staying On*, a coda to his epic *Jewel in the Crown* tetralogy. There was intense speculation after the publication of Angela Carter's novel *Wise Children* in 1991, when Carter, too, was terminally ill, that it might at least be shortlisted, but it was not. After Carter's death in February 1992, Susannah Clapp's obituary pointed out that Carter 'was never treated as the object of automatic acclaim and deference that the welter of huge obituaries might suggest . . . [S]he never won the Whitbread, was not once even shortlisted for the Booker Prize'.[23]

The near-posthumous award of the Booker Prize to Scott in 1977, and its 'withholding' from Carter in 1991 indicate something of the momentousness an award can achieve in the public eye. My own view is that the 1977 award was one of the more significant in early Booker history. Its popularity was compounded when looked at in the light of an appallingly ironic tragedy that occurred less than two years later. During the summer of 1979 the death was announced of the 1973 winner, J. G. Farrell, at the age of only 43. It was possible to link Farrell's death with his receipt of the award, for with the

---

[22]*Evening Standard*, 13 September 1990. This claim fails to take account of New Zealand and Australasian sales of titles such as Hulme's – and indeed Carey's and Keneally's. It was claimed, when the 1994 shortlist was announced, that 'David Storey's 1976 winner, *Saville*, is out of print and has been deleted by the publisher' (*Independent*, 6 September 1994).
[23]Susannah Clapp, 'Diary', *LRB*, 12 March 1992, p. 25.

money that he had won in 1973 for *The Siege of Krishnapur* Farrell had acquired a small property in Bantry Bay, Ireland. Farrell, who was slightly disabled, drowned there, it appears after being unable to rescue himself in a fishing accident. It would appear then that as a result of the deaths of Scott and Farrell, the Booker Prize was already beginning, by 1980, the year of the Golding–Burgess two-horse race, to acquire an almost mythic aura, as an award different not only in degree but also in kind from its competitors.

The Booker Prize: Eligibility and Nationality

The term 'Booker-eligibility' is widely used in the publishing world. To recapitulate: the Booker Prize is open not only to citizens of Britain and the Commonwealth (an entity which comprises a quarter of the world's population), but also to those of the Irish Republic, Pakistan and Bangladesh. South Africa had also been eligible before it rejoined the Commonwealth following the first multi-racial elections in 1994. The terms of eligibility make the award available to the majority of the world's English-speaking population (to those countries, that is, in which English is either a native or official language). The sole significant exception is the United States. The origins of these rules of eligibility have primarily to do with the way the international book market has traditionally been divided.[24]

The implications of these developments during the past fifteen years or so cannot be underestimated. Where the novel in English was formerly simply British and American in the public view, Booker-eligibility has gradually enabled the literary energy that was once at the former Empire's centre and directed outwards to the colonial periphery, by a process of post-colonial transference,

[24]The advent of the integrated European market has encouraged the founding, in 1990, of the Aristeion Prizes, as they are now known, which consist of the European Literary Prize and the European Translation Prize.

to be directed back at the enfeebled centre. The result is a literature that is significantly different in kind, tone and experience
from the mainstream serious literary American novel.

In this way, the history of the Booker Prize has been the history
of the replacement of 'the English novel' by 'the novel [published]
in Britain' since about 1980. This realization necessitates discussion of what 'Englishness' and 'Britishness' now mean in terms
of the production and consumption of fiction in Britain.

During the 1960s a number of perceptive commentators began
to express genuine pessimism about the future of the English
novel. An elegiac note is sounded in one of the best surveys of
the post-war period, Bernard Bergonzi's *The Situation of the
Novel* (1970). This book, which is still available, was reissued
in slightly updated form in 1979. Although one of its chapters
is entitled 'The Ideology of Being English', and a few writers
of the generation of Ian McEwan and Martin Amis had made
a precocious start to their careers, neither is mentioned in the
reissue. Indeed, it is sadly ironic that one of Bergonzi's few
great hopes was the Anglo-Irish writer J. G. Farrell. Proofs
of *The Singapore Grip* (1978) became available to Bergonzi
just before his reissue went to press, so allowing him a brief
impressionistic and certainly positive response to what turned
out to be Farrell's last completed novel. In the main part of his
book, however, Bergonzi was forced to concede that in the face
of fiction emanating from the United States in the 1960s Britain's
mainstream for the most part looked timid, unadventurous, reactionary, small-scale, and above all solipsistically inward-looking.
Most worryingly of all, the malaise seemed particularly to be
affecting the younger novelists, who should on any optimistic
analysis have been leading the way. For Bergonzi and others,
such an attitude contrasted all too clearly with that of (to name
but one) John Barth in the United States, some of whose most
exciting work belongs precisely to that decade.

Recently, John Sutherland has asserted that the events of
1972 (when John Berger, having won the Booker Prize but
denounced the sources of the wealth behind it), 'for all that

[Berger's speech was] mocked, have had a palpable influence in politically correcting the shortlist' ('Exceptionally Wonderful Book'). The first two Booker shortlists, in 1969 and 1970, were almost exclusively British, with the exception of the Irish writer William Trevor in 1970. In 1971, V. S. Naipaul won the prize with *In a Free State* (he would be shortlisted again in 1979 with *A Bend in the River*), and Mordecai Richler's *St Urbain's Horseman* was shortlisted. Naipaul has lived in Britain for most of his adult life; and Richler, who has retained his Canadian citizenship, was at this time also living in London (he was to be shortlisted again in 1990). In 1972, and again in 1975 and 1979, the Australian Thomas Keneally was on the shortlist, and in 1974 the South African Nadine Gordimer was joint winner. The Irish-born Brian Moore made the first of several appearances in 1976 (he would be on the list again in 1987 and 1990), as did the South African André Brink (who was shortlisted again in 1978). Probably the only writer from this group who at the time was relatively unknown in Britain was Keneally, with Gordimer, Moore and Brink occupying an intermediate category. Such developments had been noticed as early as 1975 by John Sutherland.

Things can be seen to have changed even more rapidly towards the end of the 1970s. From 1980 to 1995, ten out of seventeen Booker winners were British nationals, and they were awarded their prizes in 1980, 1981, 1984, 1986, 1987, 1989, 1990, 1992, 1994 and 1995 (these figures take account of the joint win in 1992).[25] But of these ten, two (Salman Rushdie and Kazuo Ishiguro) began life in different cultures from the one they came to settle in, and one (James Kelman), though by strict definition British, holds to an uncompromisingly nationalistic view of his citizenship.[26] By these more realistic criteria that figure of ten

[25]See Appendix A.
[26]This is a political stance. In 1989 Kelman was absent from the Guildhall and had apparently prepared a non-acceptance speech for his agent to give. He was present to receive the award in 1994, but studiously avoided the black-tie convention.

drops to seven (or eight) Britons out of seventeen – just over a third. From 1969 to 1979, out of thirteen winners (this figure takes account of the 1974 tie between Nadine Gordimer and Stanley Middleton), the only awards to non-British-born writers – apart from that to Gordimer – were made to Naipaul in 1971 and Ruth Prawer Jhabvala (*Heat and Dust*, 1975): a total of three. The development of the shortlist also reflects this pluralist trend. The shortlist was almost exclusively British until 1974. The term 'British', as already indicated, poses complex problems of definition. It is insufficient, if not insulting, to writers who are Welsh, Scottish or Irish, and it is inadequate to writers who are English. 'British' is only part of what being an 'English' writer is, despite the seat of British power being also the seat of English government. Given this point, apart from the Irish writers Jennifer Johnston, Brian Moore and William Trevor, the only writer not possessing British or Irish citizenship to be shortlisted (and not to win) prior to 1979 was André Brink (1976 and 1978). Trevor's position is the longest established of those 'home' writers mentioned here.

The first writer from the Indian subcontinent to be shortlisted was Anita Desai in 1980, and the first to win was Salman Rushdie in 1981. The first Australian to win was Thomas Keneally in 1982, and the first South African winner from an English-speaking liberal Afrikaner background (that is, a background culturally distinct from Nadine Gordimer's but similar to André Brink's) was J. M. Coetzee in 1983. The first New Zealander to win was Keri Hulme in 1985; the first black African, the Nigerian Ben Okri, won in 1991. Okri, at 31, is the youngest winner to date; Chinua Achebe, a generation older, had been the first black African to be shortlisted, in 1987. The first Canadian winner, Michael Ondaatje, shared the prize in 1992; his compatriots Alice Munro (1980), Margaret Atwood (1986 and 1989), Robertson Davies (1986) and Mordecai Richler (1971 and 1990) have all been shortlisted. The first Scot to win was James Kelman in 1994 in a year whose shortlist contained a Tanzanian writer (Abdulrazak Gurnah) and a Sri Lankan writer

(Romesh Gunesekera); Kelman had also been shortlisted in 1989. The first British writer with an African-Caribbean background to be shortlisted was Caryl Phillips in 1993. These recent postcolonial presences have prompted criticisms of 'tokenism' that are hard to rebut for a number of reasons. There is no doubt that, as John Sutherland's 1975 analysis makes clear, there was an initial disinclination to include non-British or Irish writers who were not already world names; it seems fairer to put this down to a mixture of ignorance, timidity and complacency rather than to outright prejudice. In this way, Ruth Prawer Jhabvala's success with *Heat and Dust* in 1975 becomes remarkable in itself as well as testifying to the courage of that year's judges (Angus Wilson, Peter Ackroyd, Susan Hill and Roy Fuller).

Sutherland's much more recent suggestion that Berger's 1972 outburst helped to sanitize the Britain-centredness of the Booker is certainly persuasive. At the same time, it should not be forgotten that London remains the publishing centre for the vast majority of Booker-eligible fiction. Even the most nationalist-minded Scottish and Irish novelists find it at times impossible to resist being published in London.[27] After all, each year's Booker 'winners' are not just the novelists and their books: the winners include publishers and agents who are positioned to negotiate foreign and film rights. This view has been possible since the late 1970s, but the idea that a certain kind of novelist may actually deliberately set out to write a 'generic' Booker winner was probably raised seriously for the first time as early (or as late) as 1987, with Penelope Lively's *Moon Tiger* seen to possess many of the 'epic' qualities, and much of the exotic setting (a gratuitous exoticism, it was felt by some),[28] that was to lead to

[27]For further comment on Scottish writers, see Chapter 4 below; the case about Ireland is made (controversially) in the *Bookseller*, 25 March 1994: p. 19, in the context of a discussion of Roddy Doyle's unprecedented hardback success (for a Booker Prize winner) and the dividends thereby paid off to Secker & Warburg.

[28]Malcolm Bradbury makes a similar point about the epic historical subject and the 1992 Booker Prize list; see his *The Modern British Novel* (1993; London: Penguin, 1994), pp. 452–53.

the commercial and filmic but not outright Booker success of one of the lasting shortlisted titles of its year, J. G. Ballard's *Empire of the Sun* (1984). The Spielberg movie of this title is far less faithful to the novel than is Spielberg's later *Schindler's List*, with Ballard's name very hard to pick out among the credits.

The implications of the pluralist trend sketched above are worth dwelling on briefly. The Booker winners in 1973, 1975, and particularly 1977 (when Paul Scott won with *Staying On*), all had a retrospective air of nostalgia for Britain's Raj, even though it may have been diffused through a layer of gentle and at times surreal irony, as was particularly the case with Farrell's and Scott's work. With Salman Rushdie's success in 1981 with *Midnight's Children*, a complete up-ending occurred whose implications took some time to sink in. Not only was Rushdie's novel far more experimental and internationally aware – his reading of Latin American fiction was innovative in a Booker context: of still greater significance was the fact that the viewpoint was now not British but Indian, not that of the colonizer but of the colonized. This postcolonial dimension probably only became fully apparent to Rushdie's readers after the subsequent publication of *Shame* (1983) and the polemical *Granta* essay 'Outside the Whale' (1984).[29]

The most important point, however, was that Rushdie's 1981 success created a precedent that enabled commentators to conceive of the Booker as a prize administered in Britain but offering English-speaking readers a panoramic, international and intensely *current* view of 'fiction in Britain'. In turn the events of 1981 created a climate in which the exclusion of fiction from United States writers initiated an interesting process of disconnection of British and American preoccupations and interests from each other, rather than intensifying what had become a kind of competitiveness in which British fiction

[29] This essay first appeared in *Granta* and has been collected in Salman Rushdie, *Imaginary Homelands* (London: Granta, 1991), pp. 87–101. Such remains the power of Rushdie's polemic that it is not now possible to assess Scott's work without taking account of 'Outside the Whale'.

must always lose (as it had seemed to Bernard Bergonzi in the 1970s).

All this unprecedented exposure of fiction from English-speaking countries other than the United Kingdom or the United States led to an increasingly global picture of fiction in Britain during the course of the 1980s. It is now the case that the line-up of half or more of a typical late 1980s or 1990s Booker shortlist is not centred on Britain. This reflects a new public awareness of Britain as a pluralist society, and has transformed the view that prevailed in the 1960s, that English-language fiction from 'abroad' meant fiction from the United States.

This kind of realization depends not on a view of the Commonwealth as an anachronistic construct favoured by the British sovereign and the political establishment but rather on a view of the 'postcolonial' as a dynamic cultural force with values and assumptions that compel serious attention. It can even be argued that realizing the English language as a *shared* cultural fund had to occur if 'the English novel' was to transform itself from the moribund state it had entered by the mid 1960s and arise phoenix-like from its own ashes as 'fiction [published] in Britain', part of a new global literature. Among recent consequences of this development is an accompanying need on the part of English novelists to redefine themselves in its light. 'British' is, after all, as much a mythical concept for 'English' as it is for 'Scottish', 'Irish' and 'Welsh' writers: in this sense all are equal partners under the heading 'British fiction' and contributors to the wider concept of 'fiction in Britain'.

Gender, seniority and generation are also important considerations in a section that has emphasized the increase in pluralism, and the related controversy concerning 'tokenism'. Of the twenty-nine winners (including joint winners) between 1969 and 1995, ten (about a third) have been women. There have been all-male shortlists in 1976 and (more controversially) in

1991. Although the 1973 shortlist consisted of three women out of a total of four names, the award went to the one male, J. G. Farrell. Subsequently, shortlisted women have been in a majority only in 1985: these were the winner Keri Hulme, Doris Lessing, Jan Morris and Iris Murdoch.[30]

Since the standardization of the shortlist in 1982, three Chairs have been women (Fay Weldon in 1983, P. D. James in 1987 and Victoria Glendinning in 1992); in only one of these years was the winner a woman: Penelope Lively in 1987. Although women are clearly under-represented on the shortlists and as Chairs, there is somewhat less inequality if one takes the judging panel as a whole. Looking at each year's judges, again for consistency's sake since 1982, when each year's panel has consisted of five judges including the Chair, we can see that out of the seventy-four, forty-three have been male and thirty-two female.[31] In ten years men have been in a majority, in five they have been in a minority. It is troubling to have to note that the gender ratio in women's favour has recently *decreased*, with only one year, 1990, containing more female than male judges between 1988 and 1995. In those eight years, out of forty judges twenty-six have been male.[32]

The overall decrease in women judges is really the only trend that can be deduced since 1988. In fact it is impossible to draw any conclusions other than to point to trends. The 1994 Management panel consisted of six men and three women; of the four members representing Booker plc two were men and two women. While it is true that the majority of London's

[30]Although in 1984, 1987, 1989 and 1990 three women and three men were shortlisted. In every other year, male writers have dominated the shortlist.
[31]Up to and including the announcement of the 1995 Booker Prize committee. In fact there have been five judges since 1977; in the period 1977 to 1981, the Chair was male in each case, and the panel contained one or two women. No 'trend' in this respect is really discernible before 1982.
[32]In three of those years, 1988, 1993 and 1994, women have been outnumbered four to one. Prior to 1988, this imbalance occurred in only one year, 1984, and between 1982 and 1987 women were in a majority on four out of six occasions, in 1986 by four to one.

fiction publishers are men, the gender balance among literary agents is less unfavourable to women. It would be foolish in the extreme to argue that all women are equally likely to press the claims of all women writers, but in 1985, the only year in which shortlisted women were in a majority, at least two and arguably all three women judges could be regarded as sympathetic to the claims of women writers. Yet the 1983 panel was chaired by Fay Weldon, one of its members was Angela Carter, and the shortlist contained five male authors. Yet again, the 1986 four-women-to-one-man panel could not be regarded as 'progressive' in gender-political terms as had been those of 1983 and 1985. It is accordingly less surprising to find that only one woman was shortlisted in 1986. The biggest gender-political controversy came in fact in 1989, when there was serious disagreement about Martin Amis's *London Fields*. Amis's book was not shortlisted, according to the then Chair, David Lodge, 'due to the strong objections of two members of the jury'. It is now clear that these objections came from the two women, Maggie Gee and Helen McNeil, but subsequent accounts of the proceedings from those concerned have been hard to reconcile with one another. Lodge has been frankest in recording his 'great regret' at Amis's non-inclusion.[33]

It seems then, to sum up, that charges of 'tokenism' apply more to race than gender; that women (let alone women of colour) are damagingly under-represented on shortlists (twenty-five out of eighty-three since 1982) and as Chairs (three out of fourteen since 1982), less so as judges; that even as judges go a new era of male domination seems to have dawned; and that correlations between judging panels and shortlists that take account of gender can support a number of contradictory conclusions.

Turning to the issue of generation, we can observe that, in 1978 and 1980, the Booker went to two of Britain's most distinguished senior novelists, Iris Murdoch and William

---

[33]David Lodge, 'The Novelist Today: Still at the Crossroads?', in Malcolm Bradbury and Judy Cooke, eds., *New Writing Today* (London: Minerva in association with the British Council, 1992), p. 208.

Golding respectively. The award in 1980 was of particular interest, not only because it heralded the impact of Booker success on actual sales, but because it was (as indicated above) the first to be seen as a two-horse race. Golding was apparently strongly challenged by only one other novelist of comparable stature, Anthony Burgess, whose *Earthly Powers* then went on to win the *Yorkshire Post* Book Award. This public interest was further galvanized by the 1981 list, which was perhaps overall the strongest in Booker history. In 1985 Iris Murdoch and Doris Lessing were both shortlisted even though neither won. Although Kingsley Amis won in 1986, the 1980 clash of the Titans now seems increasingly remote. Yet 1980 and to a lesser extent 1985 and 1986 were salutary reminders that the Booker Prize was not merely concerned to notice younger, promising but less well-established writers.

Competition: The Trask Awards, the Whitbread Awards, the *Sunday Express* Award, the Commonwealth Writers Prize and Others

From about 1975 until the early 1980s, with a particular boost in the high-profile years 1980 and 1981, no other prize could rival the Booker financially. However, in 1983 the Society of Authors announced the death of the reclusive Betty Trask. With this came the astonishing news that Trask had bequeathed the bulk of an estate valued at around £400,000 to the Society, subject to the creation of a charitable trust for the purpose of providing a literary prize to a young author below the age of 35. This prize would be awarded 'on the strength of a romantic novel or other novel of a traditional rather than experimental nature'.

Trask had been a member of the Society of Authors; little was known about her except that she lived frugally in the Somerset town of Frome. Certainly not even those who professed acquaintance with her had guessed at the extent of her wealth, which was largely inherited. The Trask award money was to be used for a period or periods of foreign travel. Unpublished typescripts could be included for consideration.

It was soon afterwards being speculated in the press that the prize might be worth up to £40,000 annually. The Society of Authors took a more cautious line and suggested that, if the estate were sensibly invested, the total prize money might be around £25,000. This indeed proved to be the case.

In its first years the Trask award money was shared by more than one winner, with the maximum awarded to any one successful candidate never amounting to more than half this figure. There were four winners in 1990, and even though a single award was made in 1991, the Betty Trask Awards attracted little public attention after 1984. Even so, joint winners have included writers such as Candia McWilliam, for *A Case of Knives* (1988), and Nicholas Shakespeare, for *The Vision of Eleanor Silves* (1989). Amit Chaudhuri was the single Trask winner in 1991 with *A Strange and Sublime Address*.

A more significant development, one exercising a subtler effect on Britain's literary prize culture during the mid 1980s, was the emergence of the Whitbread Awards. In 1985 the hitherto modest prize money allocated to the Whitbread Awards was raised substantially so that the overall winner would receive £17,500. At the same time the old Whitbread categories were expanded from three to five: biography or autobiography, fiction, poetry, first novel, and children's fiction. It seems that Whitbread were looking for a 'rival' formula, and the one that most fits the bill is that under which the American Pulitzer Prizes are administered. By 1995, the total Pulitzer prize money stood at over $60,000, but only $3,000 goes to the winner in any one category, and only one of the categories is for 'distinguished fiction by an American author, preferably dealing with American life'.[34] There are three Pulitzer categories: Prizes in Journalism (fourteen awards), Prizes

[34]Source: 'The Pulitzer Prizes: Plan of Award', Columbia University, New York, NY 10027 (May 1995).

in Letters (six awards), and a single Prize in Music. There is no overall category winner, however.

From 1985, the Whitbread category winners would be announced in November, after the Booker Prize had been awarded, and in effect constituted, in contrast to the Pulitzer Prizes, a shortlist for the Whitbread Book of the Year. The overall prize work, which is therefore not necessarily a novel, would collect the £17,500 prize money in January of the year following; the other four writers would enjoy the prestige of having won in their category and a consolation prize of £1,000.

In 1986 the poet Douglas Dunn was the first winner of the big £17,500 prize with his collection *Elegies*. In 1987 Kazuo Ishiguro won with *An Artist of the Floating World*. Ishiguro's novel had also been on the 1986 Booker shortlist – was the Whitbread committee attempting to upstage the Booker Prize? Debate on this point was suspended in 1988, when the Ulster writer Christopher Nolan, who has suffered cerebral palsy from birth, won with his autobiography *Under the Eye of the Clock*. Like all his work, this book had been painstakingly produced: his mother would hold his head steady while with a stick attached to his forehead Nolan would type letter by letter. Nolan was closely pursued by a fellow Irishman, the poet Seamus Heaney, for his collection *The Haw Lantern*, and by Ian McEwan, for *The Child in Time*. That novel had been widely tipped for the 1987 Booker Prize but did not even appear on what was generally considered the least adventurous Booker shortlist since 1984. By the early 1990s it seemed that one of the roles of the Whitbread was to offer the possibility of challenging the Booker in what might in the public view be regarded as a 'weak' Booker year. In 1987 the Whitbread money was raised to £18,000, while the Booker Prize remained unchanged at £15,000 until 1989; in 1995 the Booker Prize money stood at £20,000, while the Whitbread category winners now each won £2,000, with the overall prize winner taking an extra £21,000.

What lay behind the Whitbread changes of 1985? The 1984

Booker shortlist was unusually conservative in character, all the more so since from 1980 onwards the expectation had gradually gained ground that the shortlist really was increasingly becoming a kind of clearing-house for what was new and in some sense definitive in fiction in Britain. There was a widespread feeling that in a 'strong' Booker year only J. G. Ballard's *Empire of the Sun* (the Ladbroke's favourite), and Julian Barnes's *Flaubert's Parrot* would have made it to the shortlist, and that the others did not really deserve their place there. There were muted voices from the academic and quality-reviewing community endorsing the prize-winner, *Hotel du Lac* (a novel that was later televised) by Anita Brookner, a distinguished art-historian turned novelist; but in general it was felt that the 1984 events represented a retrograde step in the direction of the small-scale, parochial type of English novel that seemed an unlikely advertisement for the new mood of the mid 1980s. Even authoritative admirers of Brookner's work such as Frank Kermode apparently do not regard *Hotel du Lac* as her best.[35]

Among the more disturbing omissions from the 1984 list were a major new novel, *The Only Problem*, by Muriel Spark; and more worryingly still the most ambitious novels to date by two younger writers: Angela Carter's *Nights at the Circus* and Martin Amis's *Money: A Suicide Note*. These last two were almost certainly too sexually explicit for the 1984 judges, but have since received academic discussion as extensive as any of their competitors with the exception of Barnes.[36] It would probably be fair to conclude that the reputations of Brookner and Barnes were consolidated, commercially as well as artistically, for the

[35]See Frank Kermode, 'Losers' [first published *LRB*, 5 September 1985], in *The Uses of Error* (Cambridge MA: Harvard UP, 1991), pp. 369–75.
[36]It is significant that, in a wonderfully perceptive comparative account urging the influence of Virginia Woolf on Angela Carter, Isobel Armstrong, in 'Woolf by the Lake, Woolf at the Circus: Carter and Tradition', sets up a contrast between Carter and Brookner in the apparent – but mistaken – belief that both writers were shortlisted for the 1984 Booker Prize. See Lorna Sage, ed., *Flesh and the Mirror: Essays on the Art of Angela Carter* (London: Virago, 1994), pp. 257ff.

first time by their inclusion on the 1984 shortlist, and that those of Amis and Carter were equally so, precisely because of their omission.

If 1984 can be thought to have represented an opportunity missed by the judges, it could be argued that the Whitbread committee used the modest outcry to move enterprisingly into the field by each year allowing the suggestion to grow that the overall Whitbread Award might go to a novel that had been shortlisted for the Booker but had not won, or had not even been shortlisted – or it might go to some other category of writing altogether.[37]

Here, again, it is useful to turn briefly for comparative purposes to France and Italy. Until recently it was not possible for the Goncourt winner to be awarded any other prize (or vice versa). In France the two 'rival' prizes would by general consent be the Prix Médicis and the Prix Femina. Italy has had no such stipulation, and the two 'rival' prizes to the Strega are the Premio Viareggio, which is awarded in Venice, and the Premio Campiello, which is awarded in Rome. It is not unknown for one novel to win both of these Italian prizes in a particular year. They, together with their French counterparts, are perhaps awarded to even more 'serious' literary fiction (understood here as potentially challenging and

[37]In recent years The Netherlands has established an award – the AKO prize – that combines features of the Booker and the Whitbread. Since 1992, an initial 'long shortlist' of around twenty or so titles has been released about three months before the due date, an idea that has from time to time been mooted as a Booker possibility. The AKO list is followed up six weeks later by a shortlist consisting of six titles. The winner, announced at a TV dinner ceremony, is invariably leaked and generically the award is not confined to fiction. AKO lacks the Whitbread emphasis on categorization, and unlike the Whitbread it allows travel writing to be considered. It may be best thought of as finding its way towards an optimal formula at the present moment, rather like the evolution of the Booker during the 1970s; however, the 1994 organizers seem to have gone for a kind of Eurovision or Olympic format, with points being awarded by each judge. For a language-area consisting of only about 20 million speakers (Flemish literature is also eligible), AKO permits a remarkably high number of titles – well over 100 – to be admitted to the first round. The 1993 winner, Margriet de Moor's *First Grey, Then White, Then Blue*, was the first AKO Prize winner to be translated into English.

difficult) than the Goncourt or Strega, but even so, winners of these 'rival' prizes can command sales as high as 400,000 or more in each country. Again, their financial value is nothing like the five-figure sterling prizes under review here.

In January 1988 the first *Sunday Express* Award was made: at that time it topped the list financially, standing at £20,000 until the Booker Prize money was raised to the same level. The *Sunday Express* Award profiles itself, in a fashion not wholly complimentary to its winners, as more downmarket, more explicitly as what it has termed a less 'snooty' version of the Booker. It tends to go for genre-fiction titles, the 1988 winner, Brian Moore's *The Colour of Blood*, one of the 1987 Booker Prize shortlisted writers, being a distinguished example.

By 1990, the Booker, Trask, Whitbread and *Sunday Express* awards had been joined by several other competitors. These included the Commonwealth Writers Prize, which was founded in 1987 and is administered from Guelph, Ontario; and the *Irish Times*-Aer Lingus Literary Prizes, administered from Dublin, which were founded in 1989.

In 1990 the Commonwealth Writers Prize Best Book category, standing at £10,000, was won by the Booker-shortlisted Mordecai Richler with *Solomon Gursky Was Here*. The overall prize is the winner out of a number of regional categories (Africa; Canada and the Caribbean; South-East Asia and the South Pacific; and Eurasia), all of which are awarded £1,000. There is also a Best First Book award of £3,000.

As we have seen, the 1990 *Irish Times*-Aer Lingus International Fiction Prize (IR£25,000) went to the Booker Prize winner of that year, A. S. Byatt with *Possession*. John McGahern, also tipped for the 1990 Booker Prize, did, however, win the *Irish Times* Irish Literature Prize in the fiction category, an award amounting to IR£10,000. Although the writer must be Irish, the winning Irish Literature Prize title itself can have been published in Ireland, Britain or the United States; the terms of the *Irish Times*-Aer Lingus International Fiction Prize included Irish, British and United States authors: the first such award in 1989 had gone to Don DeLillo for *Libra*. By 1994 this latter award had become the *Irish Times* International Fiction Prize, with the same terms of eligibility as for the former *Irish Times*-Aer Lingus Literary Prizes – but as a result of the withdrawal of Aer Lingus the prize money had dropped from IR£25,000 to IR£10,000.

Another prize (not in the same financial category but enjoying a prestige exceeded only by the Booker and the Whitbread) that negotiates the space between profiling itself distinctively and picking up Booker 'leavings' is the *Guardian* Prize for Fiction (£2,000). Interestingly, it went to Pat Barker's *The Eye in the Door* in 1993, two years before Barker won the Booker with *The Ghost Road*. The *Yorkshire Post* Literary Award was most famously made for fiction in 1980, when it went to Anthony Burgess for *Earthly Powers*, apparently as a consolation prize for Burgess having lost the Booker to William Golding's *Rites of Passage*.

Also deserving of mention is a prize that will become increasingly important as the 1990s proceed. The European Literary and Translation Awards were founded in 1990 and permit member countries of the EU to nominate their best works of literature and translation over the past three years. The award money is a relatively modest 20,000 ecus (about £14,000).[38] The awards now constitute the more elegantly named Aristeion Prize. Claus Bech's *Besættelse*, the Danish translation of A. S. Byatt's *Possession*, was recently shortlisted for this award, the citation describing it as 'brilliant and satisfying', and asserting that it 'sets a new standard for the translation of literature into Danish'.

To this list may be added a new financial record-breaker: the David Cohen British Literature Prize in the English Language, which is awarded biennially. The Cohen Prize, worth £30,000, went to V. S. Naipaul in its first year (1993) and to Harold

---

[38]Sources: *Writers' & Artists' Yearbook 1992* (London: A & C. Black, 1992), pp. 560–85; Barry Turner, ed., *The Writer's Handbook 1992* (London: Macmillan, 1991), pp. 507–40. Nominated fiction titles from Britain for the 1992 award included Martin Amis's *London Fields* and A. S. Byatt's *Possession*. Neither won.

Pinter in its second (1995). It carries an interesting clause: the winner receives an extra £10,000 to commission new work with the aim of encouraging younger writers and readers.[39]

To quote from the announcement made early in 1994 before the Mitsubishi withdrawal, the Uni Prize 'has grown out of the dissatisfaction of senior women in the book world – publishers, agents, literary editors, booksellers, journalists and writers – with the neglect of women writers shown by the major fiction prizes'.[40] The Booker 'gender analysis' given above certainly lends credence to that dissatisfaction.

An all-women fiction prize, designed along the terms of the ill-fated Uni Prize, was finally revived in January 1996. Financed by an anonymous donor and sponsored by the mobile telephone company Orange (Hutchison Telecommunications [UK] Ltd) the £30,000 annual prize is administered by Book Trust. There is no nationality criterion, unlike most of the other prizes discussed in this chapter: the only conditions are that the work must be in English and have been published in the UK between 1 April and the following 31 March.

Press discussion ranged from hostile protestations about tokenism to embarrassment about timeliness – the Orange Prize was, after all, launched within a week of Kate Atkinson having won the 1996 Whitbread Book of the Year with her debut *Behind the Scenes at the Museum* (and thus having inflicted a second defeat on Salman Rushdie's *The Moor's Last Sigh*, shortlisted as Best Novel as well as for the 1995 Booker Prize). Indeed, even the most sympathetic commentators wondered whether, with a woman having won the Booker in 1995, the Whitbread in 1996, and the Chair of the Booker judges for 1996 having been announced as Carmen Callil, it could really be claimed that women were as disadvantaged as the Uni announcement quoted above was asserting. Controversy was exacerbated by widely

---

[39]Source: Barry Turner, ed., *The Writer's Handbook 1995* (London: Macmillan, 1994), p. 549. Naipaul requested the Society of Authors to draw up a shortlist for him to select from.
[40]*Bookseller*, 28 January 1994, p. 7.

quoted comments by two of the judges apparently deploring the low standard of many of the submissions. However, the winning novel, *A Spell of Winter* by Helen Dunmore, received an enthusiastic press.

While it is evident that the Orange, the Commonwealth and the Irish awards are responding quite directly to Booker success, it is too early to make any serious judgement about the impact they are likely to exert during the next few years – most particularly about the extent to which (given their different conditions of eligibility) they will identify themselves with the texts that get shortlisted for the Booker Prize. Certainly they do not, at present, have much primary impact on sales. Still, the presence of more than half-a-dozen fiction prizes all yielding five-figure sterling amounts in 1996, all of which are open to British nationals (and five to Irish or Commonwealth nationals), contrasts strikingly with the situation as recently as 1985, when there had been only one. While it may be pointless to speculate on how prizes of this kind will develop, it cannot be denied that they have certainly done more than could possibly have been expected in 1980 to bring serious literary fiction in English to public attention. I have suggested that lowering the prize money and transforming the publicity aspect might be one way forward if the primary aim is to sell books and increase the consumer's horizons and enjoyment, but each prize's aim is clearly different. What is not so clear is how those aims are conveyed to the reading public. Whatever the truth of the matter, the commercial climate within which the prize culture has flourished in Britain over the past fifteen years will be my next topic.

3

Canon and Commerce

The purpose of the previous chapter's account of the Booker Prize as Britain's best-known literary award for fiction was to emphasize its leading role in profiling serious literary fiction – a role that could not have been foreseen twenty years ago. The Booker has evolved in powerful and unpredictable ways; in some years it has been clearly perceived as an artistic and/or commercial success, in others as a failure in either category, and very rarely as both. Yet even as a failure – of whatever sort – it has exercised a galvanic effect on the book trade, by encouraging other prizes to emerge or re-profile themselves, by stimulating generic promotions, or simply by extending the terms of reference of the novel in Britain. In every sense, Booker's role has been integral to the mechanics of (on the one hand) commerce and (on the other) the formation of a particular kind of literary canon.

If the discussion so far has focused on the Booker, the aim here is to take a wider view, from a number of related commercial perspectives, of the culture within which serious literary fiction is produced, purchased and read. We need to examine Booker's impact on hardback and paperback sales, bearing in mind the test case of A. S. Byatt's *Possession*. The effects of Booker as a cultural phenomenon worth attention can only be fully realized, however, when one assesses the changes undergone by the book trade from the mid 1970s to the demise of the Net Book Agreement (NBA) in September 1995, and examines the policies and practice of Britain's two major chains (Dillons as a subsidiary, until March 1995, of the Pentos Group; Waterstone's as a subsidiary, since

1989, of W. H. Smith). These will be scrutinized in the second part of this chapter.

It is now clear, for instance, that Waterstone's Book of the Month (this need not necessarily be a novel, of course) exerts an immediate and palpable influence on book sales – as in its own way did Dillons' erratic flouting of the NBA under its then managing director Terry Maher.[1] Waterstone's Book of the Month is not imposed 'from above' but chosen on the basis of polls conducted among all Waterstone's branches, and takes account of critical reception in the major broadsheets as well as book programmes on the radio.

Waterstone's Book of the Month was instituted in June 1990, apparently in response to the appearance of Nicholas Mosley's *Hopeful Monsters* (1989), a title that strongly captured the imaginations of Tim Waterstone and John Mitchinson:[2] 1991 titles included *The Redundancy of Courage* by Timothy Mo, *Talking It Over* by Julian Barnes, *The Van* by Roddy Doyle, and *Murther & Walking Spirits* by Robertson Davies; among the 1992 titles were *The Famished Road* by Ben Okri, *Ever After* by Graham Swift, *Wise Children* by Angela Carter, *Black Dogs* by Ian McEwan, *Lemprière's Dictionary* by Lawrence Norfolk, *The English Patient* by Michael Ondaatje; 1993 titles included *Sacred Hunger* by Barry Unsworth, *A Suitable Boy* by Vikram

[1]Maher was forced to resign from the Pentos Group in September 1993, twenty-one years after he had founded it, and eighteen months before the Group's collapse into bankruptcy and receivership. See 'How Pentos passed its sell-by date', *Financial Times*, Weekend 4/5 March 1995, 'Weekend Money', p. 5. There is a succinct and balanced account of the case for and against (primarily against) the NBA by Barry Turner, 'Free to Trade: The Decline and Fall of the Net Book Agreement', in his edition of *The Writers' Handbook 1995* (London, Macmillan, 1994), pp. 150–51. Clearly, events will lead to a due assessment of that case. See also Terry Maher's account of his time with the Pentos Group, *Against My Better Judgement: Adventures in the City and in the Book Trade* (London: Sinclair-Stevenson, 1994) and John Sutherland's review of it, 'From Clogs to Books', *TLS*, 30 September 1994, p. 32. See also Sutherland's polemic 'Cheapened Classics', *TLS*, 2 September 1994, p. 9.

[2]I am extremely grateful to John Mitchinson for providing information, answering queries and correcting some errors in this section.

Seth, *Ulverton* by Adam Thorpe, *Paddy Clarke Ha Ha Ha* by Roddy Doyle; among the 1994 titles were *The Stone Diaries* by Carol Shields and *Birdsong* by Sebastian Faulks; and among the 1995 titles *High Fidelity* by Nick Hornby, *Felicia's Journey* by William Trevor and *The Moor's Last Sigh* by Salman Rushdie. John Mitchinson, who has tracked the Waterstone's Book of the Month since its inception, believes that the real breakthrough as manifested in substantially increased sales came with Doyle's *The Van* in August 1991 when it is estimated that, as Book of the Month, Waterstone's sales of *The Van* increased by a third during that month. By 1993, Waterstone's Books of the Month were consistently never less than doubling, and sometimes as much as trebling, the market for the chosen books. In this way, commercial promotion worked to the mutual benefit of author, publisher and purchaser or reader.

The effects of the Waterstone's Book of the Month initiative are a telling indication of the current state of book promotion in general.[3] There seems to be a consensus that booksellers have entered the equation in such a way that publicity departments and marketing personnel must devote just as much energy in trying to reach the bookshops as they spend in reaching the media. For this reason, a brief indication of how serious literary fiction is now promoted during the mid 1990s is in place here.

Publishers of literary fiction now make no secret of their practice of dividing their lists into 'lead' and 'non-lead' titles. Only the former are 'seriously' promoted – that is, are allocated a substantial marketing and publicity budget. A lead title will be by a novelist who has a record of strong sales or by a lesser-known figure in whom the publisher in question ardently believes. The mechanism thus begins with a publisher's passionate conviction that a book is so special that it merits gambling with the company's money. At this early stage, word-of-mouth contact between publisher and what Dan Franklin of Jonathan Cape

[3]In what follows I am indebted to a correspondence with Gail Lynch, and have drawn on Kate Figes, 'Those Crucial Six Weeks', The Sunday Review, *Independent on Sunday*, 12 November 1995, pp. 32–33.

calls 'three or four key scouts in London' is crucial (Figes, p. 32). While this informal but high-level lobbying is going on outside, the lead title must equally convincingly be promoted within the publishing house itself, because both publisher and editor must sell the book to their own sales force for the dream to become reality. Here it is clear how important the role of bookstores has become: the aim of marketing and publicity personnel is now twofold. They must get the title into the shop in the form of a saleable product, and they must then get it into the customers' hands and so out of the shop. If, despite all the sales people's best efforts, the title is not in the shop by publication day, all the planning, and a great deal of money, will have been wasted.

About nine months before publication a promotional portfolio is assembled. This will be geared to the nature of the book. It consists principally of what is known as a 'presenter', a colour brochure usually four to twelve pages in length featuring a photograph and biographical details of the author, sales figures of previous titles, and other promotional material specific to the lead title in question and including a colour photograph known as a 'packshot', showing the book, the poster, and other related items. This is presented at regular sales conferences by the publisher, traditionally to sales representatives, although it is thought likely that the role of representatives will decrease as information technology becomes sophisticated enough to permit publishers to interact with bookstores directly. Other promotional material takes the form of posters and stickers, but these, being cheap to produce and thus myriad, must be really eye-catching to make any serious impact. Clearly, if the lead title is chosen as the cover for the publisher's catalogue, all the better.

If the author's presence will definitely enhance the sales conference, she or he is invited too. This applies to high-profile established names, as well as to younger writers such as Will Self, who are regarded as interestingly off-beat performers. Certainly an author's presence tends to enhance a lead title's prospects within the bookstore itself, so that drinks parties involving *all* levels of store personnel prior to publication are seen as a good investment (of course, the publisher pays). The author's role may be extended further: a personal letter to sales representatives or booksellers can translate into sales too. In turn, the author's own morale can be boosted by the production of postcards featuring a jacket design, the thinking behind this kind of promotion being that a sense of established success before the event is crucial.

Lead titles are first circulated as bound proofs: 100 to 200 is a typical run; and 500 to 1,000 is by no means unknown. A thousand bound proofs of Salman Rushdie's *The Moor's Last Sigh* were issued in the spring of 1995, all numbered and signed, as is now increasingly customary. About five months before publication these bound proofs are sent to what are known as 'long lead' magazines (middle-brow glossies, literary journals) and their reviewers, freelance journalists, and TV and radio contacts. Here again, the word-of-mouth element is important.

Trade promotions are directed at both bookstores and the book trade in general. A lead title may be selected for advertisement in W. H. Smith's *Bookcase* magazine, or editorial coverage in *Dillons Review*. (The policy of Waterstone's newly launched *W Magazine* is unclear at the time of writing.) If these slots are expensive (in some cases up to £3,000 per page), investment in Christmas catalogues can be more so. Waterstone's Book of the Month promotions are also expensive, but cost around £1,500. As to the publishing world, a front cover of the *Bookseller* can cost as much as £4,000 and a small panel in *Publishing News* as little as £200.

Six months ahead of publication the media are approached: BBC2's *Bookmark*, BBC1's *Omnibus* and ITV's *South Bank Show* are the obvious full-length TV programmes to aim for. Lesser slots include BBC2's *Late Review* and Channel 4's *Book Choice*. Radio at present plays an increasing role: Radio 4's *Books & Company*, Radio 3's *Book of the Month*, and a wide range of national and local chat shows offer attractive promotional possibilities, as do serializations on *Book at*

Bedtime or *Woman's Hour*. Author interviews in the daily and Sunday broadsheets, and promotional tours organized by bookstores, complete the picture.

Such outlets are generally felt by publishers to have rather more impact than literary reviews, which are only slightly less evanescent than the events described above, even if it is generally felt that in recent years review space may once more be on the increase. Perhaps the major change of which the publishing world has become aware since the late 1980s has been the development of a 'meet-the-author' culture. Some novelists have become skilful at handling lucrative promotional events from which sales can benefit remarkably. This cultural shift has in turn led to a remarkable efflorescence of home-based reading-groups held during weekday evenings, principally amongst middle-class women.

The really striking and paradoxical aspect of the whole business of promotion of serious literary fiction at the present time is the disjunction between the amount of planning that goes into promoting a lead title in the year prior to its publication, and the sense the reading public has of instant exposure. It is true that the first six to eight weeks after publication are often crucial to the success of a lead title (or indeed any title that is fortunate enough to be noticed despite having the promotional odds stacked against it), but a second bite at the cherry can be unusually successful too, as when, for instance, paperback publication follows on the heels of a reading on *Woman's Hour*. But despite a public view of instant success, it simply is not possible to promote a lead title within a few days. A great deal has gone on behind the scenes in the months before the final product is purchased by the customer who has been so skilfully and assiduously targeted. The entire exercise has been focused at that particular customer in such a way that a sense of excitement, already encouraged by word-of-mouth promotion, as it were clicks into place once the customer is in the bookstore.

A successful lead title enters the 'canon' by virtue of a

multiplicity of cultural forces that are as commercial as they are 'literary'. We may think of more conventionally literary forms of 'canon' – that dense mass of consensus and its surrounding, ever-changing, swirl of debate – by recalling the proscriptive, combative views of F. R. Leavis in the 1930s and 1940s. Leavis came to regard Jane Austen, George Eliot, some of Charles Dickens, most of Henry James and Joseph Conrad, and all of D. H. Lawrence, as exemplifying alone the 'great tradition' of English literature. More recently Harold Bloom's *The Western Canon* (1994) has been criticized as being provocatively patriarchal. My point here is that the canon with which I am dealing rests on many of the same assumptions about literary canon, chief amongst which is that what is left out but considered worth discussing – the penumbra – is, as always, just as important as what is admitted to the canon. The fact that my 'canon' is commercial as well as literary (what's 'in'? what's everybody reading this season?) by no means implies that the two kinds are mutually exclusive: indeed, both carry a sense of elitism that may not be to everyone's taste.

Neither Booker shortlists nor Waterstone's Book of the Month promotions provide the only guidance to the reader of today's serious literary fiction. In 1983 Desmond Clark of the Book Marketing Council (BMC) came up with the idea of the 'Best of Young British Novelists' and under Bill Buford's robust editorship a selection of work by twenty writers was published in *Granta* in the same year. Anthony Burgess's selection, *99 Novels*, appearing a year later and in direct and angry response to a BMC promotion of the 13 best novels since the Second World War, contributed to a general atmosphere of contemporary canon-formation. *Granta* produced a follow-up, 'Best of Young British Novelists 2', that appeared in 1993. A significant number of the original *Granta* writers have since made their names, one of the most striking success stories being that of Pat Barker, the 1995 Booker Prize winner. Others in that first selection were Martin Amis, Julian Barnes, William Boyd, Maggie Gee, Kazuo Ishiguro, Ian

McEwan, Adam Mars-Jones, Timothy Mo, Salman Rushdie, Graham Swift and Rose Tremain. William Boyd excepted, the selection seemed disinclined to pay attention to writing by Scots, an omission that was rectified in the 1993 selection with the inclusion of Candia McWilliam, A. L. Kennedy and Iain Banks. To look back at the 1983 selection is to realize, indeed, how many of its writers (more than half) were male, white and English; Ishiguro, Mo, the already famous Rushdie, the Nigerian-born Buchi Emecheta and the late Shiva Naipaul were the only representatives of the huge growth of British-based international English-language fiction that was already starting to be noticed.

Significant in this context is the changing role of the British Council in the promotion of British fiction at home and abroad. Topics here would include the British Council's sponsoring of international seminars featuring contemporary writers such as its annual summer meeting in Cambridge, which attracts many participants (academics, and increasingly publishers and journalists) from around the world (perhaps forty or fifty from as many countries). Since 1990 the British Council has co-published what have become substantial annual anthologies of new writing that supplement its other material relating to contemporary writing, ranging from the short Contemporary Writers leaflets produced in association with Book Trust to the relevant volumes in the newly relaunched Writers and their Work series.[4]

[4]The relaunched Writers and their Work series is being co-published by Northcote House, Plymouth. The 1995 New Writing 4 anthology included several writers, such as Louis de Bernières, Tibor Fischer, A. L. Kennedy, Candia McWilliam and Lawrence Norfolk, who were selected as part of the 1993 Granta 'Twenty Best of Young British Novelists' list. In addition to the British Council New Writing series, see the University of East Anglia's matrix anthologies (University of East Anglia: Centre for the Creative and Performing Arts [CCPA]). One might also mention here the British Council's quarterly newsletter Literature Matters, a particularly useful source of information for those living and working overseas. I am grateful to Kate Bostock, who edits Literature Matters, for up-to-date information on these various British Council initiatives.

The Booker Prize and Related Sales: Expectations and Disappointments

Whatever the truth of claims that by the mid 1980s a Booker winner might expect up to 80,000 extra hardback sales as a direct result of the prize itself, the point such claims illustrate is the fact that at some stage between the late 1970s and the mid 1980s the Booker laureate's dividends, direct or indirect, came dramatically to exceed the monetary value of the prize itself.[5] Two *Bookseller* articles referred to in the Introduction above give an idea of a pattern that was becoming established in the early 1980s. The 700-page manuscript of Salman Rushdie's *Midnight's Children* was delivered to Liz Calder, then at Jonathan Cape, in July 1979. The book was published on 23 April 1981 to a 'heartwarming critical response' (in considerable contrast to the 1975 reception of *Grimus*).[6] On publication, 650 copies of *Midnight's Children* had been allocated by subscription. The 1,000 mark had been passed by June and at the time of the announcement of the shortlist on 11 September, sales stood at 2,252. Within the next month another 900 copies were sold and, as Calder puts it, '[a] provocative article by Brian Aldiss in the *Guardian*, and a feature by Hunter Davies on the Booker in the *Sunday Times* helped stir up a groundswell of excitement'. As we have seen, the titanic clash between William Golding's *Rites of Passage* and Anthony Burgess's *Earthly Powers* had taken place only the year before, but it was evident that Booker winners, as well as some shortlisted titles, were now beginning to command impressive sales. Yet it is clear that in these relatively early days publishers were

[5]In his contribution ('The Novelist Today: Still at the Crossroads?') to Malcolm Bradbury and Judy Cooke, eds., *New Writing* (London: Minerva in association with the British Council), p. 210, David Lodge argues that the Booker Prize 'had made little or no impact on sales during the 1970s', perhaps slightly overrating the watershed nature of events in 1980 and 1981.

[6]Liz Calder, 'Bandwagon Blues', *Bookseller*, 20 February 1982, pp. 640–43.

still extremely nervous by today's standards about risking high Booker-related print-runs. The Rushdie problem was intensified by the presence of two other, more established, Cape authors – Doris Lessing and Ian McEwan – on the 1981 shortlist, as well as that of D. M. Thomas's *The White Hotel*, which had broken spectacularly into the US market, selling hundreds of thousands of copies in its first year.

In the event demand for *Midnight's Children* initially outstripped supply. The prize was announced on 20 October 1981; although a 10,000-copy reprint had been ordered in the standby eventuality of Rushdie's winning, the go-ahead was not given until the prize was safely in. By 23 October, with sales standing at 4,353, stocks were exhausted, and a further 2,338 copies had been ordered before the reprint finally arrived two weeks after the prize announcement. By 13 November, sales stood at 10,072: 'in one week 5,738 copies were invoiced' (Calder, p. 643). In the immediate run-up to Christmas 1981, nearly 2,000 copies were sold per week, and by the end of January 1982 Cape had sold over 21,000 copies of *Midnight's Children*.

In the case of Thomas Keneally's *Schindler's Ark* the principal problem facing Hodder & Stoughton was that the publication date had originally been scheduled for 1 November 1982.[7] Ion Trewin's attractively self-deprecating account of the 1982 success shows particularly interestingly how early Booker hype could catch publishers by surprise if they had other targets in their sights:

> When the Booker shortlist came in mid September I was, I think, the last person in Hodder to appreciate the significance. So convinced was I of the book's power that the Booker at first seemed an irrelevance. But others at Hodder, more concerned with subscribing and selling [*Schindler's Ark*], had absorbed the lessons of the two previous years when not only William

[7]See Ion Trewin, 'Handling a High-Flying Winner', *Bookseller*, 5 March 1983, pp. 816–18.

Golding and Salman Rushdie, successive winners, had sold exceptionally well, but Anthony Burgess and D. M. Thomas, the runners-up, had done so too.[8]

In the event, the publication date of *Schindler's Ark* was moved forward to 18 October, with review copies initially going out as 'folded, collated and jacketed sheets . . . with the promise of bound copies to follow' (Trewin, p. 817). Keneally had been on the Booker shortlist three times before, 'and the nature of his subject would [Trewin felt sure] guarantee major press coverage' (Trewin, p. 817). Although the first print-run amounted to 17,000, 11,500 of these had been earmarked by Book Club Associates (BCA) on the strength of Keneally's previous track record. Yet even though *Schindler's Ark* had also received positive endorsements from Graham Greene and Alan Sillitoe in July 1982, it was clearly still felt, by Trewin if not by some of his colleagues, that the Booker was going to have little impact one way or the other on sales. On the morning after the Booker Prize was announced, 'Hodder's sales office was besieged, with orders for some 5,000 copies taken in one day' (Trewin, p. 817). By the end of October 1982, sales were over 17,000; the 30,000 mark was passed less than a month later; and on 31 January 1983 sales stood at over 40,000. A significant statistic is that on the same date, Australian sales were at an *additional* 17,500. Trewin's story ends with the news that 'BCA's reprint book club, World Books, has made [*Schindler's Ark*] a main book, which means approximately another 80,000 copies' (Trewin, p. 818).

These available accounts of how in the early 1980s Booker

---

[8]Trewin, p. 816. Note how the 'runners-up' terminology, as we have seen alien to the Booker's terms of reference, is beginning to become common parlance. Trewin's self-mocking sense of obliviousness to Booker's commercial potential is all the more fascinating in view of the fact that he had himself chaired the adjudication board in 1974, when Nadine Gordimer and Stanley Middleton had shared the prize.

success could catch even experienced and established publishers
on the hop are fascinating. Even so, by the end of the decade hardback sales of *Midnight's Children*, although clearly
well into five figures, were low by 1980s Booker standards
as a whole. In fact, as we have seen, the title that did
the best in hardback between 1981 and 1988 has turned
out to be *Schindler's Ark*. Despite scepticism from within
Britain, the surprising commercial success of Keri Hulme's
The Bone People (1985) suggests that titles such as Hulme's
and Keneally's did unusually well not just in the United
States but, much more significantly, in Australia and New
Zealand.

A winner of Rushdie's kind took longer than is sometimes
thought to achieve real commercial success and enter academe: a remarkably high proportion of sales of *Midnight's
Children* have been in paperback. What is still not widely
appreciated, perhaps, is that it took the *Satanic Verses* affair
to benefit every back title by Rushdie and all subsequent
titles too, especially in the US. Rushdie's retrospective and
later success has been even more dramatically affected by
the *Satanic Verses* affair than the sales of all A. S. Byatt's
work were by the success of *Possession*. A longer-term and
more controlled view has to be taken of Rushdie's success
if one compares it to that of *Schindler's Ark*. At·the time
of Trewin's account, published less than six months after
Keneally's novel appeared, *Schindler's Ark* had grossed in
hardback sales alone between twenty-five and thirty times
the value of the prize itself. Although the reissue as a paperback tie-in to the Spielberg movie has elevated that figure vastly further (worldwide tie-in sales of *Schindler's List*
during 1994 were in the millions rather than in the tens
of thousands), that success occurred more than a decade
after the first publication of Keneally's novel as *Schindler's
Ark*.

For data for 1983 and 1984 we must turn to Martyn Goff,
according to whom J. M. Coetzee's 5,910 hardback sales for

Life & Times of Michael K in the months prior to September 1983 increased by more than another 5,000 on being shortlisted and a further 34,000 on winning in October 1983. Sales of Anita Brookner's titles had been averaging between 2,000 and 3,000 'despite excellent reviews and publicity'; a print-run of 4,000 was ordered for *Hotel du Lac*, but by the end of 1984, the novel had sold 50,000.[9]

After these high hardback sales had begun to level off (if we are to credit the 50,000 figure), there was now the prospect of still higher paperback sales. This certainly seems true of Anita Brookner's fortunes in 1984. If 1984 was, as was suggested above, a 'poor' Booker year in terms of public and media opinions of what serious literary fiction ought to be, it must nevertheless be remembered that winning the Booker with whatever title seemed – by the mid 1980s – to have become a guarantee of success for author, publisher and agent. During the late 1980s Brookner, publishing a novel annually, settled down to capture a steady annual share of the quality paperback market, even if her hardback novels appear not to have matched her 1984 success.

If we look at more recent events as noted in the résumés accompanying Alex Hamilton's paperback fastseller lists for 1991, 1992, 1993 and 1994, we can gauge fairly accurately what the paperback impact of the Booker has been a decade after its commercial breakthrough in the early 1980s.[10] The period encompasses the worst recession to have occurred in the years covered by this book: even so, the 96th title on Hamilton's 1991 and 1992 lists managed to sell more than 100,000 copies, the 98th title on his 1993 list was as successful

[9]Martyn Goff, ed., *Prize Writing* (London: Hodder & Stoughton/Sceptre, 1989), p. 22. These figures should probably be regarded as erring on the side of generosity, in view of what we have seen above.
[10]The period separating paperback reissue and hardback original has shortened from more than two years in the late 1970s, through eighteen months in the early 1980s to less than a year by the 1990s.

as these, and by 1994 all 100 titles once more exceeded 100,000 sales.[11]

Hamilton's figures for 1991 show that A. S. Byatt's *Possession* (the 1990 Booker Prize winner) came 26th with more than 250,000 sales, William Boyd's *Brazzaville Beach* 62nd with nearly 139,000, and Ian McEwan's *The Innocent* 79th with 117,000. Boyd and McEwan had both been tipped for the Booker shortlist; neither made it but both did better than any shortlisted title. These are probably the only titles in the list of one hundred that could be considered as falling under the heading 'serious literary fiction'.

In 1992, the paperback of Ben Okri's *The Famished Road* (the 1991 Booker Prize winner) came 37th with more than 187,000 sales; David Lodge's *Paradise News* came 41st with 173,000, Julian Barnes's *Talking It Over* was 71st with 117,000, Roddy Doyle's *The Van* 88th with 103,000 and Angela Carter's *Wise Children* 94th with just short of 101,000. Booker laureation, whatever the degree to which that is reflected in hardback success, was by now ensuring a place in the paperback top fifty, with paperback sales approaching or exceeding 200,000.

The other successes can be ascribed to a variety of factors that support one's sense of how promotional activity as discussed above affects consumer behaviour. All but the Lodge title were also Waterstone's Book of the Month in 1991 and 1992. Lodge has now become a high-selling author with virtually whatever title is promoted – if we wish to seek a reason for the specific

[11]In 1991 only the top 2 titles exceeded 750,000 copies; in 1992 the first 3 titles were past this post; and although in 1993 the 750,000 level was once more passed by only 2 titles, those 2 sold far better than their counterparts in 1991 and 1992. In 1994, again the top 3 titles made it past the 750,000 level with the next 3 – that is, the top 6 altogether – close behind above the 650,000 mark (a feat managed only by the top 3 titles in 1991 and 1993). The fastest selling 1993 title (*Jurassic Park*) exceeded 1,010,000 copies – with number 2 (*Wild Swans*) not far behind at over 940,000. In 1994 *Wild Swans* sold another 685,000. Half-million or more sales were managed by the top 8 1991 titles, the top 10 1992 titles, the top 8 1993 titles and the top 7 1994 titles; sales of 250,000 or more were managed by the top 26 titles in 1991 and 1992, the top 36 in 1993 and the top 30 in 1994.

success of *Paradise News*, that success seems attributable to the TV adaptation of *Nice Work*, an effect indicated by earlier sales of that title and compounded by reader appetite for an experience already enjoyed. Barnes capitalizes on earlier success, as we shall see in a moment. Doyle, of these writers perhaps the most popular and widely read Irish writer of his generation in Britain, offers a more extreme case than Lodge of a writer benefiting from TV serialization. Carter's posthumous success is of a piece with the unexpectedly widespread public reaction to her death in February 1992, when Virago sold out of all her backlisted titles. Carter is now widely read and studied in Britain's universities.

How would the sharing of the Booker Prize in 1992 affect paperback sales? In 1993 the paperback of Michael Ondaatje's *The English Patient* (joint 1992 Booker winner) came 64th with nearly 142,000 and Iain Banks's *The Crow Road* (not shortlisted) 89th with over 110,000 sales.[12] Barry Unsworth's *Sacred Hunger* (joint 1992 Booker winner) did not feature on the list but achieved about 80,000, so that aggregate paperback sales of both titles amount to over 220,000 – more than Okri but slightly fewer than Byatt.[13] The dire predictions as to what would happen in the event of the first tie since 1974 (and only the second in Booker history) do not appear to have been fulfilled, as we also saw with the hardback sales of these novels in the last chapter. Both the Ondaatje and the Unsworth titles, it should be said, were Waterstone's Books of the Month.

The 1993 sales of Roddy Doyle's *Paddy Clarke Ha Ha Ha* as a Booker winner were the most spectacular to date. The paperback fastseller reached 20th place (6 places higher than the previous best Booker winner, A. S. Byatt's *Possession* in 1991). Doyle's novel sold nearly 355,000 in 1994. In Doyle's

[12]Sources: Alex Hamilton's 1991 Chart reprinted in *The Writers' & Artists' Yearbook 1993* (London: A. & C. Black, 1992), pp. 241–47; Hamilton, 'Tales of Gloom', *Guardian*, 12 January 1993; Hamilton, 'Clogs by the Aga', *Guardian*, 11 January 1994, reprinted in expanded form in his 1993 Chart, *The Writers' & Artists' Yearbook 1995* (London: A. & C. Black, 1994), pp. 255–61.
[13]Alex Hamilton, 'Clogs by the Aga', *Guardian*, 11 January 1994.

case the initial hardback sales, as we have seen, were also remarkably high.

Other Booker-eligible titles, or titles hovering in the wings, achieving high paperback sales in 1994 were more numerous than for many years; they include Vikram Seth's *A Suitable Boy* (22nd with more than 330,000), Sebastian Faulks's *Birdsong* (47th with nearly 176,000), Iain Banks's *Complicity* (62nd with 139,000), Elizabeth Jane Howard's *Confusion*, the last part of a sequence (75th with more than 121,000) and William Boyd's *Blue Afternoon* (92nd with just over 110,000).

Most remarkable in a year remarkable for tie-ins was (as already indicated) the 1994 paperback success of Thomas Keneally's *Schindler's List*, which sold more than 873,000, grossing well over £5m, in the UK and export markets.[14] Although these figures now make Keneally's title by far the most commercially successful Booker winner ever, by far the greater proportion of that success – as reflected in vast American sales – must be attributed to its reissue as a tie-in to the Spielberg movie. Although Doyle's title has been the most successful winner 'on its own merits' over a much shorter time-span, Keneally's original paperback fastseller managed over 300,000 in 1983.

Going a little further back than 1991, we can see that the 1990 paperback fastseller figures were in many ways comparable, although they show more vigour, suggesting that the recession did not really begin to affect sales of serious literary fiction in paperback until 1991.[15] The top 10 in 1990 included a title by John le Carré, whose novels remain among those suspended uneasily between the serious and the genre-fiction categories. At 36th place was Julian Barnes's *A History of the World in 10½ Chapters*. This title was not included on the 1989 Booker shortlist but had been strongly promoted and favourably

[14]Source: *Guardian*, 10 January 1995; *Bookseller*, 13 January 1995, pp. 19–22.
[15]Source: the *Guardian*'s 'Top Hundred Chart of 1988 Paperback Fastsellers', compiled by Alex Hamilton, and reprinted in *The Writers' & Artists' Yearbook 1990* (London: A. & C. Black, 1989), pp. 232–37.

reviewed. At 42nd place in 1990 was the 1989 Booker winner, Kazuo Ishiguro's *The Remains of the Day*. It was with his 1990 title that Ishiguro moved to a peculiarly English kind of subject-matter, even though many reviewers seemed incapable of avoiding a need to consider the *treatment* of this subject-matter in terms of the *japonaiserie* of his first two novels.[16] Total sales of each title exceeded 200,000 in 1990; each had appeared in paperback in the summer of that year. Just below the 200,000 mark, at 46th place, was Martin Amis's *London Fields*, which had only been available in paperback since September 1990. In 1990, as in 1988, a Drabble and a Weldon title made it into the top 100, but only just: *A Natural Curiosity* came in 94th and *The Cloning of Joanna May* scraped in at 100th place, respectively. The other interesting feature of the 1990 list was the presence, at 90th place, of Bruce Chatwin's posthumously assembled collection *What Am I Doing Here?* It is hard to know what to make of a success such as Chatwin's: on the one hand there is no doubt that it both testifies to his ability and reflects the reader's enjoyment of previous work, notably *Utz*, which had been on the 1987 Booker shortlist; on the other (as with Angela Carter) there is a sense of both nostalgia and regret – as well as of a career closed and thus assimilable.[17]

The kinds of success demonstrated by the paperback fortunes of serious literary fiction titles from the late 1980s onwards is noteworthy. The caution of the early 1980s had

[16]Cf. Ishiguro's own comment on this tendency: 'These stereotypes are all right as part of a publicity game. Where it gets irritating is when people read your work in a particular kind of way: it seems my Japanese novels are so exotic and remote that I could have written bizarre Marquezian or Kafkaesque stuff and people would still have taken it as straight realism. I've always had to struggle against this literal-minded tendency in British audiences.' Quoted by Blake Morrison in the *Observer*, 29 October 1989, p. 35. The mixed reception accorded Ishiguro's lengthy and, as many readers felt, truly Kafkaesque *The Unconsoled* (1995) bears out this *cri de coeur*.

[17]Source: Alex Hamilton's 1990 paperback fastseller chart, reprinted in *The Writers' & Artists' Yearbook 1992* (London: A. & C. Black, 1991), pp. 213–19. Waterstone's November 1993 Book of the Month was a collection entitled *The Photographs and Notebooks of Bruce Chatwin*.

been transformed, within the space of three or four years, to confidence leading almost to hubris. A glimpse at the advances paid to the kinds of novelist with which this book is concerned may help to make the point as well as stress what a high-risk strategy the payment of substantial advances in this sector of the market continues to be. None of what follows allays one's uneasy sense that authors, agents and publishers of serious literary fiction, many of whom might have been expected to have been hostile to the political and financial climate engendering the Lawson boom of the later 1980s, were swept along in its wake, long after its demise. Indeed, given the left of centre, Charter 88 political leanings of so many figures in the book world, this buoyancy oddly reflected the new assurance of the Thatcherite meritocracy.

Of course, high advances (often multiple advances for several titles over a longer period) have been paid to bestselling writers ever since the advent of the paperback market and before: a sense of what had by the mid 1980s become possible for a genre-fiction writer is indicated by the events of 1986, when in the United States the $5m barrier for a publishers' advance was broken for the first time for James Clavell's *Whirlwind*. Advances for serious literary novelists have naturally been much lower, but six-figure sums (whether in dollars or pounds sterling) are not now unknown, whereas they would have been unheard of – certainly in Britain – at the beginning of the 1980s.

After the impressive commercial success of *Waterland*, which made it to the Booker shortlist in 1983, Graham Swift was reported in 1987 to have received an advance of £125,000 for *Out of This World*, which appeared the following year; not long afterwards the same publishing conglomerate, Viking, paid Salman Rushdie an advance of $850,000 for the US rights to *The Satanic Verses* (1988). This astonishing figure was brokered by the controversial American agent Andrew Wylie, who had managed to lure Rushdie away from his British agent Deborah Rogers and – as things turned out – from his British publisher

Jonathan Cape. (Rushdie returned to Cape with *The Moor's Last Sigh* in 1995.) At the end of the 1980s Ian McEwan was in a position to ask for and receive from Cape an advance of £250,000 for *The Innocent.*[19] By December 1994, the McEwan advance for *The Innocent* could be seen as one of several milestones on the way to Martin Amis's post-recession record of around £480,000 or (if one is to believe the highest estimate) £505,000 for serious literary fiction for *The Information* from HarperCollins in 1995. Following his Booker and commercial success with *The Famished Road*, Ben Okri also received an advance of £250,000 from Jonathan Cape for the sequel *Songs of Enchantment*, and Vikram Seth received the same amount in advance of *A Suitable Boy* from Orion as we shall see below. Recent multiple advances include the late [Sir] Kingsley Amis's two-book £300,000 (HarperCollins) and Jim Crace's three-book £400,000 (Viking).

The implications of advances of this magnitude on the fortunes of peers of Martin Amis as well as younger writers are complex. Positions were staked out, with A. S. Byatt threatening to leave Chatto & Windus should its owner Random House UK Ltd offer Amis the desired advance, arguing that she always earned out her advances and that a sum of this magnitude could only be to the disadvantage of first-time writers. Others, in contrast, felt that, although the sum was unlikely to be recouped (or only just), Amis was 'worth it' as a loss leader to a big conglomerate such as HarperCollins. The Faber publishing director Robert McCrum put the Amis advance in the broader context of the really serious money swirling around in the popular genre-fiction world nearly a decade after the Clavell $5m:

[19]It took some while for news of this deal to emerge, but the details seem to have been generally known by the time of the appearance of two articles by Melvyn Bragg that appeared in the *Sunday Times* of 10 and 17 December 1989. I am grateful to John Peereboom for drawing my attention to these. For a while around the end of the 1980s and the beginning of the 1990s Cape's advances became legendary.

Publishers hate to admit that they write off unearned advances, and resort to various subterfuges to disguise their mistakes. Some merrily transfer unearned advances into 'intangible assets'. Others, like HarperCollins, will coyly admit to an ambiguous category of advances neither earned-out nor written off, a figure which now stands at a stupendous £27.2 million. A substantial part of this colossal figure must include the absurd £20 million paid to Lord [Jeffrey] Archer for a three-book contract, a figure that makes the Amis half-million look like pocket-money.[20]

Indeed, by the late 1980s (with the quite remarkable exception of Viking in the case of Rushdie's *Satanic Verses*[21]) advances of the magnitude being offered for serious literary fiction titles certainly could not have been recouped on hardback sales alone. This represents a fact about 'vertical' publishing, the arrangement whereby an author receives 100 per cent of the paperback royalties when the original hardback publisher issues a paperback under a wholly-owned imprint (e.s. Cape hardback/Vintage paperback) (as contrasted with an author who under sub-licence from the original hardback publisher to a paperbacker typically receives about 60 per cent of those royalties). Paperback success (in effect a relaunch as little as six to nine months after the initial hardback release) would then justify the advance. In principle, this kind of commercial

[20]Robert McCrum, 'Lunatics and suits', *Guardian Weekend*, 4 March 1995, p. 24.

[21]It seems reasonable to guess that sales receipts to date must be in the region of several million dollars. For the first three years following the Khomeini *fatwah* of 14 February 1989, Rushdie refused to allow the book to appear in paperback, but by the third anniversary of his confinement in February 1992 he apparently relented, feeling in a position to put under pressure those Western governments that had necessarily if undesirably linked his fate to those of the Lebanese hostages. Rushdie used this opportunity to call a halt to censorship through the state-sanctioned terrorism pursued by Iran, since the Lebanese hostage crisis had in any case finally been resolved in the closing months of 1991.

calculation has been the case ever since the advent of paperback publishing. If one calculates a 10 per cent royalty on sales below 2,500 rising through 12.5 per cent to 15 per cent on sales above 10,000, even if hardback sales were to reach the unusually high figure of 20,000 or more (for a serious literary fiction title costing – say – £12 per copy in hardback in 1988), the total royalty payable would have been around £30,000 (see Introduction, n.17). Even in the most optimistic of scenarios – an auspicious publication achievement early in the calendar year followed by Booker success boosting sales by a further 40,000 to 80,000 hardback copies – the extra hardback royalty gained would have been £108,000 at most.[22] Paperback sales of 200,000 or more, assuming a 7.5 per cent royalty, perhaps rising to 8.5 per cent on a title costing £4 per copy at late 1980s prices, would have added less than half again to that figure, and could over a period of two or three years eventually make up the difference. The sales of translation and film rights –

[22]Bookwatch Ltd's EPOS figures for the period 1987–95 tell a rather different story. They suggest that under optimum conditions the Booker Prize enhanced sales of the winner by a surprisingly consistent 20,000 to 30,000 throughout this period: this figure is based on EPOS data from the week of the announcement of the award until the following mid-January, by when the Booker effect has largely evaporated. Only Roddy Doyle's *Paddy Clarke Ha Ha Ha* stands out, achieving something like two to three times this figure. As has been noted, the combined figures resulting from the Ondaatje–Unsworth tie in 1992 were little affected, and the Kelman win in 1994 was about a quarter of the 1987–95 average. The data for the average shortlisted hardback title simply do not bear out the high claims made in the early 1980s: a generous estimate suggests that EPOS recorded sales stood at (at most) 20 per cent of the average of such sales of the winning title throughout this period. Sales figures are compiled on a 'sale or return' basis. Because this term is often misunderstood, I am particularly grateful to Philip Flamank of the Publishers Association for clarifying to me its legal meaning, which is that under its terms given retailers do not own the books they stock, nor do they pay for them prior to retailing them. Other terms customarily used in the retail trade are 'come and go', 'see safe', and 'swap', all of which indicate the contractual boundaries of what is loosely termed 'sale or return'. This practice no doubt also accounts to some extent for the discrepancy between EPOS data and the higher figures supplied in the media and elsewhere. Yet all the data cited here suggest that a higher proportion of royalties on Booker titles is now earned through paperback sales than is generally believed.

if part of the publisher's rights package – would have to be added as well to be on the safe side, but an enormous gamble would have been taken. Translation rights (like film rights) are proportionately more lucrative for the author than are royalties on home or export sales, but much harder to be assured of.

In the case of the Amis advance, it was pointed out that *London Fields* was unique among the *oeuvre* to date in having been hyped in the American market in a way no other Amis title had been before; *London Fields* was quoted as having sold 40,000 in hardback and more than 250,000 in paperback (e.g. the *Guardian*, 16 December 1994) and as being by far Amis's most successful title to date in commercial terms, but most of these sales were in and around London itself. Bearing in mind the usual provisos about hardback figures quoted in the media, *London Fields* would, on the basis of figures like this, have earned a total royalty in the region of £200,000. One can see why Cape, even in its most adventurous frame of mind, was unwilling to go beyond £300,000 for *The Information*.

Yet even so, the high-risk high-advance strategy does sometimes work. In 1992 Phoenix House paid Vikram Seth £250,000 for his 600,000-word epic *A Suitable Boy*, which was published in hardback at £20, a price considerably above the 1993 £15 threshold. *A Suitable Boy* was quite legitimately promoted as a serious literary novel, but more provocatively than this as '[an] epic of post-independence India . . . a worthy successor . . . to *Vanity Fair, Middlemarch* and *War and Peace*'. By the end of 1993 it was evident that the gamble had paid off: the book may be between twice and three times the length of Rushdie's *Midnight's Children*, but it is a more straightforward read. *A Suitable Boy* failed to make it to the Booker shortlist – the 1993 Chairman Lord [Grey] Gowrie, former Arts Minister to Margaret Thatcher, offering some caustic advice about editing it down – nor was Seth successful in winning any of the other major literary prizes. Despite all this, Gowrie's view was not shared by influential quality reviewers, Peter Kemp's *Sunday*

Times notice being particularly favourable; indeed the very length of the novel became its main selling point, a challenge to the general readership. By the end of 1993 *A Suitable Boy* had sold 120,000 hardback copies.[23] Again, assuming a 10 per cent royalty rising to 12.5 per cent or even 15 per cent we may assume that the hardback success alone will have justified the advance and indeed have earned its author 30 per cent to 40 per cent on top; in 1994 the 1,475-page paperback, retailing at £8.99, was billed as 'The Number One Bestseller'. Later that year, and in time for the Christmas rush, *A Suitable Boy* was made available as a three-volume boxed *de luxe* paperback set actually costing more than the original hardback. Paperback sales in 1994 of the single-volume version, as we have seen, exceeded 330,000 and the novel grossed nearly £3m, from which we may cautiously deduce that Seth's total earnings from this title (bearing high discount sales in mind) have been in excess of £500,000 and are set to go further. But this is a special case in which the length of the novel affected its high unit cost, and in which hardback sales, at more than a third of the total, formed an unusually high proportion of that total – and it is, ultimately, high hardback sales that earn the money. (In contrast, hardback sales of *London Fields* were less than one seventh of the total, which is a more typical picture.)

Many of today's big advances for serious literary fiction are direct responses to the commercial successes of their authors' previous work, so that Graham Swift's advance for *Out of This World* must be seen as riding on the back of the wide and international acclaim for *Waterland*. As the 1990s have progressed, the size of advances has increased as the Seth case may suggest. John Banville, who has a full-time post as literary editor of the *Irish Times*, received an undisclosed offer for two books from Picador which seems at least partly to have been made to lure Banville away from Secker & Warburg, with

[23]Source: '1993 – Hardbacks Go Mega', *Bookseller*, 24/31 December 1993, p. 27.

whom he has been publishing for twenty years (his *The Book of Evidence* was Booker-shortlisted in 1989). Banville's comment was interestingly downbeat, and characterizes the more sober mood of the post-recession mid 1990s:

> You have to realize that two books is a minimum of five years' work and if you actually divide the figure up [reputed to be £300,000], it's not all that much.[24]

If the late 1980s onwards, then, were characterized by one single commercial pattern as far as high-profile novelists are concerned, that would be the spectacular increase in the amounts of money changing hands: between publishers, authors, and their agents; and between authors and publishers, booksellers and the general public. Although all have been affected by the recession, none of these parties seems willing or even able to contemplate a return to the lower-key commercial realities of the 1970s or mid 1980s. The role of agents, in particular, has become commensurately more high-profile within the last two decades. Whereas formerly it would have been regarded as a breach of protocol for an agent to submit the same manuscript to more than one publisher simultaneously – and this is a course of action many first-time authors are still customarily counselled to avoid – 'multi-agenting' (that is, giving as many as ten different publishers a simultaneous option on a manuscript) is now the norm.

Between 1986 and 1990 the choice of Booker winner kept most people content. Publishers saw huge returns on their investments, the book trade was lively and the reader's expectation of pleasure was largely satisfied. The paperback sales figures tell their own story. By the time of the recession, expectations had become unrealistically high. In just over six months of appearing in

---

[24]*Bookseller*, 28 January 1994, p. 7. Martin Amis similarly pointed out in his *South Bank Show* interview with Melvyn Bragg (ITV, 19 March 1995) that *The Information* had taken him five years to write.

paperback in 1990, Kazuo Ishiguro's *The Remains of the Day* had sold over 200,000, and the title had grossed over £1 million in paperback by the end of 1990. The 1990 Booker winner, A. S. Byatt, broke more decisively than any of her predecessors into the American market, as we have seen, with the exception of Thomas Keneally's resurrected *Schindler's List* as paperback tie-in to the Spielberg movie.

More recent events initially surpassed all expectations or precedent. The 1993 Booker winner Roddy Doyle's *Paddy Clarke Ha Ha Ha* grossed over £6m in hardback and paperback within a year of his winning the prize. By early 1995, Doyle would have earned in royalties alone a figure over twenty times the prize money he had been awarded fifteen months earlier.

Several features account for this quite unusual success. The hardback price was, at £12.99, relatively low for 1993. The subject-matter and tone of the book seem to have attracted many readers by word of mouth. Doyle's TV serial screenplay of *The Family* was transmitted by BBC1 in the early months of 1994. On the basis of the earlier sales figures for *The Van*, it seems reasonable to infer, as has already been suggested, that Doyle's readership is unusually geographically and socio-economically widely spread for a writer of serious literary fiction, an inference that would support the high TV ratings that in turn fed back into sales of *Paddy Clarke Ha Ha Ha*. All the same, it had become evident from the Ishiguro and Byatt titles that under consistent optimal conditions, gross revenue from hardback and paperback publication of a Booker winner would amount within two years of initial publication to many times more than the prize money itself. In contrast, it is unlikely that James Kelman's royalty-based earnings will substantially exceed the cash value of the prize. Such volatility contrasts with Anita Brookner's success a decade previously: her hardback royalty would have been between four and five times the value of the prize, and that proportion would have increased to perhaps seven or eight times the value of the prize after paperback publication had brought in the major part of its gross revenue. But that result, a third of what it might potentially become ten years later, would have been reached more slowly a decade earlier – within two to three years rather than fifteen months.

It is clear from the Kelman win in 1994 that a Booker win does not necessarily guarantee vast sales, but it can lead to quite spectacular success. The more consistent and predictable pattern observable during the period 1986–90 is doubtless preferred by those in the book trade. Yet there are clearly years in which by some mysterious chemistry both commercial success and recognition for a hitherto underrated or unknown novelist come together, and naturally this is the most satisfactory outcome for all concerned.

It is also the case that booksellers do continue to run risks in stocking little-known or low-selling shortlisted authors in large numbers,[25] particularly after the surprises (in book-trade terms) of 1983 and 1984, their follow-up in the period 1986 to 1990, Roddy Doyle's 1993–94 *annus mirabilis* and the Kelman 'flop' of 1994–95. Even then, it would be fair to say that those Booker winners that have given rise to less enthusiasm, even to gloom, in the book trade – Keri Hulme's *The Bone People* (1985), Ben Okri's *The Famished Road* (1991), the joint win between Michael Ondaatje and Barry Unsworth in 1992, and James Kelman's *How Late It Was, How Late* in 1994 – have tended to recoup sales in paperback at least. A fact overlooked by the more complacently London-oriented elements in the publishing and even retailing world is quite simply, as we have seen, that a writer such as Keri Hulme sold exceptionally well in New Zealand and Australasia; on the evidence simply of walking into major retail outlets in Glasgow it can be seen that Kelman, similarly, has clearly done better in Scotland than in the south.

In those years in which deafness to commercial and artistic

[25]The present Managing Director of Waterstone's, Alan Giles, is on record as saying that by late 1994 Waterstone's had largely brought its stocking problem of the earlier 1990s under control; see 'The consolidation of Waterstone's – to kill or cure', *Bookseller*, 24 March 1995, pp. 12–14.

response in non-metropolitan areas has been more prevalent than usual, the higher-profiled Booker-shortlisted authors will take up some of the commercial slack once they have appeared in paperback. This can be ascertained by checking the figures for the paperback fastsellers for the year 'Booker plus two'.[26] But the evidence presented so far suggests that those titles that, in the public perception, ought to have made it to the shortlist but did not may do just as well if not better.

One might even be able to relate the success of such writers to the nature of the winner, or the shortlist, although this argument can cut both ways. But it does seem significant that, in the year of Byatt's success, none of the other shortlisted titles approached the paperback success of two unshortlisted novelists: William Boyd, with *Brazzaville Beach*, and Ian McEwan, with *The Innocent*. Both titles had been expected to make it to the 1990 shortlist, failed to do so, and nevertheless sold well, as we have seen. Boyd's name-recognition derives partly from his inclusion on the 1982 Booker shortlist with *An Ice-Cream War*, whereas McEwan had been Booker shortlisted in 1981 with *The Comfort of Strangers*, and had expected to be in 1987, with *The Child in Time*. McEwan's status remains fascinatingly harder to define on account of his subsequent shortlisting with *Black Dogs* in 1992, a title that will surely turn out to be one of the most memorable novels of the decade.

Waterstone's, Dillons and the Retail Book Trade

A shift in emphasis is now due, away from the promotion and laureation of serious literary fiction in the mid 1990s, and more specifically towards how it is actually publicized and sold. The retail outlets available to the reader of serious literary fiction in

[26]The 1990 winner, *Possession*, appeared in paperback as early as February 1991; sales figures relating to the whole of 1991 could thus only be released at the beginning of 1992 at the earliest.

the mid 1970s were very different from what they have become two decades later. One way of comprehending the change of climate is to pause momentarily to reflect the price differential between hardback and paperback fiction. Whereas in 1994 the average hardback novel was retailing at £14.99 and the average paperback novel at £5.99 – that is, the hardback was, on average, less than three times the price of the paperback – that ratio in the 1960s and 1970s was more likely to be in the region ten to one. It is not that hardbacks have become cheaper – paperbacks, and above all B-format trade paperbacks, have actually become more expensive. But there has always been a threshold to be crossed before a paperback buyer becomes a hardback buyer; the demise of the NBA looks like demolishing this threshold, especially since Alex Hamilton reported early in 1996 that he 'couldn't find any publisher who believes that there is any point to discounting paperbacks'.[27]

Formerly, however, there was a greater polarization between the paperback buyer and the hardback buyer. At the risk of caricaturing the two ends of the market, one could say that the former would have been more likely to look to station and airport bookstores, or general retailers such as John Menzies or W. H. Smith, than would the latter. Whereas the paperback buyer would have accepted that the outlets she or he was patronizing were lightly and patchily stocked, these limitations were clearly preferable to the chaos of Foyle's in Charing Cross Road, or the patrician atmosphere of specialist stores such as Dillons University Bookshop in London, Blackwells in Oxford or Heffers in Cambridge. All well stocked with contemporary hardback and paperback fiction, they were clearly in whatever way seen as elitist in their appeal to the consumer's pocket – to say nothing of the consumer's time, as in the case of Foyle's with its Byzantine invoicing system. The sense of elitism had much to do with the locations of these specialist stores: the axis

[27] Alex Hamilton, 'The paperback bestsellers of 1995', *Bookseller*, 12 January 1996, p. 27.

was London and Oxbridge (although Blackwells Books had been expanding for a long time and by 1995 owned eighty bookstores in the UK). To be sure, other university campuses and other towns had their specialist bookstores too, but these tended to be chains such as Hudsons, Mowbray's, and what later became Sherratt & Hughes. There were, of course, many more local independent stores, but they were for the most part inferior to the rapidly diminishing number of their 1990s counterparts.

In the 1980s a revolution took place in the retail book trade that amounted to a dramatic extension of the book-buyer's franchise. It took the form of what can only be termed a shake-up of the entire system. The two single biggest changes were, firstly, the acquisition by the Pentos Group, under its then director Terry Maher, of Dillons University Bookshop from the University of London in 1977 for £650,000,[28] and secondly, the founding of Waterstone & Co. Ltd in 1982, and the rapid branching out of both concerns across the UK. The competition that ensued between the two enterprises exercised a ripple-outwards effect on the entire specialist retail book trade in Britain. It is hard to convey to any reader under about the age of 30 the magnitude of these changes in terms of what one encounters when one walks into any of the 250 or so bookstores associated with Dillons or Waterstone's today. Nevertheless it is important to try to do so because, contrary to much popular perception, the British book-buyer has never had it so good.

Until the Pentos Group's final collapse in March 1995, the division that included Dillons the Bookstore (as it is now officially known) also comprised, among others, Hatchards,[29] Mowbray's Bookshop, Claude Gill and the Hodges Figgis bookstore in Dublin (the Dillons division's only store outside the UK). To some consternation, the Athena cards and poster chain, another

[28]See 'How Pentos passed its sell-by date', *FT* 4/5 March 1995, 'Weekend Money', p. 5.
[29]The original John Hatchard first opened his bookseller's and publisher's in Piccadilly in 1797; see Roy Porter, *London: A Social History* (London: Hamish Hamilton, 1994) p. 143.

division of the Pentos Group, had closed down in January 1995; the Pentos Group's failure to intervene on that occasion was seen by some as a sinister harbinger of what might happen should other divisions of the Group prove equally unprofitable. In the event, the Pentos Group's division that includes Dillons was bought up by Thorn EMI for £36m at the beginning of March 1995, within twenty-four hours of Pentos's declaration of insolvency, a confident move that was widely interpreted as proving the high regard in which Dillons is held in the high-street retail trade.

Although before the Pentos Group collapse Dillons claimed to have almost 150 branches throughout the UK, this figure incorporated a large number of associated bookstores: only about thirty Dillons' branches were listed as 'major', and another fifty or so at most carried the distinctive blue-and-gold logo. There are another half-dozen Hatchards (a Dillons Bookstore) apart from the Piccadilly branch, all confined to the South-East. There were 103 branches of Waterstone's in the UK and Ireland at the beginning of 1996 with seven more planned by the end of the year. Trying to assess Waterstone's position in relation to its parent company is the more straightforward business: at the present time Waterstone's stock turnover represents 10 per cent of that of W. H. Smith for books in general and nearer 15 or 20 per cent for serious literary fiction.[30]

The most objective account would have to concede that since 1982 Waterstone's has taken the lead in many aspects of the book retail trade, with Dillons following close behind as the main competitor. Together these two enterprises have utterly transformed the face of bookselling in Britain, and it is worth noting the main changes that have occurred, not least because they have become linked with related activities in the publishing world. In 1989 Waterstone's & Co. Ltd merged with Sherratt & Hughes, then the specialist bookselling division of W. H.

[30]Source: John Mitchinson (private conversation).

Smith Ltd, to form Waterstone's Booksellers.[31] At that time 20
per cent of the new company was made up of shareholders of
the previous Waterstone's (including many employees) with the
remaining 80 per cent passing to W. H. Smith, which acquired
total control of the company in May 1993. At about this time Tim
Waterstone, who had founded the original company, sold
his share of it and began a new career as a novelist. By 1994,
store turnover of the W. H. Smith group in its entirety exceeded
£2bn annually at more than 600 outlets; this contrasted with
approximately £250m (one eighth of the W. H. Smith figure)
at more than 400 outlets for the Pentos Group.[32]

From its inception, Waterstone's policy was seen as unusually
aggressive in terms of what had traditionally been the standards
of the specialist retail book trade. The sites sought were large
(the company quotes a minimum requirement for a new store of
700 square metres, with a preference for 1,000 square metres)
and the venues attractive, that is to say, situated in town and
city centres, reachable by foot or public transport rather than
by car. By late 1994 Dillons, in contrast, had chosen a much
wider variety of sites, moving into out-of-town shopping malls
while at the same time retaining its stores in the high street,
expanding on to campus sites, and opening a flagship store at
London's Science Museum in South Kensington.[33]

Waterstone's, in particular, transformed the retail book trade
by making it a priority to employ energetic, enthusiastic and
knowledgeable staff. Many branches are open seven days a
week and on every weekday evening. Dress code is extremely

---

[31]A useful retrospective from five of the original team, marking the tenth
anniversary of Waterstone's and giving considerable insight into the policy
and philosophy underlying the enterprise, appeared in the *Bookseller*, 28
August 1992, pp. 559–62.

[32]Source: *Independent on Sunday*, Business Section, 6 November 1994.

[33]Source: information kindly supplied by Karen Tomlinson, Merchandise
Controller, Dillons. A preference for out-of-town sites has marked recent
(mid 1990s) developments in the electronics and hardware retail sector, to
the detriment of stores within that sector that have remained in the high
street. It is by no means evident that book-buyers' preferences have been
reflected in these developments.

informal: this may be off-putting to some customers but clearly attracts a larger number. Waterstone's staff do now wear the distinctive (and as from late 1994 redesigned) 'W' logo in order to be recognized in the store. A popular perception characterizes the difference between Waterstone's and Dillons as that between clutter on the one hand and a cleanliness verging on the clinical on the other. It's sometimes said that Waterstone's are booksellers who happen to be in the specialist book trade whereas Dillons are specialist retailers who also make money out of books.[34] Ideally, of course, the market ought to be able to accommodate both kinds of business, although recent events suggest that it may not be able to do so indefinitely: it is generally felt that in recent years Dillons expanded too quickly over far too wide a range of sites. Not surprisingly the Thorn EMI take-over of Dillons in March 1995 led rapidly to a slimming-down operation, and within a month it was announced that as many as forty of the least profitable stores were to close, with job losses exceeding 2,000.

Dillons' expressed aim of attracting customers who are traditionally put off by bookshops is a noble one, but it seems clear that the concept simply has not sustained enough customer revenue to guarantee a secure long-term future. From the present vantage point it does seem that in the event of a real high-street war between the two stores at some time in the foreseeable future, Waterstone's would be the more likely to survive because of its willingness to manage a vast budget reflected in massive but increasingly controlled stocking, coupled with its more cost-effective staff ratio and its clearer sense of the kind of book-buying customer it is setting out to attract.

The demise of the NBA has naturally made the future harder to predict, with Dillons immediately following a riskier course than Waterstone's in offering bigger discounts on a wider range of titles. Indeed, the month after the NBA collapse saw a ferocious price-war, with sales soaring by almost 50 per cent in the first four weeks, a rise clearly insufficient to make up the money being

---

[34] Another analogy has Waterstone's playing Sainsbury's to Dillons' Tesco's.

lost by retailers. Later reports suggested a more focused and selectively targeted policy of price-cutting by both stores, and their competitors, just before the run-up to Christmas 1995.[35]

The most crucial difference between the two chains is in their stocking policy. Observation suggests that an average branch of Waterstone's displays more of its stock 'face out' (as opposed to 'spine on') than does its competitor. Among the effects of a policy such as this are the challenges posed not just to competitors but to publishers themselves: an eye-catching cover design can be the single most influential feature persuading a customer to buy a book, thus paying its way and enhancing the reputation of the designer.

Of the 500,000 titles in print in Britain, Waterstone's claims that its larger branches carry between 80,000 and 100,000, a quantity matched by no other competitor. Accessing stock has been fully computerized for some while. Waterstone's is (at the time of writing) introducing its own state-of-the-art computer system *ULYSSES* at an estimated cost of £20m. *ULYSSES* will be able to access well over a million titles (more or less all British and American titles in print combined) using 150 fields of enquiry. This kind of foresight is giving Waterstone's the edge in ordering unstocked titles, and will continue to do so. The preceding discussion highlights a sad paradox. The tremendous dynamism Waterstone's and Dillons have brought to the book trade can only be good for consumers of fiction. At the same time, that very dynamism will continue to place many good small independent bookshops under threat, unless these are able to profile themselves very distinctly, such as the London-based Books Etc., whose fourteen stores include one at Gatwick Airport.

All the developments discussed above have raised the profile of serious literary fiction to levels that could not have been foreseen a quarter of a century ago. These developments are, I believe, self-perpetuating: that is, perceived success implies a success formula,

[35]'Book sales soar but prices fall', *Guardian*, 2 November 1995, p. 1; 'Booksellers breathe again as "price war" proves damp squib', *Independent*, 4 December 1995, p. 5.

which it is clearly attractive to attempt to emulate, refashion or upstage. The production of fiction as a commodity affects the ways both aspiring and established novelists do business with their agents and publishers, and the ways in which they aim to attract their readers. The purpose of the next section will be to explore the relationship between this commercial context and the chosen literary themes of the writers in question.

My assumption is that the novelists I discuss have worked in an increasingly intensified atmosphere, one in which both the promotion and the reception of serious literary fiction have become steadily more consumer-oriented. How many of even the most interesting postcolonial writers of recent years, for example, are – however subconsciously, with whatever desire to say something new – now responding both aesthetically and commercially to the 1980s as 'the Rushdie decade'? Or – likewise – how many slush-pile literary detective novels with a double historical time-scheme has A. S. Byatt's *Possession* spawned?

Such self-conscious commercial categorization offers a real challenge to today's novelists, agents, publishers and readers. The preoccupations discussed in this book's next section will be considered with such pressures in mind.

II

PREOCCUPATIONS:
MARGIN
AND
PRIVILEGE

4

New Fiction from Scotland

Since the 1980s a number of events have combined to bring
Scottish fiction to the attention of the world outside. Observers
have come to express the view that not since the 'Scottish
Renaissance' of the 1920s and 1930s, and indeed, arguably
not since the time of Scott and Burns at the turn of the
eighteenth and nineteenth centuries, has the national literature
of this part of the British Isles achieved so high a profile in the
global English-speaking community. In support of this view,
the editors of *The Scottish Novel since the Seventies* (1993)
emphasize their survey's innovatory character by pointing out
that its two immediate predecessors were published in 1978
and 1984 respectively, and that Alasdair Gray's groundbreaking
Lanark (1981) – now surely indispensable to any discussion of
Scottish fiction since the 1980s – is discussed only as the tenth
and final chapter of the latter.[1]

Anyone attempting to convey a picture of Scottish fiction
since 1981 is faced with difficult choices. The selection of three
novelists, Alasdair Gray, Iain Banks and A. L. Kennedy, might on
the surface be open to question, in view of the concentration on
urban life. However, the new realities of the Scotland presented
in this chapter are certainly those of a country much of whose
notable recent writing constitutes a nationalist and socialist,
and often strikingly co-operative, enterprise, and my choices

---

[1]See Gavin Wallace and Randall Stevenson, eds., *The Scottish Novel since
the Seventies* (Edinburgh: Edinburgh UP, 1993), p. 5. The predecessors
were Francis Russell Hart's *The Scottish Novel: A Critical Survey* (1978)
and Isobel Murray and Bob Tait's *Ten Modern Scottish Novels* (1984).

reflect those realities. I hope that Banks's non-science fiction work, set mainly in and around Edinburgh and the Firth of Forth, serves to correct an otherwise Glaswegian if not actually 'Red Clydeside' perspective. In any case the Glaswegian urban socialism represented in the fiction discussed here breaks away from the traditional macho culture with which it is usually associated, with much of the writing self-consciously adopting an interesting and complexly enlightened gender politics. This is as true of James Kelman's Booker Prize-winning *How Late It Was, How Late* as it is of that novel's predecessor *A Disaffection*; both novels affirm the voices of women, or rather (as with the newer novel) their absence, in delineating the inadequacies of Kelman's men. The 'controversial' label has stuck to Kelman largely because of his uncompromisingly in-your-face use of a Glaswegian patois that causes offence to middle-class Anglophile Scottishry.[2]

A dilemma facing Scottish writers (and this applies equally to Irish, Welsh or distinctly regional writers on the British mainland) is the decision whether to support local small presses or surrender to the London publishers' marketing muscle in order to reach a potentially global audience. Many Scottish writers feel torn between loyalty to their own national roots and the desire for wider recognition. Alasdair Gray's debut novel *Lanark: A Life in Four Books* (1981) is an extremely unusual instance of a novel published by a small publisher, in this case Edinburgh's Canongate Press, yet going on to make an international reputation. Since then Gray has alternated between

[2]Even that sympathetic and humane *doyen* of Scottish literature and culture, Edwin Morgan, seems uneasy about this aspect of Kelman's writing: see Morgan's 'Tradition and Experiment in the Scottish Novel', in Wallace and Stevenson, p. 96. However, it is worth pointing out here that David Lodge, who chaired the 1989 Booker committee that shortlisted *A Disaffection*, is on record as saying that he does not regard Kelman's novel as 'formally adventurous': 'Its aesthetic motivation is entirely mimetic. It challenges the reader primarily by its content and use of Glaswegian dialect, not by its narrative form'; see Lodge's 'The Novelist Today', in Malcolm Bradbury and Judy Cooke, eds., *New Writing* (London: Minerva in association with the British Council, 1992), p. 209.

his London publishers Cape and then Bloomsbury, and smaller Scottish presses such as Canongate or Glasgow's Dog & Bone. But it is more usual to find London publishers 'poaching' as many as 75 to 80 per cent of Scottish fiction debuts, and the true figure may be even higher.[3] A. L. Kennedy's first publication, her short-story collection *Night Geometry and the Garscadden Trains* (1990), appeared with Polygon in Edinburgh; but her debut novel *Looking for the Possible Dance* was published by Secker in 1993, and she moved to Cape for her second, *So I Am Glad* (1995).[4] In this case, Kennedy's move almost certainly represents loyalty to her compatriot editor Robin Robertson, who together with Dan Franklin left Secker for Cape in 1994, the year of publication of Kennedy's second short-story collection *Now That You're Back*.

Looking back over the past decade and a half, one might single out the following as events which taken together help to form the picture I am trying to sketch: in 1981, Alasdair Gray's *Lanark* appeared to spectacular critical acclaim when its author (until then known principally as a painter) was in his late forties and was hailed as Scotland's answer to James Joyce; in 1984 a much younger writer, Iain Banks, made a notorious debut with *The Wasp Factory*, a striking augmentation of the 'nasty' genre that placed him briefly in the company of such male English counterparts as the Ian McEwan and Martin Amis of the 1970s; and in 1993 A. L. Kennedy was chosen as the youngest of *Granta* magazine's twenty 'Best of Young British Novelists 2'.

As we have seen, Kennedy was one of three Scots in this selection, the others being Iain Banks and Candia McWilliam, author of *A Case of Knives* (1987), *A Little Stranger* (1989) and *Debatable Land* (1994). Kennedy's *Looking for the Possible*

[3]See Alison Lumsden, 'The Scottish Novel since 1970: A Bibliography', in Wallace and Stevenson, pp. 232–43, from which the above estimate is made.
[4]It is a telling sign of London's parochialism that the copyright page of the 1994 Minerva reprint of *Looking for the Possible Dance* reads: 'The author has asserted his [*sic*] moral rights'. Cape rectifies the error with *So I Am Glad*.

Dance won a Scottish Arts Council Book Award, as did both Banks's *The Bridge* (1986) and Kelman's *A Disaffection*. The latter novel was also awarded the James Tait Black Memorial Prize (an award that since 1979 has been supported by the Scottish Arts Council).

Although (in retrospect surprisingly) *Lanark* did not make it to the Booker shortlist in 1981 (the year Salman Rushdie's *Midnight Children* won the prize, and Doris Lessing, Ian McEwan, Muriel Spark[5] and D. M. Thomas were among the writers shortlisted), Gray has nonetheless won more major prizes than his Scottish colleagues mentioned here. But he has never even been shortlisted for the Booker.[6] *Lanark*, in addition to winning a Scottish Arts Council Award, was selected as the Scottish Book of the Year; and prize-winning acclaim from south of the border eventually came when *Poor Things* (1992) received both the *Guardian* Fiction Award and the Whitbread Novel of the Year Award (although not the overall Book of the Year award).

The pattern from outside Scotland may be characterized as one of sporadic recognition during the first half of the 1980s, with a real breakthrough in terms of the novel in Scotland as a collective and indeed at times collaborative enterprise coming only at the end of that decade and persisting into the 1990s. This is the moment to emphasize a compelling connection between the remarkable efflorescence of indigenous cultural activity that began to take place in 1980s Scotland and a crisis arising out of an almost desperate response to external political events.

In 1979 a narrow majority of Scots voted against continued

[5]Inclusion of the half-English Spark in this chapter might have strengthened the view from Edinburgh, where she grew up (see the first volume of her autobiography *Curriculum Vitae* [1992]). However, Spark's novels since the mid-1970s have focused on Italy, France and the London of the earliest part of her career.
[6]James Kelman is the only Scottish writer to have won the Booker Prize to date. Kelman, again, is one of the writers Robin Robertson edited at Secker, also publishers of the 1993 Whitbread Book of the Year, Jeff Torrington's debut *Swing Hammer Swing!* (1992), which carries a warm endorsement from Kelman, Torrington's friend and fellow-Glaswegian, as well as claims from English critics that Torrington, too, is Glasgow's new James Joyce.

central government from Westminster in what was nevertheless an unexpectedly conservative response to the real possibility of parliamentary devolution for the first time since the 1707 Act of Union. Under the conditions of this referendum, however, the majority was not sufficient to alter the status quo. The result exacerbated a clear dissatisfaction among Tory voters at the low level of public funding in Scotland's commercial and industrial infrastructure; the hostile response from the Scottish left to the events of 1979 has been wholly justified in terms of its fear of a rise in an already high level of inner-city unemployment and social disadvantage.

The right wing of the Scottish electorate seems to have been insufficiently persuaded that Scotland could achieve or sustain economic self-sufficiency. The only really imaginable conservative defence of the continuation of the Union in its present form, from the Scottish point of view, is the truly disenchanted belief that given the choice between an Edinburgh- and a Westminster-based bureaucracy, it was better to stick with the devil you knew. The reaction among Scotland's left-wing intelligentsia to both 1979 polls (the devolution referendum and the General Election that brought Margaret Thatcher to power) was bitter and uncomprehending; it is best expressed in its own words in a characteristic passage from Banks's *The Bridge*:

> The Fabulous Make-Your-Mind-Up Referendum was, effectively, pochled – rigged, in English. A lot of carpentry work in the old High School went to waste [. . .]
>
> 'Oooohh, shit,' he said, as they sat up in bed in the small hours watching the election results come in. Andrea shook her head, reached for the Black Label on the bedside cabinet [. . .]
>
> 'Well . . . at least she's a woman,' he said glumly.
>
> 'She may be a woman,' Andrea said, 'but she ain't no fucking sister.'
>
> Scotland voted for Labour, with the SNP a close third.

What it actually got was the right honourable Margaret Thatcher, MP.

He shook his head again. 'Oooohh, shit.'[7]

The ensuing period of Conservative political domination in the UK as a whole needs to be seen against the backdrop of the 1979 referendum in Scotland and the remarkable erosion of Tory support outside the traditional Labour strongholds in Lowland Scotland since the late 1980s. This process culminated in the virtual extinction of Tory-held councils in the 1995 local elections. Today, the Scottish electorate must choose between four parties whose power bases are much more evenly divided numerically (although not regionally) than in England. Three opposition parties – Labour, Scottish Nationalist (SNP) and Liberal Democrat – now claim a complex mixture of both strongly regional and widely popular support. The inner-city socialist of Clydeside must be set against the fringe liberalism of the highlands and islands (the Liberal Democrats are despised in the world of *The Bridge*), with all three opposition parties representing varying strengths of separatism. However, as the Banks extract makes clear, Scotland in the 1980s got what England voted for.

A further, shared, phenomenon ought to be taken into account in any discussion of recent fiction in Scotland. It concerns the role of Glasgow as the 1990 'European City of Culture'. It is true that in the European context this event put Glasgow 'on the map', culturally speaking, but the mixed reactions it triggered within the city and country itself are not widely understood.

Many Scottish writers and artists expressed hostility – in direct proportion to strength of nationalist feeling – to an enterprise they found it hard to see as anything other than an expression of cultural hegemony imposed upon them from a complexly perceived 'outside'. Comparison with Ireland may help here. Although the point is often made that Ireland shows

[7]Iain Banks, *The Bridge* (1986; London: Futura, 1989), pp. 239–41. Further page-references to this edition in the text above.

in its literature and culture many more affinities with Western Europe than does England, it is not usually appreciated how different Scottish attitudes to Europe are from English ones (and I mean 'English' rather than 'British' here).

Part, but only part, of the reason lies in the radical differences between the legal, educational and religious establishments in Scotland and England. Many people are aware of the existence of the 'Auld Alliance' between Scotland and France against England that persisted over several centuries. To this day educated Scots (like their Irish counterparts) tend to acclimatize to everyday life in mainland Europe better than the English, mainly because as speakers of a non-standard form of English, standard English is to them already, sociolinguistically speaking, a 'foreign' tongue.

One expression of the complexity of Scottish attitudes to cultural hegemony from outside may conveniently be found in Alasdair Gray's *Lanark* itself. Duncan Thaw is explaining to Kenneth McAlpin why in his opinion no one ever notices how magnificent a city Glasgow is, in contrast to other world cities:

> ... if a city hasn't been used by an artist not even the inhabitants live there imaginatively. What is Glasgow to most of us? A house, the place we work, a football park or golf course, some pubs and connecting streets. That's all. No, I'm wrong, there's also the cinema and library. And when our imagination needs exercise, we use these to visit London, Paris, Rome under the Caesars, the American West at the turn of the century, anywhere but here and now. Imaginatively Glasgow exists as a music-hall song and a few bad novels. That's all we've given to the world outside. It's all we've given to ourselves.[8]

[8]Alasdair Gray, *Lanark: A Life in Four Books* (1981; London: Granada/Panther, 1982), p. 243. Further references to this edition in the text above. The passage is discussed perceptively by Angus Calder, *Revolving Cultures: Notes from the Scottish Republic* (London & New York: I. B. Tauris, 1994), pp. 204–205.

This insight into Scottish lack of cultural confidence, which we will see strikingly restated by A. L. Kennedy, came into uneasy confrontation in 1990 with the longstanding cultural clichés variously known as 'Tartanry' or 'Kailyardism' (or 'Kailyairdism'). Kailyardism and what its practitioners practise were famously described by Neil Gunn in 1929 as 'the parochial, sentimental, local-associative way of treating Scotland and the Scots'. In contrast, the true 'Renascent Scot':

> ... wants to treat of Scotland as rock and sea and land – a unique and wonderful rock and sea and land – and he wants to treat of Scotsmen as real projections of *Homo sapiens* (rather than as kirk-elderish grannies), and he wants to complete his picture in such a way that will not only make self-satisfied Scotsmen sit up but will make the cultured of the world take notice.[9]

The 1990 confrontation over Glasgow as 'European City of Culture' seemed to take the form of a potent distillation of national and cultural pride and self-abasement. Perhaps it is an inevitable feature of the small nation. But as we shall see, this confrontation is fascinatingly plotted (how consciously it is hard to say) by A. L. Kennedy in *Looking for the Possible Dance*, with its juxtaposition of the heritage-industry cliché of the *ceilidh* (whisky set to dance) with a far grimmer internecine cliché of violence and self-hatred taking the form of crucifixion on a wooden floor, the Glaswegian equivalent of the 'concrete overcoat' of London's East End gangsters, or the 'knee-capping' of the IRA.

A brief sharpening of the focus on my chosen writers against this politico-cultural background will serve to preface a fuller

[9]Gunn's polemic was reprinted in the *Scottish Literary Journal* 4/2 (December 1977), p. 60, and is cited in Isobel Murray and Bob Tait, *Ten Modern Scottish Novels* (Aberdeen: Aberdeen UP, 1984), p. 3. The survey by Murray and Tait is that referred to in note 1 above.

discussion of their work. Alasdair Gray's impressive start proved hard to sustain, although *1982, Janine* (1984) was clearly helped by the success of *Lanark*. When Gray visited Amsterdam in 1988 to take part in an arts festival marking the impending passing-on of the 'European City of Culture' torch, he disarmingly introduced himself by saying that each of his novels seemed to be half the length of its predecessor. Not until *Poor Things* did Gray produce a novel that was not in some way contrasted unfavourably with *Lanark*.

Banks is to date the most prolific of these writers: soon after the appearance of *The Wasp Factory* he 'bifurcated', as John Sutherland has put it, into the literary novelist Iain Banks and the science-fiction writer of 'space operas' Iain M. Banks.[10] By 1995 Banks had produced fourteen novels in total. Although there is not complete agreement as to which category some of Banks's novels fall into, his distinct pen names suggest a certainty about his own view of his writing. Those stories that are indubitably science fiction have appeared under the Orbit imprint, whereas the literary fiction, which also includes formally challenging works such as *Walking on Glass* (1986), from a very early stage appeared in paperback in a characteristic black-and-white design specially marketed for this part of the Banks *oeuvre* by Futura (now Abacus).[11] Banks himself has famously said that he could not have written his own favourite among his novels, the much acclaimed *The Bridge* (1986), had the nightmare sections of *Lanark* not already been available as an influence.[12] One of the informing aspects of *The Bridge* is obvious yet easy to

[10]John Sutherland, 'Binarisms', *London Review of Books*, 18 November 1993, pp. 24–25.
[11]This is the Little, Brown (formerly Macdonald) imprint that has also published Stephen King and Ellis Peters.
[12]Cited by Thom Nairn in Wallace and Stevenson, p. 129 and by Roderick J. Lyall, 'Postmodernist otherworld, postcalvinist purgatory: An approach to *Lanark* and *The Bridge*', *Etudes écossaises* 2 (1993), p. 43. Lyall explores the idea that both novels exemplify a secularization of the means of social control substituted by Scottish Calvinism ('public confession and disgrace [the "cutty stool"]' [Lyall, p. 42]) for Catholic Purgatory.

ignore, and that is that the novel actually celebrates one of Scotland's rare – and thus all the more prized – triumphs of twentieth-century engineering, the Forth Road Bridge and the foreign (i.e. English) investment it represents. The Forth Road Bridge appears in 'concrete' form on the contents page if this is turned 90° to the right.[13]

A. L. Kennedy's *Looking for the Possible Dance* contains a remarkable passage that articulates as clearly as any of her contemporaries the lack of Scottish cultural self-confidence which I believe sets recent Scottish writing apart from the long, assured, independent tradition to be observed in Ireland. 'THE SCOTTISH METHOD (FOR THE PERFECTION OF CHILDREN)' is portrayed as a scarring process, something its heroine Margaret Hamilton, 'like many others, will take the rest of her life to recover from'. Two of the tenets of this grimly Calvinist catechism are its second and its tenth (and final) ones: 'The history, language and culture of Scotland do not exist. If they did, they would be of no importance and might as well not'; and 'Nothing in a country which is nothing, we are only defined by what we are not. Our elders and betters are also nothing: we must remember this makes them bitter and dangerous'.[14] These dogmas fire the mixed Glaswegian clichés of *ceilidh* and crucifixion with their obscurely impervious power, and contribute to what have been termed Kennedy's unusual 'downbeat but telling and [. . .] subtle' talents.[15] Kennedy shows how Scottish identity is thwarted by education, yet affirms Margaret's power through the course of the novel.

[13]I owe this observation to Roderick Lyall (private communication). Banks himself seems to make a similar point in interview with T. Donaghue, 'Iain Banks: "Thatcherism, and the 80s and all that sort of stuff"', in *57° north*, November 1994, p. 3: 'There's a sort of template structure with *The Bridge*: the template of the bridge, the Forth Road Bridge, then there's an imposed structure.' I am grateful to Alan Bisset for the reference.
[14]A. L. Kennedy, *Looking for the Possible Dance* (1993; London: Minerva, 1994), pp. 15–16. Further references to this edition in the text above.
[15]The description is borrowed from Edwin Morgan, Wallace and Stevenson, p. 91.

Experiment and Collectivism: Alasdair Gray

When it first appeared in 1981, *Lanark* was applauded as one of the most original and fascinating publications to come out of Scotland this century. The work had clearly been nurtured for more than two decades, part of it having appeared in print as early as 1958, as the acknowledgements page testifies. In view of the time it took to appear, *Lanark* itself was followed by a remarkable flurry of activity in which a Gray publication appeared almost annually between 1981 and 1986. In addition to *1982, Janine*, another novel, *The Fall of Kelvin Walker*, appeared in 1985, to be revised in 1986, and a collection of shorter fiction, *Unlikely Stories, Mostly*, in 1983 – three of these pieces had also first appeared in print during the 1950s.

Lanark is self-consciously constructed as an epic, and claims a place in the international vernacular epic tradition. As its subtitle indicates, *Lanark* consists of four Books. At first sight their numbering, in the order Three, One, Two, Four, appears subversive, but a completed reading reveals that what we have is recognizable as a double epic in which the formula of commencement 'in the middle of things', and the use of flashback, have been subjected to unusually close scrutiny. For Books One and Two are not simply flashback but constitute another story altogether, one that looks at first very much like a *Bildungsroman*. These parts no doubt encouraged the comparison with the Joyce of *A Portrait of the Artist as a Young Man*, but as a whole *Lanark* is a more nightmarish and fantasy-driven achievement. Isobel Murray and Bob Tait have written perceptively of 'the contrast [. . .] between the starkness of much of [*Lanark*'s] content and the vitality of the creative performance'.[16] Books One and Two relate the life of Duncan Thaw as a Glaswegian portrait of the young man as an art student up until his mysterious death, disappearance or suicide.

[16]Murray and Tait, *Ten Scottish Novels*, p. 222.

The narrative of Books One and Two is told to the eponymous consciousness Lanark (who is never given a first name) at a crucial point in his purgatorial after-life in the city-world of Unthank – a world on which the sun never shines – by the Beckett-like voice of an 'oracle'. The briefly included life-history of this unnameable voice relates, in a transitional passage between Books Three and One, how it rejected its body and indeed the entire physical world. The oracle tells Lanark:

> By describing your life I will escape from the trap of my own. From my station in nonentity everything existent, everything *not me*, looks worthwhile and splendid [. . .] Your past is safe with me. (*Lanark*, p. 116)

The oracle's 'station in nonentity' is typographically suggested by an absence of quotation marks whenever it speaks.

The main question posed and ultimately unanswered by the form and content of *Lanark* is to be found in the relationship between its two halves. Even though Books One and Two are sandwiched between them, Books Three and Four offer a continuation *and* a mirroring of the 'earlier' books. The purgatorial and surrealistic afterlife Lanark experiences first in Unthank, and then Provan, to which he journeys, both reflect and refract the experiences Duncan Thaw has undergone in Glasgow.

There is space to indicate only a few examples here. The world of Unthank and Provan bears a nightmarish relation to the deprived topography of Thaw's *Glasgow*, yet after Thaw's disappearance Lanark achieves the consummation with Rima that Thaw had failed to achieve with Marjory Laidlaw, the last in Thaw's series of admired but unavailingly lusted-after princesses lointaines. The relationship with Rima is maturer, too, in terms of the politics of gender.

The theme of sexual frustration and fantasy recurs in *1982, Janine* and *Something Leather*. In *Lanark* the progression from sexual frustration to fulfilment prefigures the way in which

Thaw's private, domestic, dissident and even anti-social or anti-societal concerns are replaced by Lanark's increasingly publicly and municipally minded ones. Still, towards the progressively quest-like end of Book Four it becomes evident that Lanark's struggle has been against an established system or order that he has discovered during the course of Books Three and Four but – like the reader – has been unable to make much sense of.

The extent to which Lanark's life is to be seen as a linear continuation of Thaw's, or a cyclic purgatorial re-enactment of it, is unclear, but there is considerable duplication. The characters' names are distinctly unusual. Moreover, those relating to characters and places in the novel's two halves seem to be deliberately unmatched, so that the topographical name Lanark is applied to a character whose name elsewhere, Thaw, challenges us to find some kind of significance in it.[17] Similarly we seem invited to juxtapose the topographical name Glasgow with the resonances offered by their fantasy counterparts Provan and particularly Unthank. Lanark's son's name, Alexander, is etymologically related to Alasdair.

The duplication is worth pointing up because it partakes, as Angus Calder cogently argues, in the 'doubleness' so widespread in Scottish literature.[18] It recurs in a strange episode towards the end of Book Four, where Lanark encounters his author, who

[17]In addition to its sense of unfreezing, the name can be read as an anagram of 'what'. As such it forms an existential question mark – and even, arguably, a homophone (in standard English, though not in Gray's own) of the Beckettian 'Watt'. One recalls James Joyce's Stephen Dedalus musing on his unusual name.

[18]Among Calder's examples are James Hogg's *Justified Sinner* (1824) and R. L. Stevenson's *Dr Jekyll and Mr Hyde* (1886), sparked by a discussion of his fellow Scot Karl Miller's study *Doubles* (1985) (*Revolving Culture*, p. 191). Hogg's novel has itself been rewritten and feminized by Emma Tennant in *The Bad Sister* (1978). In his discussion of *Lanark*, Calder usefully highlights the European span of Gray's influence: thus to William Blake Calder adds the illustrators Piero di Cosimo and Hieronymus Bosch, Aubrey Beardsley and Edward Burra. Indeed, Calder's entire catalogue of influences includes many sources about which Gray's 'Index of Plagiarisms' is silent (*Revolving Culture*, pp. 201–205).

is named Nastler. The odd name strikes the reader like Thaw as anagrammatic, but in this case insolubly or even inscrutably so. The entire section is entitled 'Epilogue' but it actually forms the conclusion to Chapter 40, and is followed by four more chapters. At first presented as Provan's king, Nastler is revealed also to be a conjuror when the bookshelves and canvases that Lanark impetuously overturns, in the studio-like room in which the encounter takes place, mysteriously right themselves.

Nastler is attended by a girl who is completing some of the more tedious detail to one of Nastler's canvases: she leaves after a short altercation about payment, an exchange in which Nastler's tightfistedness becomes evident, and Nastler and Lanark begin the discussion that forms the bulk of the Epilogue. Lanark's predicament is compared and contrasted with those of the major European epics from Homer to Tolstoy. In this way Gray asserts his claim to a long tradition as the writer of the first modern Scottish epic, but the story starts to fissure as various accompanying voices, including a querulous annotator Sidney Workman, undermine this claim. One footnote, for instance, reads:

> But the fact remains that the plots of the Thaw and Lanark sections are independent of each other and cemented by typological contrivances rather than formal necessity. A possible explanation is that the author thinks a heavy book will make a bigger splash than two light ones. (*Lanark*, p. 493, note 8)

The author, Alasdair Gray, thus appears to have an alter ego in Nastler – yet at the same time, Nastler is speaking to Lanark about his (Nastler's) creation of Duncan Thaw, who would seem in many respects to be an autobiographical version of Gray. As if such a resonating echo-chamber were not enough, the words of Sidney Workman (or whoever it is that provides the footnotes), intervene to disrupt this complex set of connections. The question of the relationship between the two 'halves' of *Lanark* is raised yet left unanswered; indeed it is not capable of determination, in view of and because of the fracturing that surrounds and accompanies the encounter between the character Lanark and his fictive creator Nastler. The various voices all sabotage each other. A note comments on the Index of Plagiarisms that it 'proves that *Lanark* is erected upon an infantile foundation of Victorian nursery tales, though the final shape derives from English-language fiction printed between the '40's and '60's of the present century', and goes on to attribute to Nastler – and then to undermine – the claim that he has been 'summarizing a great tradition which culminates in himself!' (*Lanark*, pp. 489–90, note 6)

Much has been written about *Lanark*, and I shall mention only the last of the Epilogue's footnotes because it relates to a little episode already referred to, which concerns the girl who has been assisting Nastler with the more tedious details of a particular canvas:

> As this 'Epilogue' has performed the office of an introduction to the work as a whole (the so-called 'Prologue' being no prologue at all, but a separate short story), it is saddening to find the 'conjurer' omitting the courtesies appropriate to such an addendum. Mrs Florence Allan typed and retyped his manuscripts, and often waited many months without payment and without complaining . . . (*Lanark*, p. 499, note 13)

This passage comprises the most bizarre of what has come to be seen, since *Lanark*'s appearance, as Gray's tendency towards acknowledgements that are fulsome if not obsessive in their gestures towards collaborativeness. At the end of *1982, Janine*, for instance, Gray supplies an 'Epilogue for the discerning critic', in which various literary debts are mentioned.

Because *Poor Things* (1992), the novel generally considered Gray's most significant achievement since *Lanark*, has received much less attention, I shall conclude this section on Alasdair Gray with a short account of those aspects of *Poor Things*

that are foreshadowed in the extended acknowledgements of
Lanark. What was playful in *Lanark* has become much more
seriously and overtly politicized in *Poor Things*. Like *Lanark*,
too, *Poor Things* raises genuinely existential questions posed,
not just thematically in terms of 'rebirth', but formally in terms
of a Chinese-box construction that negotiates the space between
fiction and reality.

If *Lanark* comprises a distinctly Scottish rewriting of the
entire epic tradition with a *Bildungsroman* embedded within
it, *Poor Things* may be seen as a subversively Scottish and
feminist rewriting of the Frankenstein's monster narrative,
offering itself as a text edited by Gray. (A case could be
made for the more distant presence of James Hogg.) The
documents in the case consist of a posthumously discovered
package left by Scotland's first, and controversial, woman
physician, Dr Victoria McCandless, who had died in 1946
and stipulated that the package – addressed to a putative
grandchild or great-grandchild – should remain unopened
until 1974. The main part of the narrative consists of the
privately printed memoirs of her feckless husband, Archibald
McCandless. From this narrative it would appear that Victoria
is a freak: Archibald's grotesque mentor Godwin Baxter has
revived the drowned corpse of a pregnant woman and replaced
her brain with that of her unborn foetus. The editor Gray seems
to accept this explanation, reckoning that on her death in 1946
Victoria's brain (born in 1880) was 66 but her body (born 'in
a Manchester slum in 1854') was 92.[19] In Archibald's account,
'Bella Baxter' (as she is known) elopes prior to her marriage
to him with the hapless Duncan Wedderburn, who is driven
insane by her sexual demands. Travelling through Europe she is
mistaken for a Lady Blessington. Victoria's own (much briefer)
account upends Archibald's by positing an alternative narrative
whereby she has escaped to Baxter's house from the brutalizing

[19] Alasdair Gray, *Poor Things* (London: Bloomsbury, 1992), p. 317. Further
references in the text to this edition.

sexual demands of her first husband, the blimpish stereotype General Sir Aubrey de la Pole Blessington.

The male narrative thus posits the woman as reborn as a result of Godwin Baxter's experimental surgery, but its 'authoritative' voice falls silent on Archibald McCandless's death in 1911 (Baxter has already died in 1884 and Blessington had apparently committed suicide the previous year). The female narrative posits a more sadly conventional story of husbandly brutality and uxorial escape. Gray's seeming editorial endorsement of the male narrative is frivolously deflected by a double publisher's blurb on the inside jacket flap, one for 'a high-class hardback' (in which Gray claims to have 'shrugged off his postmodernist label') and one for 'a popular hardback'. More seriously, any account of *Poor Things* must take on board Gray's keen factual interest in the enlightened socialism of Dr Victoria McCandless. In earlier life she has run an abortion clinic, and a post-retirement correspondence with the real-life communist poet Hugh MacDiarmid (C. M. Grieve) (1892–1978), also one-time co-founder of the SNP, forms part of Gray's editorial apparatus. Alongside Gray's persistently contentious political comment on the Scottish professional establishment, there are lighter touches: at one point the national broadsheet the *Scotsman* is described as 'an Edinburgh journal' (p. 285).

In his recent work Gray has taken his artistic collectivism to new lengths. In *Something Leather* (1990) Gray acknowledges – to an unpublished story by James Kelman – his use of subversive orthographic marking to indicate standard English 'because I enjoy its weird music'.[20] It is certainly true that the result ('I do not wish to deprive you of a bedroom wha you have slept fo nialy faw yias, Harriet' [*Something Leather*, p. 139]) can be seen as challenging analogues to Alison Lee's remarks on the distancing effect of Scottish words in the realist sections of *Lanark*:

---

[20]Alasdair Gray, *Something Leather* (1990; London: Picador, 1991), p. 251. Further references in the text to this edition.

Words such as 'dauner' (walk or stroll), 'keeked' (peeked), and 'midden-rakes' (garbage pickers) make Glasgow as distant and fictional a world [to the non-Glaswegian] as Unthank.[21]

Yet anyone writing in an English dialect can orthographically represent standard English, as Gray does in *Something Leather*: the acknowledgement to Kelman seems almost headstrong.

This perverseness characterizes the frame surrounding the case documents comprising the bulk of *Poor Things*. The frame is again presented collectively, as an argument between Gray and the man who has actually discovered the McCandless documents, Michael Donnelly. The point of contention between these two 'authorities' is that in 'editing' the documents discovered by Donnelly, Gray has allegedly destroyed their binding in the interests of reproducing their handsome etchings by a William Strang – these 'etchings' are familiar to readers of Gray's other work as his own illustrations, and they are supplemented by *genuine* anatomical etchings reproduced from the medical textbook of Gray's namesake – before mislaying them altogether ('These mistakes are continually happening in book production, and nobody regrets them more than I do' [*Poor Things*, p. xiv]). In this way, the only authority for what the reader ends up reading is Gray's own, and the rival claims of historical fact and fictional pastiche remain indeterminate.

Justifying the 'Nasty': Iain Banks

For the most part, England's critical establishment reacted to Iain Banks's *The Wasp Factory* with hostility; not all of this was completely undisguised, however. At the silly end of the spectrum was the view that the manuscript might have been submitted in jest 'to fool literary London into respect for rubbish' (*The*

[21]Alison Lee, *Realism and Power: Postmodern British Fiction* (London & New York: Routledge, 1990), p. 103.

Times), with the *Times Literary Supplement* considering it a cynical attempt to make an impact with a first novel and the *Sunday Express* regarding it as the literary equivalent of the video nasty. These responses can be seen partly as a knee-jerk failure to read the mood of the time, and more interestingly as a failure to come to terms with how the reading public was beginning to respond as consumer of the literary fiction of its time. Here, the self-importance of 'literary London' undoubtedly played a role. Perhaps most significantly of all, these responses failed to appreciate the stylishness that other reviews, while by no means applauding the subject-matter, regarded as a – or perhaps the – redeeming feature ('Iain Banks must be given credit for a polished debut. Enjoy it I did not' [*Sunday Telegraph*]). All the same, there were a few positive reactions, one of the most unqualified coming from Selina Hastings in the *Daily Telegraph*:

> Iain Banks has written one of the most brilliant first novels I have come across for some time. His study of an obsessive personality is extraordinary, written with a clarity and attention to detail that is most impressive.

All these responses and many more are reproduced, in what was standard practice for the time, on the cover and opening pages of the 1985 Futura reprint. But in this case the responses were so at variance with each other that they can be read as playing into the hands of both Banks's and Futura's marketing personnel by suggesting not simply that controversy was to be the main selling point of this novel, but that the reviewing establishment had been confronted with something it could not handle. The implication was that author and publisher were prepared liberally to tolerate a far wider range of expression than were those who condemned them. Differences of taste are one thing (one can 'enjoy' a novel of this kind or not) – but it is hard to believe that 'crassly explicit language' (*The Times*) and 'control', 'assurance' and 'originality' (the *Financial Times*) amount to descriptions of the same book. This original approach to the blurb-bite strategy paid off: subsequent Futura/Abacus reprints reflect the increasingly positive assessment of Banks's total achievement. The paperback reprint of *Complicity*, which first appeared nearly a decade later in 1993, even quotes a send-up blurb by Banks himself: 'A bit like *The Wasp Factory* except without the happy ending and redeeming air of cheerfulness'.

Selina Hastings' *Daily Telegraph* review noticed what can be seen in retrospect as two constants in Banks's writing: a highly developed interest in obsessively psychopathological states of mind, and a remarkable talent for the deft verbal description of complex mechanical and technological processes and locales, a talent that implies a highly visual imagination on the writer's part. To these qualities may be added the violence and nastiness noted by practically every reviewer of *The Wasp Factory*; and the central critical question must, I suppose, be whether the entire brew can be justified. A brief subsequent account of *Complicity* demonstrates my view that, in the intervening decade, the talent discernible in *The Wasp Factory* fully justifies the nature of the subject-matter, however nasty this may be felt to be.

Both *The Wasp Factory* and *Complicity* work with the 'double' once again recognizable from the Scottish Gothic tradition: in each case the double stands in relation to the narrator as a displaced sibling. Frank Cauldhame in *The Wasp Factory* is assailed by grotesque phone calls apparently charting the physical approach of his maniacal half-brother Eric, who has escaped from the institution in which he is being held. In *Complicity* the 'journo' Cameron Colley becomes involved with the investigation of the bizarre tortures and deaths of a series of establishment figures.

Frank Cauldhame lives with his father on an island, apparently situated in the Firth of Forth. Although the precise location is never made clear, both house and environment are described with adroit yet obsessive accuracy. Eric has been institutionalized after witnessing a horrific sight (in due course unflinchingly described) in the basement of the teaching hospital in which retarded children are being housed and where he has been carrying out a vacation job. The description of that incident is introduced with all the suspense an experienced practitioner of horror can generate, but in retrospect it is Frank's description of Eric's insanity that is striking for what it reveals about Frank's own maturity of insight, although some readers might regard this as a shortcoming on a first-time novelist's part, a failure to disguise himself as author sufficiently. Nevertheless, to Frank, Eric is:

> . . . an adult damaged and dangerous, confused and pathetic and manic all at once. He reminded me of a hologram, shattered; with the whole image contained within one spear-like shard, at once splinter and entirety.[22]

Sitting beside this degree of seasoned objectivity is a paradox uniting the half-brothers. Eric has been declared a danger to society: his aberration chiefly takes the form of torturing, killing and eating dogs. Frank, however, on his own admission, has committed three childhood murders, and appears to live undetected in the relative if unusual comfort of his own home, accorded a remarkable degree of independence (he is still below drinking age). Frank describes his murders with the lack of passion of the true psychopath, and this aspect of his character is counterpointed by his early admission that, since his birth has never been officially registered, he must remain hidden away on the island, one of society's secrets – his lack of schooling contrasting with Eric's considerable scholarly achievements. Nevertheless, Frank appears remarkably intelligent, articulate, resourceful and self-knowing. The murders themselves ('It was just a stage I was going through' [*Wasp Factory*, p. 42]) involve complex planning and an ability to act quickly and spontaneously when the right moment presents itself. But the

[22]Iain Banks, *The Wasp Factory* (1984; London & Sydney: Futura, 1985), p. 139. Further references to this edition in the text above.

destruction of the wasps means more: it is a kind of religion to Frank. It is accompanied by various rituals and incantations, and incorporates an important element of chance. The most noticeable feature of the Wasp Factory, a complicated death machine, is a clock face formerly belonging to the Royal Bank of Scotland and dated 1864:

> I watched the wasp come out of the jar, under a photograph of Eric I had placed face down on the glass. The insect wasted no time; it was on the face of the Factory in seconds. It crawled over the maker's name and the year the clock was born, ignored the wasp candles totally, and went more or less straight for the big XII, over that and through the door opposite, which snicked quietly closed behind it. It went at a fast crawl down the corridor, through the lobster-pot funnel made from thread which would stop it from turning back, then entered the highly polished steel funnel and slipped down into the glass-covered chamber where it would die. (*Wasp Factory*, pp. 122–23)

Frank's control over his environment extends to his insight that the island on which he lives has significant potential. At one point he reflects that 'all our lives are symbols' (*Wasp Factory*, p. 117), and when off the island he knows that 'it is good to remove oneself sometimes and get a sense of perspective from a little farther away' (*Wasp Factory*, p. 136). He, just as much as the reader, is wrong-footed by the revelation of the real use to which his father has put a childhood accident in which Frank is supposed to have been castrated by a dog. We discover that Frank's father has actually *constructed* Frank with the same kind of irresponsible spontaneity later to be exhibited by his offspring, who in reality turns out to be Frances Lesley Cauldhame. Her father, who always does the cooking, has feigned the castration and dosed her ever since with male hormones. Unable to procreate – but not for the reasons she and the reader have hitherto believed – Frances immediately reconstructs her symbolic understanding of the narrative closure that is really hers:

> Believing in my great hurt, my literal cutting off from society's mainland, it seems to me that I took life in a sense too seriously, and the lives of others, for the same reason, too lightly. The murders were my own conception; my sex. The Factory was my attempt to construct life, to replace the involvement which otherwise I did not want. (*Wasp Factory*, p. 183)

It is important to be clear that this revelation uses the 'nasty' to relate Frances's 'reconstruction' of herself to chaos theory, to both the implications of randomness and the task of the novelist or fiction-maker to impose sense on senselessness.

The idea that 'all our lives are symbols' can be both meaningful and ludicrous in Banks's world. This combination is nicely caught in a motif from *Complicity*, in which one of Cameron's journo colleagues tries entering Scots place-names into his spell-checker: thus 'Colonsay' becomes 'Colonic'; 'Carnoustie', 'Carousing'; and so on. Although this is not as hilariously funny to Cameron as it is to his colleague Frank Soare, there are in fact two simultaneous jokes here: spell-checks can present bizarre solutions to intractable problems (this can often be more amusing in itself than Frank's examples suggest), and spell-checks can be seen by a particularly paranoid kind of Scot to have been designed, like so much other computer software, with the cultural hegemony of standard UK or US English inherent in their default settings. The simultaneity is a fitting emblem of the way words and episodes in Banks's fiction can be interpreted in terms of an apparent randomness that may, perhaps, after all, turn out to be significant.

Cameron's investigation into the events that constitute the story of *Complicity* actually implicates him in those events. The narrative begins with an episode of the kind that punctuates it until Cameron's and the reader's discovery that he is being held in police custody and used as bait for the real offender. However, the identity of the offender, even though the alert reader may guess it before long, is implicated with Cameron's own in a number of ways. Although the main part of *Complicity* is a first-person narration, the unusual second-person form is used for the sadistic, obsessively technical and descriptively presented episodes of torture and murder. This narrative device, while it may rule out Cameron as the offender, certainly plants in the reader's mind the distinct possibility that Cameron may be carrying out these attacks while high on crack and oblivious of them afterwards, since he is candid about his coke-sniffing, joint-rolling and drinking, as well as his fast driving while high.

Cameron also has a predilection for sado-masochism and acts out his fantasies with Yvonne, the wife of one of his friends. One particularly vivid scene involving the bondage, rape and buggery of a woman (presumably Yvonne by Cameron) is presented without a 'frame' before disclosing itself at the end as a planned fantasy that is then seen to counterpoint an earlier bondage episode in which Yvonne has dominated Cameron. Cameron is further implicated by his previous concoction of a spoof feature, 'Radical Equaliser?', in which the idea of taking revenge in kind on over-zealous police chiefs and judges, profiteers and arms smugglers (who may be government ministers), and ruthless tycoons and industrial chiefs, is aired. While under initial interrogation, in England where the laws of custody allow greater freedom for police investigation than in Scotland, Cameron reflects:

> . . . this is ghastly. I can't believe they're actually asking me this sort of stuff. They can't really think I'm a murderer, can they? I'm a journalist; cynical and hard-bitten and all that shit and I do drugs and I drive too fast and I hate the Tories and all their accomplices, but I'm not a fucking *murderer* . . .[23]

[23]Iain Banks, *Complicity* (1993; London: Abacus, 1994), pp. 109–110. Further references to this edition in the text above.

The real culprit turns out, as the reader has suspected and if not guessed, then at least passionately hoped, not to be Cameron, but a childhood friend with whom Cameron has identified intensely and closely, one of the unexamined heroes of the Falklands-Malvinas offensive of 1982 – a man who by the time of the novel's present has tipped into insanity. Banks gives the by now conventional idea of postmodernist self-reflexiveness an original twist by suggesting that the real complicity is between those who connive at society's ills not simply by allowing them to happen, but by reading about them in – and writing about them for – the media. Banks's world-picture is rescued from dreary adolescent rebelliousness of the we-are-all-guilty sort by the liveliness and lightness of touch that characterizes all his best writing.

At the end of *Complicity* Cameron recalls an incident in which he has visited one of Edinburgh's historical horror-spots, Mary King's Close, 'abandoned and covered over in the sixteenth century, left just as it was, untouched, because so many people had died of the plague in that part of the old town's swarming tenement-warrens' (*Complicity*, p. 309). The soon-to-be culprit has accompanied Cameron and as a practical joke arranges to have the lights switched off. This dry run for the novel's avenging crimes compounds the idea of complicity through the technical device of using the second-person narrative of or for Cameron himself:

... in those moments of blackness you stood there, as though you yourself were made of stone like the stunted, buried buildings around you, and for all your educated cynicism, for all your late twentieth-century materialist Western maleness and your fierce despisal of all things superstitious, you felt a touch of true and absolute terror, a consummately feral dread of the dark; [. . .] and in that primaeval mirror of the soul, that shaft of self-conscious understanding which sounded both the depths of your collective history and your own individual being, you glimpsed – during that extended, petrified moment – something that was you and not you, was a threat and not a threat, an enemy and not an enemy, but possessed of a final, expediently functional indifference more horrifying than evil. (*Complicity*, p. 310)

Contrasting with everything that has preceded it by for once descending under the facile morality, the computer-game violence and the novel's glitzy 1990s designer surface, yet at the same time contriving to show how Banks has Cameron perceive his darker double self, the tone of this passage is brilliantly suspended between portentous profundity and genuine cleverness – these are after all the words of a journalist who has to sell those words. At his best, Banks cannot be fingered for either frivolity or pessimism about the late twentieth-century human state, but his irruption into recognition in the English-speaking world as one of Scotland's most fluent fictional voices of the 1980s and 1990s has been remarkably hard for some of his non-compatriot readers to appreciate. The writer who began with such technical brilliance but failed consistently to distance himself sufficiently from his protagonist is now at the height of his powers: it is not technique alone, but his understanding of the genuine moral ambiguities his use of language compels that justifies Iain Banks's subject-matter.

Ironic Betrayal: A. L. Kennedy

If the storyline of A. L. Kennedy's *Looking for the Possible Dance* is straightforward, its plot and narrative are not. The young heroine, Margaret Hamilton, leaves Glasgow for London after being fired from her position at the local Community Link Centre, also known by those working there (despite its repressive regime) as the 'Fun Factory'. In a novel of quiet humour but strange and sometimes sinister echoes, it will transpire that the loss of Margaret's job is part of a general climax characterized by an unexpected outburst of violence. The various courses taken by Margaret's personal relationships with two males, and the nature of her professional relationship with a third, seem in their totality to comprise her reasons for leaving Glasgow. On the train journey, she meets a fourth male, severely disabled and described in terms that imaginatively and sympathetically reflect his physical limitations. The novel charts the course of this journey; Kennedy's technical achievement here is to imagine herself and her readers into the mind of the ironically named paraplegic listener, James Watt; the journey is interspersed with various kinds of flashback that, at the novel's conclusion, fit jaggedly together, offering the suggestion of a falling into place of all the pieces but at the same time leaving the ending remarkably open.

The personal relationships are those with Margaret's late father Edward (Ted) Alisdair Hamilton and boyfriend Colin McCoag, like Margaret a Scot. Colin and Margaret have met while studying English literature together at an unnamed university 'down south'. Margaret shows an external conformity that is tempered by a rich and drily amused recollective and fantasy life, by communal participation at student demonstrations and dope-smoking sessions, as well as by her own reference to the loss of her virginity 'in the third week of the second term. To Colin. He took it away to wherever virginity goes' (*Possible Dance*, p. 40). In a strange ritual before this last-named event, the couple have their hair cut: early in the morning of her departure from Glasgow Central Station, Margaret has intriguedly observed two drunks trying to cut each other's hair before being removed by the police. Margaret's professional relationship is with Mr Lawrence, who runs the Community Link Centre. These relationships, all very different, are nevertheless connected in subtle ways.

The novel opens with a childhood scene recollected with an unjudgemental generosity of spirit that is to colour the rest of Margaret's life: that scene takes place outside the only dance she can recall her father taking her to, 'the never repeated Anniversary Ceilidh at the Methodist Church Hall and the blue light it called to her father's eyes' (*Possible Dance*, p. 3), while in a gently maudlin but by no means stotious way he assures her that 'Everything else [other than the moon and the stars] is a waste of time' (*Possible Dance*, p. 1). At this moment, Ted Hamilton achieves a kind of heroism in his daughter's eyes that is to be found nowhere in his behaviour as subsequently described. Although there is genuinely poignant compassion, instanced in a childhood memory of the father's gently applying iodine to Margaret's bleeding knees, it is not hard to see elsewhere in the relationship between father and daughter a role-reversal whereby Margaret comes to replace the absent mother. Ted is unemployed, but he keeps the best garden in the close. There is one moment at which Ted appears to drop his guard ('She didn't die, she fucking left me. Did you think I would tell you that? [. . .] She ran away the first chance she got because I was no bloody good' [*Possible Dance*, p. 66]), but these words are uttered in distress at the prospect of Margaret's relocating permanently 'back down south', and he regrets them the very next morning.

The relationships with her father and Colin are ones that Margaret can for the most part set the agenda for, even though Colin's presence is intermittent. More than once the solitariness of both Margaret and Colin is rendered in terms of one observing the other without the other's being aware of this. The device serves to intensify the unexpectedness of the climax as it involves Colin, who at one point exposes a loan shark in front of the Fun Factory's clientèle and pays a terrible price for doing so, in effect being unwittingly betrayed by Margaret. The delicacy of Kennedy's treatment of this sequence of events lies not least in the way she invites the reader to associate the rather unpredictable Colin's innocent predilection for acupuncture with the repellent Glaswegian gangland revenge cliché in which he is crucified by being nailed to a wooden floor. Colin survives this ordeal but is scarred by it in a way that reminds us of the equally baleful effects of Margaret's schooling on her sense of self. The portrayals of both relationships, with Ted and with Colin, are shot through with a wholly original mix of vulnerability and mutual incomprehension.

In this sense nothing could be more different than the professional relationship with Mr Lawrence, the director of the community centre, not least because he refuses to accept the sanctioned boundaries to that relationship. All three men, Ted, Colin and Mr Lawrence, reveal themselves as dependent in various ways on Margaret. Despite plenty of machismo among the Fun Factory's characters there is a strong quiet feminism at work in Margaret that allows her portrayal as a kind of wise fool, whose intelligence is on a completely different level from that of the other characters.

In the case of Mr Lawrence, the only palpable 'elder' and 'better', there is a constant hint at unwanted intimacy on his part that situates him uneasily and unhealthily in that area occupied neither by parent nor by partner. Characteristically Mr Lawrence is seen as repulsive for only as long as the reason for his behaviour remains unaccounted for. When his dipsomaniac wife Daisy appears on the scene, the repulsion is replaced – both for the reader and those characters privy to the scandal that is just about avoided at the Community Link Centre's truly unique *ceilidh* – by feelings of pity and incomprehension that a relationship such as that between the Lawrences should have been allowed to reach such a deep pitch of misery.

Added to those feelings is a sense of anger in the book, which the reader comes to share, at the isolation of the individual by the debased values of a ruined society. In Kennedy's portrayal of Glasgow, individuals can remain so ignorant of each other's despair that when the chance to show human concern arises, by listening to and plumbing its depths, even a sympathetic character such as Margaret is impotent to salve that despair. Early in the novel there is a harrowing little episode when Heather, one of the Centre's café helpers, drops a jar of sliced peaches: the ensuing outburst allows us a glimpse into an otherwise unnoticed life of virtually unalleviated misery and social deprivation. The vignette economically contrives to remind us that abuse of children may not be limited to the physical:

> 'I feel like it's my fault. It must be my fault. I mean, she's only six, she's just a wee lassie. "I'll batter her cunt in," she says. "I'll batter her effing cunt in." She's only six. I've no idea who she was talking about [. . .].
> 'I don't speak like that. Not in front of her [. . .]. It's the kids round here. [. . .] You think you're doing right to send her to school, you've got to do that, you think she'll be safe, and she comes back talking like a whore.' (*Possible Dance*, pp. 27–28)

The real rhetorical artistry with which the episode involving the Lawrences is handled is shown to be incalculably more effective than inarticulate anger would have been. Margaret is browbeaten into retrieving a semi-comatose Daisy from the Ladies' and into Mr Lawrence's car. Mr Lawrence later returns, frustrating any possible charges of sexual harassment that Margaret might, in her desperation, have wanted to bring, for Margaret is faced with a deliberate piece of moral blackmail on Mr Lawrence's part. It transpires that in the period that Mr Lawrence had returned to the *ceilidh*, Daisy has died at their home through inhalation of her own vomit.

Margaret lacks the power to resist the tables being turned on her: Mr Lawrence's version of affairs, in which Margaret, in playing hard to get, has been demurely offering a series of come-ons, will be the one to gain authority; it is enhanced by a fellow-worker's frightened treachery, and Margaret's career as a social worker is effectively destroyed.

What is striking about the plotting of Kennedy's novel is that Mr Lawrence's version of events, in which Margaret has in effect been at least partly responsible for Daisy's death, turns out to prefigure what we discover to be Margaret's betrayal of Colin. Ironically, that betrayal is something Margaret never even discovers, although the attentive reader will return to pick up some clues that have been dropped earlier in the book. It would be doing an injustice to the tone of the entire episode leading up to Margaret's sacking, however, not to quote from her last words on the episode:

> 'Mr Lawrence, all of this has nothing to do with me. Not even your slimy, wee fantasies have anything to do with me. I hope your new Centre does well. For the sake of some people here who are my friends. And, more than anything, I hope that none of the women who work for you will ever have to come in contact with that thing you call your mind.'
> 'Is that all?'
> 'That's all.'
> 'I take it we'll agree to differ, then.'
> 'And I'll go quietly, yes. What's the point in anything else. Pardon me if I don't shake your hand. Oh, and Mr Lawrence.'
> 'Yes?'
> 'Take a running fuck to yourself. Good morning.' (*Possible Dance*, pp. 225–26)

The political background against which the novels discussed in this chapter have been written has stoked up the resurgence of Scottish fiction. I have tried to indicate something of the range of this resurgence. If there is one single achievement on which all else rests it is Alasdair Gray's, for he has managed to do what even MacDiarmid failed to, which is to bring experimental writing into the Scottish and thus European mainstream, and to free Scottish literature from the exclusively realist and other limitations it had laboured under till then.

It is for this reason that in selecting a Celtic culture within the British Isles (the term is used here to include Ireland), I decided to concentrate on Scotland. Yet it would have been misleading to exclude Ireland from discussion altogether. Irish writing has long enjoyed a more favoured and prominent position than its Scottish counterpart. Experimental and/or international Irish writing

(Joyce, Beckett, Flann O'Brien, John Banville) has a strong established European history. Even though the greater part of Ireland (unlike Scotland) has been an independent republic for much of the twentieth century, Ireland (like Scotland) is still striving to come to terms with a definition of itself that has to a large extent been imposed in complicity with the cultural oppressor: the Tartanry of Scotland has an inexact but relevant counterpart in the 'blarney' of Ireland. Still, for many years mainstream Irish fiction has included rural realism (John McGahern, William Trevor, Jennifer Johnston) and, since the late 1970s, the harsher and quite often black-comic sides of urban reality as well (Dermot Bolger, Roddy Doyle). A fascinating recent novel, Dermot Healy's *A Goat's Song* (1994), combines both into a new kind of all-Ireland novel.

The nationalism of the Scottish fiction I've found myself drawn to in this chapter presents us with an interesting paradox. On the one hand it is confident in nature, and has shown itself to be capable of reaching an international readership. On the other hand, the nationalism of Scotland is plagued by a characteristic common to that of all small European nations. A revealing passage in Irvine Welsh's recent cult novel *Trainspotting* makes the point vividly, anarchically, and desolately; the speaker is in London:

> The pub sign is a new one, but its message is old. The Britannia. Rule Britannia. Ah've never felt British, because ah'm not. It's ugly and artificial. Ah've never really felt Scottish either, though. Scotland the brave, ma arse; Scotland the shitein cunt. We'd throttle the life oot ay each other fir the privilege ay rimmin some English aristocrat's piles. Ah've never felt a fuckin thing aboot countries, other than total disgust. They should abolish the fuckin lot ay them. Kill every fuckin parasite politician that ever stood up and mouthed lies and fascist platitudes in a suit and smarmy smile.[24]

[24]Irvine Welsh, *Trainspotting* (1993; London, Minerva, 1994), p. 228.

Scotland is faced with the unpalatable fact that what little is known about it from outside is of the 'heritage-industry' nature (what has been described above as Kailyardism or Tartanry). What the Scots know about England, or indeed the United States, is both more – and more accurate – than what those more influential countries know (or wish to know) about Scotland. The result: nationalist pride jars against a sense of inferiority.

When the Union finally disintegrates and Scotland becomes either a properly devolved country with its own assembly, or a truly independent nation (whether the republic most people now realistically expect, or the Catholic European state dreamed of by the Stuart monarchists), this problem of self-definition will be the most pressing facing Scottish nationalism. The literary resurgence of the past decade may well prove to have been the great preparation for that exciting prospect.

5

Fantasies of London: Past and Present

Born, for the most part brought up, and entirely schooled in London – the London on what Angela Carter might (legitimately) have called the 'right' side of the tracks (its affluent north-western suburbs) – I have watched the city of my birth and youth become the focus for a quite extraordinary burst of creative energy since the 1980s. Like many others I have been appalled by London's socio-economic decline over the same period. Many Londoners share, with others whose love of this city is deep, a sense that the 1980s witnessed one of the worst collapses in London's civic and communal health, both physical and spiritual.

This chapter focuses on some of the most interesting fictional responses to that decline, responses that have frequently taken the form of non-realistic or surrealistic explorations of London's past, present and future. One has to look back over the longer term, to T. S. Eliot, to Oscar Wilde, to R. L. Stevenson, to Charles Dickens, to find any really vital parallel for the London writing that has been appearing since the 1980s. A lively contribution to this dynamism has been that of writers such as the English-born Hanif Kureishi, whose fascinating hybrid London novels of the 1990s, *The Buddha of Suburbia* (1991) and *The Black Album* (1995), reflect his own part-English, part-Pakistani parentage, and show how London now appears to recent incomers. Work such as Kureishi's is the home-grown version of the enlarged international franchise of the novel in Britain today. It fuses concerns of ethnicity and identity with attention to London's unfashionable suburbs versus its throbbing heart – as well as (in the latter novel) offering interesting insight into the forces driving young British Muslim fundamentalists.

Of the generation of novelists that began publishing fiction in the 1950s, it seems to me that only one, Iris Murdoch, has succeeded in imaginatively constructing a London of her own, a fantastic cityscape unlike any other. Yet recently she has been joined, in different but absorbing ways, by writers such as Peter Ackroyd, Martin Amis, Angela Carter and Iain Sinclair. In the novels I have recently found myself drawn to, the present is rarely the present without being suffused, sometimes terrifyingly, sometimes comically, always arrestingly, with the past; place is haunted by voices and presences, some harmless and some baneful; and the realism of the action has become a realism of excess, of magic or of the dreaming world.

Roy Porter's splendidly energetic and informative *London: A Social History* (1994) shows how during the 1980s London was dealt a severe if not fatal thrashing. Many events have buffeted London in its two millennia of existence. Not least among these has been the threat of depopulation and sheer physical destruction in the 1660s and again in the 1940s. Only the massive numbers of people migrating to London from all parts in the eighteenth and nineteenth centuries saved the city – with its scarcely credible death rates, levels that for periods substantially exceeded birth rates – from terminal decline.

Porter goes further, however, and strongly emphasizes the unenviably unique position London has found itself in since 1986. In that year the Greater London Council (GLC) was abolished, leaving this extraordinary city alone among the great cities of the industrialized world in possessing no central political and administrative body. The abolition of the traditionally radical though often irritatingly ineffective GLC, successor to the nineteenth-century London County Council (LCC), has been seen as consistent with the view of an administration headed throughout the 1980s by a prime minister who appears genuinely to have believed that 'There is no such thing as society'. This has encouraged a socio-demographic crisis from which London is in serious danger of imploding beyond repair. Even though a future Labour administration is committed to some kind of regeneration of central elected civic authority, the damage already done may be irreparable.

London threatens to become – perhaps in some senses has already become – a Third World city. Habitats of 'fabulous, luxurious, ostentatious wealth' occupy the same civic space as pockets of high unemployment. The evil of unemployment is a nightmare that London (unlike most of Britain's other major centres of urban population) has in the past managed to avoid, yet 'by 1990, 20 per cent of Hackney's and Haringey's population was out of work, as was 35 per cent in the King's Cross area of Camden'.[1] A new generation of London novelists has had to engage with the surreality of a city thus described by Roy Porter:

> Homelessness – eradicated by the mid twentieth century – became endemic again in the Thatcher years. Swarms of dossers and vagrants reappeared, cardboard cities sprouting in the luxuriance of yuppie affluence. An encampment of tramps and the homeless arose at the Waterloo Bridge roundabout, fifty yards from the Festival of Britain site and next to the National Theatre, while elegant Lincoln's Inn Fields became a Third World shanty town for scores of the homeless – a settlement tolerated for several years, since nobody wished to assume responsibility. As in Third World countries, thousands in London now beg by day [. . .] and sleep rough in shop doorways and church porches [. . .]. The sprouting of ghetto cultures of unemployed ethnic minorities, associated with drug-trafficking and attended by bush warfare with the police, signals a novel crisis for London; in previous centuries immigrants – Flemish weavers, Huguenot craftsmen, Irish navvies and Jewish refugees – were integrated fairly quickly

[1]Roy Porter, *London: A Social History* (London: Hamish Hamilton, 1994), pp. 387, 370.

into the community, because London was a city of economic opportunity. The availability of work always facilitated the integration of newcomers, the young and the poor.[2]

With that last point, Porter makes the case for the uniqueness of London's present predicament – which is not that it exists (for it exists elsewhere, in many American and indeed British inner cities), nor even that it is without any kind of precedent (we have been here before, with the London of Defoe, of Hogarth, of Dickens). What is terrifying about the London of the post-Thatcher era is that the political administration that has followed it has seemed unable or unwilling to finance any 'community' for the dispossessed to be integrated into. The traditional sources of work in London are no longer as available as they were throughout the Industrial Revolution and before. As Porter puts it:

> An ever-rising proportion of today's [London] population is unproductive, [. . .] chronically dependent on income support and social services. Many [. . .] are 'problem people': the aged and disabled, lone-parent families, children in care, delinquents, drop-outs, dossers. [. . .] The capital today harbours huge concentrations of the unskilled, the long-term unemployed, new migrants, drifters, offenders and others caught in the poverty trap and excluded from the mainstream.[3]

No wonder that some of the most compelling fantasies of London spawned during and after the Thatcher decade are apocalyptic in nature, or look back to other ages in which London's cityscape included poverty, squalor, loneliness and criminal depravity. The fictional London of the 1980s and 1990s, then, is a complex topographical construct. It includes what Angela Carter's Dora Chance calls 'the left-hand side,

[2]Porter, p. 372.
[3]Porter, p. 3.

the side the tourist rarely sees, the *bastard* side of Old Father Thames'.[4] We may take this to comprise the areas not just to the south of the Thames (excluding the fashionable suburbs such as Dulwich or Wimbledon) but to the east of the Lea; it also includes one of many unresolved areas to the west of the West End that (according to whom you wish to be) could be described as Holland Park or the Ladbroke Grove that runs under the highly polluted A40(M) Westway. It is that London on which this chapter focuses.

Realigning the City: Peter Ackroyd and Iain Sinclair

The publications of Peter Ackroyd between 1982 and 1994 include eight novels. Ackroyd accepts that our lives can be lived only in the present. However, he combines this acceptance with his inheritance of a sharply formulated sense of the belief associated with T. S. Eliot, who, incidentally, wrote brilliantly about London in many of his earlier poems including *The Waste Land* (1922), that our sense of the present must include a communally shared sense of the past. Ackroyd, who published a biography of Eliot in 1984, has since said:

> All previous moments exist concurrently in every present moment. Language made our world and our language now contains its own complete history. Previous words, previous styles lie embedded in the way we speak now. They are layers of language like fossil strata beneath the surface.[5]

In Ackroyd's London Weekend Television (LWT) London Lecture, 'London Luminaries and Victorian Visionaries', which he

---

[4]Angela Carter, *Wise Children* (London: Chatto & Windus, 1991), p. 1. Further references in the text are to this edition.
[5]Brian Appleyard, 'Aspects of Ackroyd', *Sunday Times Magazine*, 9 April 1989, p. 54. Cited by Luc Herman, 'Peter Ackroyd', in *Postwar Literatures in English: A Lexicon of Contemporary Authors* 7 (March 1990), p. 2.

gave at the Victoria and Albert Museum on 7 December 1993, this idea was enhanced by his description of London as 'one of the dark places of the earth' which 'has always been a shadowy and merciless city'. He went on to assert that '[t]here are parts of London [. . .] where time has actually hardened and come to an end', and later suggested 'a chronological resonance within the city itself'.[6]

None of his readers will deny Ackroyd his astonishing ear for '[p]revious words, previous styles' as expressed in a command of literary pastiche in all his work, especially since the justly acclaimed *Hawksmoor* (1985; Whitbread Novel of the Year and *Guardian* Fiction Award). Later novels include *Chatterton* (1987; shortlisted for the Booker), *English Music* (1992), *The House of Doctor Dee* (1993) and *Dan Leno and the Limehouse Golem* (1994). All demonstrate a gift for historical ventriloquy rivalling all his contemporaries: Ackroyd clearly researches his work deeply. Indeed, so vivid are these historical evocations, of language and style, and also of the social history and topography of London, built on layer by layer as the centuries have passed, that Ackroyd's present-day city seems curiously flat and impoverished. The young Timothy Harcombe, for instance, whose passage to adulthood is charted in what is in effect a spiritualist *Bildungsroman* in *English Music*, is deprived of a normal childhood in the 1920s not because his father Clement exploits him – however kindly – as a medium, but because he is friendless. This lack of friends of his own age is something Timothy himself more than once remarks on. Other forms of solitariness play similar roles in the strangely lifeless lives of the present-day Londoners of *Hawksmoor*. Charles Wychwood actually dies during the course of *Chatterton*. But there is a form of the present, in *Chatterton* particularly, that is wilfully and grotesquely alive: here it is as though Ackroyd has brought Dickens (whose life he has also written) into the present

---

[6]The last quotation appears in the edited version, 'Cockney Visionaries', reprinted in the *Independent*, 18 December 1993, p. 27.

day. Certain present-day Ackroyd characters are reminiscent of Dickensian grotesques such as Daniel Quilp, but Ackroyd makes their sexual ambiguity more explicit, prefiguring the worlds of cross-dressing, high camp and music-hall which he recreates so spectacularly in *Dan Leno and the Limehouse Golem*.

For the most part, however, Ackroyd's present-day Londoners remain physically inert, unanimated: they eat simple austere meals, often in unlit rooms that may at times be alive with whisperings and shadows, and their encounters with the numinous occur in dreams and visions, with what is often a minimum of physical exertion. Children, meaning boys, are principal characters in much of Ackroyd's fiction as they are for Dickens; many of the parents are single, and there is a high concentration of widowed or deserted fathers. Ackroyd himself was brought up as an English Catholic, and it is a peculiarly English form of lower-middle-class Catholicism (certainly not that of the literary-aristocratic convert) that suffuses much of the atmosphere. Its role seems to be to draw attention to the possibility of a world of Englishness untouched by either the Reformation or the establishment of a national, Protestant, yet episcopal State Church that has appropriated not just the hierarchical structures of the old religion but London's pre-Reformation, pre-conflagration buildings as well.[7]

Ackroyd's most recent interests are celebrated in *Dan Leno and the Limehouse Golem*, a novel in which he has developed a newly invigorated blend of historiography and linguistic 'embedding', to use his own word, to capture the most recent forms of popular entertainment not to have survived in technically recorded form.[8]

---

[7]Some of these preoccupations intersect interestingly with Kingsley Amis's *The Alteration* (1976).

[8]There is an eccentric London bookseller in *Chatterton* named Leno. This detail seems of a piece with the larger displacements by Ackroyd's Dyer of the historical *Hawksmoor*, or the wrong-footing of readerly expectations in *The Great Fire of London* (1982), a novel actually related intertextually to Dickens' *Little Dorrit* and the business of creating a film version of nineteenth-century London.

The last two novels published by Angela Carter, *Nights at the Circus* (1984) and *Wise Children* (1991) take their place, too, in celebrating the exuberance of an often unheard tradition of alternative entertainment in London, and it is in this context that I shall be considering them.

Hawksmoor (1985) has quickly become, to the world of academe, a much discussed international postmodernist text, but none of the commentators who approach it in this way seem interested in considering it as part of a wider literary programme (shared by most of the other writers treated in this chapter) of what Patrick Wright has termed 'realigning the city'.[9] Nicholas Dyer's Hawksmoor churches are deliberately sited. Here, Ackroyd's imagination has been powerfully fired by his fellow-writer the poet and novelist Iain Sinclair, whose remarkable prose-poem *Lud Heat* (1975) was reissued by Vintage in 1995.

An attempt to 'reconstruct' *Hawksmoor* realistically would run roughly as follows: in 1711 the architect Nicholas Dyer begins work on the construction of seven new London churches to replace those destroyed in the Great Fire of 1666. Dyer has been involved with a satanic cult since the deaths of his parents during the plague of 1665; he consecrates each of the seven churches he builds during 1711 and (it is to be assumed) 1715 with the sacrifice, or murder, depending on one's point of view, of a male virgin, usually a young boy. In twentieth-century London, the detective Hawksmoor investigates a series of murders that appear to be occurring on the sites of Dyer's churches. Ackroyd outdoes the *nouveau romancier* Alain Robbe-Grillet in *Les gommes* (1953; *The Erasers*, 1964), creating in Hawksmoor a figure who is at once murderer, detective, and – finally – victim.[10]

[9]Patrick Wright, *A Journey through Ruins* (1992; London: Flamingo, 1993), pp. 253ff.
[10]I owe this insight to Nicole Slagter, diss., 'Worlds made of words: a response to Brian McHale's postmodernist fiction' (Amsterdam, Vrije Universiteit, September 1989), pp. 71–75.

Ackroyd's construction of the alternative history is explicit.[11] If in terms of architectural career the fictional Dyer conforms to the historical Nicholas Hawksmoor, there are some significant deviations. Like the historical Hawksmoor, Dyer is a pupil of Sir Christopher Wren. But the satanism is Dyer's own, and as to observable topographical fact, Dyer's seventh and last church, Little St Hugh's beside Moorfields, does not actually exist, whereas the other six do. The broad outlines of Ackroyd's present-day London could be reconstructed from any A–Z street map. Yet closer examination shows that Ackroyd has kept to the street plans of the London of 1711–15, so that some of the smaller streets down which the detective Hawksmoor walks no longer actually exist, even though the main thoroughfares are still to be found.

Late in the narrative, Hawksmoor appears to be researching his case by consulting 'DYER, Nicholas' in an encyclopaedia, where Dyer's dates are given as '1654-c.1715' [sic]. The dating is worth remarking; Hawksmoor reads: "'[Dyer] died in London in the winter of 1715, it is thought of the gout, although the records of his death and burial have been lost'".[12] The point of the doubt in the case of Dyer's biography is that in the alternative universe of Hawksmoor, Dyer's death must still take place: that is, it and that of Hawksmoor come together at the moment each meet and blend in the unspoken rendezvous in the fictional seventh church, Little St Hugh's ('And when they spoke they spoke with one voice') (Hawksmoor, p. 217). St Hugh is traditionally identified with the young virgin boy martyr or sacrificial victim: his tale is told, for instance, by Chaucer's Prioress.

Ackroyd's alternative world is not a socially privileged one. There is an extended passage on the life of a tramp later to be one of the murder victims; there are references to the gay underworld of, and a sinister portrayal of a lunatic asylum in,

[11]Cf. Brian McHale, *Postmodernist Fiction* (London & New York: Methuen, 1987), pp. 41–130, etc.
[12]Peter Ackroyd, *Hawksmoor* (1985; London: Sphere/ Abacus, 1986), p. 214. Page-references in the text above to this edition.

early eighteenth-century London. The latter culminates in one of the book's most deliberately perplexing puzzles:

> At this I laugh'd and the Madman turned to me crying: What more Death still Nick, Nick, Nick, you are my own! At this I was terribly astounded, for he could in no wise have known my name. And in his Madness he called out to me again: Hark ye, you boy! I'll tell you somewhat, one Hawksmoor will this day terribly shake you. Then his Tongue rolled inwards all in a Lump, and his Eye-balls turned backwards, nothing but the White of them being seen. And the Gaoler made Signs for us to leave. (*Hawksmoor*, p. 100)

Perhaps most strikingly there is the presence, almost as a *leitmotif* connecting the novel's two aberrant worlds, of a children's culture of songs, rhymes, jingles and charms that (as in the real world) are passed on orally yet remain marginal to the world of the prevailing (adult) culture.

Iain Sinclair's first novel, *White Chappell, Scarlet Tracings*, was published in 1987, the same year as Ackroyd's *Chatterton*. *White Chappell, Scarlet Tracings* is a virtuoso conception that on one of its many levels merges the first Sherlock Holmes fiction, 'A Study in Scarlet' (1881), with the real Jack the Ripper – or Whitechapel – killings of late 1888.[13] Watson begins his tale famously thus:

> In the year 1878 I took my degree of Doctor of Medicine of the University of London, and proceeded to Nettley to go through the course prescribed for surgeons in the army . . .

Sinclair's bookseller narrator treats the first page of this story (as he puts it) 'like a prison censor, carefully blacking out, to uncover the mantic tremble beneath':

[13]Sinclair is not the first writer to have linked Sherlock Holmes with the Whitechapel killings; see, for example, Michael Dibdin, *The Last Sherlock Holmes Story* (1978; London: Faber, 1990).

[BLACK] I took my [BLACK] Doctor [BLACK], and [BLACK] Netley [BLACK] through the course prescribed for surgeons . . .[14]

In this way, one of the more ingenious but eccentric Ripper theories is vigorously restated. 'My Doctor' becomes Sir William Gull, the royal surgeon who in real life is supposed to have lobotomized the Catholic prostitute Annie Elizabeth Crook after she had given birth to a daughter, Alice Crook, in April 1885. This child had allegedly been fathered by the feebleminded and sickly Prince Albert Victor, Duke of Clarence (eldest brother of the future George V), who until his early death in 1892 was – after the future Edward VII – next in line to the throne. Clarence (so the theory goes) had met Annie Crook (who was later institutionalized and died in 1920) at the instigation of Walter Sickert. Sickert was later alleged to have fathered a son, Joseph, by Alice Crook. In the 1980s a 'Joseph Sickert' promoted an elaborate fraud linking his own origins as a natural son of Walter Sickert to the rumour that Alice Crook's nanny had passed the story of the Gull lobotomy on to a group of Whitechapel prostitutes who had attempted to blackmail Gull by attributing the death of the first five Ripper victims to his surgical expertise. Gull's factotum had been another character from real life, his coachman John Netley. In the Holmes story, Nettley is the (similarly real-life) name of the Royal Victoria Military Hospital near Southampton, founded after the Crimean War of 1856, where military surgeons were trained. The Holmes story involves the discovery of a body in a Whitechapel room that shows no external signs of injury, although the room itself is spattered with blood that is not the victim's. Sinclair invigorates

[14]Iain Sinclair, *White Chappell, Scarlet Tracings* (1987; London: Paladin, 1988), p. 59). Further page-references to this edition. There is a Borgesian moment on p. 25 in which the bookseller narrator finds 'some version of the legendary Christmas Annual with the first printing of the first appearance of Sherlock Holmes, *A Study in Scarlet* [, in which t]he date "1878" had been altered to "1888". The word "Nettley" had been altered to "Netley"'.

the most ingenious of various historical attempts to link the Ripper killings with the British Royal Family.

Patrick Wright has intriguingly stressed the genuine importance of the writer Iain Sinclair's other major real-life occupation: as a bookseller 'Sinclair built up his own exotic bibliography from the exceptional volumes that floated by'.[15] The point, presumably, is that Sinclair the bookseller is likely to be more attracted to what is unorthodox than is the professional academic social historian precisely because of the fortuitous manner in which the books in question will come his way; at any rate Sinclair encountered the work of writers such as E. O. Gordon and Alfred Watkins, producing an eccentric topographical synthesis that Wright describes as follows:

> . . . the routes of the Krays, the prophetic writings of William Blake, the sites of Jack the Ripper's killings and the Ratcliffe Highway Murders, old sheep tracks crossing east London, the seepage of cholera through underground water systems, the movement of books as they drift through the street markets, fragments of alien or prehistoric belief systems from the Tarot through to ancient Egyptian cosmology, the horrors reported weekly in the dead-pan prose of the *Hackney Gazette. (ibid.)*

According to an acknowledgement in *Hawksmoor*, Sinclair's *Lud Heat* 'first directed [Ackroyd's] attention to the stranger characteristics of the London churches'. *Lud Heat* is provided with maps that argue that certain of the Hawksmoor churches are linked by leylines, lines of force that join two or more prominent points within a given topography, believed to be formed by prehistoric tracks but also possessing magical powers. Sinclair's belief in these seems far more impassioned than Ackroyd's. On the other hand, the London of Sinclair's imagination does not attempt linguistic or ventriloquial pastiche: instead its imagery

[15]Wright, *A Journey through Ruins*, p. 257.

is astonishingly idiosyncratic, its energy charged by the sheer force of Sinclair's imaginative conception of London.

Where Sinclair departs substantially from Ackroyd is in his evident view that the past is embedded in the present at a much more fantastic, even futuristic, level. *Downriver* (1991), for instance, is a fantasy that at one level follows the Thames through London to its North Sea estuary, but at another level does so with such a transgression of historical fact and such a wealth of daring wordplay that one is inclined to think away from Britain or even Europe to a writer such as Mexico's Carlos Fuentes. (Patrick Wright is, with Mike Goldsmith, a co-dedicatee of *Downriver*.) For Sinclair, the London Thames' most famous and cartographically most vivid meander becomes 'The Isle of Doges (*Vat City plc*)' [italics *sic*]. In this fantasy, Thatcherite greed and the very roots of the British constitution are bizarrely juxtaposed in a vision of national decline:

> We knew that the Isle of Dogs had been sold to the Vatican State, and we did not care. It was a natural consequence of Runcie's merger. One of the shakier assets that had to be stripped. The peg of uncircumcised land was known to the outlying squatters of Blackwall and Silverstown as 'The Isle of Doges', and to the cynics of Riverside as 'Vat City'. This deregulated isthmus of Enterprise was a new Venice, slimy with canals, barnacled *palazzi*, pillaged art, lagoons, leper hulks: a Venice overwhelmed by Gotham City, a raked grid of canyons and stuttering aerial railways. A Venice run by secret tribunals of bagmen, too slippery for Vegas; by relic-worshipping hoodlums, the gold-mouthed heads of Columbian cocaine dynasties.[16]

If this nightmare vision of Canary Wharf (the Centre Point of the 1980s and 1990s) sounds like Roy Porter in a state

[16]Iain Sinclair, *Downriver (Or, The Vessels of Wrath): A Narrative in Seven Tales* (1991; London: Paladin, 1992), p. 265.

of altered consciousness, other passages in *Downriver* give a sense of the blistering political anger that lies just under the surface of Sinclair's prose (just as much as under that of Patrick Wright), its frayed nerve-ends flapping. Indeed, the exordium to *White Chappell, Scarlet Tracings* concludes with the cry: 'Grantham's daughter, this is your vision' (p. 12), and Wright's *A Journey through Ruins* (1992) is dedicated to 'Lady Margaret Thatcher' [*sic*].

In Sinclair's *Downriver* the fictional Margaret Thatcher, like the exemplary nineteenth-century monarch and matriarch whose eponymous values she famously espoused, has been widowed, and begins each day in the hands of her image-makers ('She was a prisoner of the rituals she alone had initiated. If she ever appeared in her original skin the underclass would riot and tear her to pieces' [*Downriver*, p. 220]). It is possible that the Leaderene, 'a couple of years into her fifth term in what was now effectively a one-party state and a one-woman party' (*Downriver*, p. 220), has connived at her husband's death, but such rumours are drowned in her image-makers' propaganda that she is now married to the nation:

> The Widow wanted a fitting memorial to her Consort. It would have to achieve an epic scale (Valhalla), soar above the docks – signifying her courage in the face of adversity, and also the courage of the nation, the 'little people', Britain-can-take-it, 'Gor blimey, Guv', it's only *one* leg, ain't it?' A memorial to the spirit of the Blitz and a torch to Enterprise. It should make Prince Albert's cheesy stack look like the heap of bat guano it would, in truth, soon become. No rivals were tolerated . . . (*Downriver*, p. 224)

It is through flights of linguistically charged fantasy such as these that clichés of Victorian architectural values, or of Londoners' stoicism faced by the wreckage and mutilation of Blitz and V-bombs are simultaneously valued and mocked. Such clichés grapple anarchically with each other and with what they serve to signify by being brought into abrupt confrontation with those signifiers: the monumental white elephant of the late 1980s, Canary Wharf, or the embarrassment brought upon – and despicably evaded by – the military and political establishments as recently as 1982 by the survival, indeed the very existence, of maimed Falklands-Malvinas veterans.

Sinclair's own acknowledgements page to *Downriver* refers to his 'grimoire of rivers and railways'. What lies beneath the metropolis has also exercised its fascination, not just on Ackroyd and Sinclair himself, but on a much younger writer, Lawrence Norfolk, who would (one assumes) respond sympathetically to Ackroyd's belief in 'parts of London [. . .] where time has actually hardened and come to an end'.

Norfolk's imposingly assured debut, the 600-page *Lemprière's Dictionary* (1991), posits an alternative history of the founding of the East India Company. The modestly ineffectual hero's quest for the unattainable Juliet Casterleigh takes in a series of bizarre deaths apparently playing out episodes from Ovid's *Metamorphoses* before settling in a richly registered London replete with the social history, the privileged customs, and the everyday noise and smells of the life of the late eighteenth century.

The quest widens to take account of John Lemprière's desire for discovery of his place in Britain's imperial structure. That structure is imagined both literally as an underground labyrinth constituting the cabalistic elements of a clandestine organization, as well as metaphorically, as an oracular mystery whose solution demands Lemprière's entire comprehension of his place in it. Juxtaposed with the bustle and clamour of London's surface is a silent, coded world lying beneath that surface, a once-living organism:

> Now down through the city's tight skin to the hotch-potch of rocks and earth beneath. Through blue-grey and stiff red clay, crumbly slabs of sediment, black granite and water-bearing

formations, past fire-damp flares, shale and veins of coal to pierce a second, more secret skin and enter the body of the Beast. Here, long fluted chambers twist away into honeycombs and open into caverns the size of churches with cradles of silica hanging from brittle calcified threads, ridges, flanges and platforms all frozen in stone to wait for centuries beneath the city. Once it was a mountain of flesh, red throbbing meat and muscle. Now it is dead stone with its veins sucked dry as dust and all its arteries blown out clean by time; an ignorant monument playing host to nine, then eight men who crawl through its passages like parasites and who differ in their understandings of its chambers, tunnels and lattices, not unnaturally – it can be accounted for in so many ways.[17]

The conception of London-as-organism has intermittently been a concern of its anatomists and inhabitants. Roy Porter offers several instances of the belief that at various times in its history this particular city was seen as a malignant tumour growing out of control, or a predator that sucked increasing numbers of humans into it in order to counter and compensate for its rapacious avarice – a metaphor for the low life-expectancy and poor living conditions London offered so much of its populace.

Recapturing Popular Entertainment: Peter Ackroyd and Angela Carter

In *Dan Leno and the Limehouse Golem*, we find Peter Ackroyd associating himself with one of the other elements of Ripper mythology, the crazed midwife, although to pursue this point further would be to spoil the book for those who have yet to read

[17]Lawrence Norfolk, *Lemprière's Dictionary* (1991; London: Minerva, 1992), p. 192.

it. Ackroyd's fantasy (these murders take place in the autumn months of 1880, not 1888) is interwoven in documentary fashion with an attempt to recreate the experience of nineteenth-century music-hall. In his LWT lecture Ackroyd had drawn attention to the 'energetic display' of the 'monopolylinguists [. . .] comedians or actors who play a number of quick-change parts in the course of one performance' ('Cockney Visionaries', p. 27), and it seems useful to have this sense of performative energy in mind when considering Angela Carter's *Nights at the Circus* and *Wise Children*, too.

Dan Leno and the Limehouse Golem can be read as a demonstration of the principal thoughts underlying the 'London Luminaries, Victorian Visionaries' lecture. A patchwork of music-hall patter, diary, trial records, first-person and apparently omniscient narration, the novel is Ackroyd's most accomplished act of literary ventriloquy-cum-pastiche yet. While *Dan Leno* is a ventriloquist's creation it nevertheless contains the information the reader needs to deconstruct it – in fact it invites deconstruction and the reader is forced to engage with the story as the various 'discourses' or modes of utterance vie for further attention and belief. The styles work almost like characters in a play, who are ideally of course characterized by the language they speak, but none of whom we should mistake for the author. As ever, it is the totality that counts – and the totality of *Dan Leno* is impressive:

[Elizabeth Cree's] attention was entirely concentrated on the threadbare stage-curtain ahead of her. A very large man in the most extraordinary striped top-coat was being helped on to the raised wooden boards, and although he seemed the worse for drink he managed to stand upright and raise his arms in the air. He called, 'Silence, if you please!' in a very stern voice and Elizabeth noticed, with some surprise, that a whole bouquet of geraniums was pinned to his buttonhole. Finally, to much cheering and laughter, he began to speak. 'A keen east wind has spoiled my voice,' he bellowed out, and then had to wait for the cheers and catcalls to subside. 'I am overwhelmed by your generosity. I have never know [*sic*] so many dear boys with such perfect manners. I feel as if I am at a tea-party.' There was so much noise now that Elizabeth had to put her hands to her ears . . . [18]

This kind of writing is augmented by an almost deadpan documentary style (something of a departure for Ackroyd), and the first-time reader is forced to confront the mystery of trying to figure out the relationship between the journals of Elizabeth Cree and her husband John. This mystery deepens on a second reading as one peruses once more the narrator's account of John Cree's labours in the British Museum Reading Room and his unawareness of his proximity to the historical presence and significance of Karl Marx and George Gissing. Interspersed with these various voices are the trial depositions of a case of murder, the verdict in which is certain but puzzling.

The book opens with an account of the hanging of Elizabeth Cree in Camberwell Prison on 6 April 1881, ostensibly documentary and straightforward in nature but with one chillingly inscrutable enigma, towards a solution of which the entire novel beckons:

> While [Elizabeth Cree] stared down at the official witnesses, the rope was placed round her neck (the executioner, knowing her precise size and weight, had measured the hemp exactly). She spoke only once before he pulled the lever and the wooden trapdoor opened beneath her. She said, 'Here we are again!' Her eyes were still upon them as she fell. (*Dan Leno*, p. 2)

Reviewing *Dan Leno* (none too warmly), Iain Sinclair remarked that the hanging of Elizabeth Cree 'is like something cranked in a

---

[18]Peter Ackroyd, *Dan Leno and the Limehouse Golem* (London: Sinclair-Stevenson, 1994), p. 18. Further references in the text to this edition.

penny slot-machine'.[19] The point is taken as long as the sense of execution as performance is stressed, along with the idea that the line dividing it and music-hall is perceived as terrifyingly and farcically thin. Among the red herrings of Ackroyd's novel is what is suggested in the full title: that is, the mass-hysterical scapegoat view that the Limehouse murders of the autumn of 1880 are being committed by a golem, which, according to one of the victims-to-be, '[o]ur ancestors thought of [. . .] as an homunculus, a material created by magic, a piece of red clay brought to life in the sorcerer's laboratory'. This 'fearful thing [. . .] sustains its life by ingesting the spirit or soul of a human being'.[20]

Attribution of the Limehouse murders to a golem accounts for the xenophobic anti-Semitism rife both in the world of *Dan Leno* and in that of the Ripper killings. Another of Ackroyd's red herrings is the fascination of at least two of his characters (a fascination shared with both the historical Thomas de Quincey and, in our own time, by Iain Sinclair and, it would seem, P. D. James) with the Ratcliffe Highway Murders of 1811. It is consistent with Ackroyd's beliefs that the spirit of place of these murders continues to haunt the 1880s London of *Dan Leno and the Limehouse Golem*.

London at the turn of the nineteenth and twentieth century is the site of the first part of Angela Carter's *Nights at the Circus*, a performance of deliberate buoyancy and technical verve. Much has been written about Carter's work,[21] but her last two novels have not (to my knowledge) been juxtaposed with other fictional

---

[19]Iain Sinclair, 'The Cadaver Club', *LRB*, 22 December 1994, p. 21.

[20]*Dan Leno*, p. 68. There is another fictional disquisition on the golem in Bruce Chatwin's *Utz* (1987).

[21]In the introduction to her edition of essays on Carter, *Flesh and the Mirror* (London: Virago, 1994), Lorna Sage quotes the President of the British Academy, Sir Keith Thomas, as having informed her that in 1992–93 'there were more than forty applicants wanting to do doctorates on Carter, making her by far the most popular twentieth-century topic' (Sage, p. 3).

reworkings of 'the side [of London] the tourist rarely sees'.[22] In *Nights at the Circus* the sceptical young American journalist Jack Walser is forced, as John Haffenden put it in interview with Carter, 'to go through various degrading hoops'.[23] The last of these is figured in Walser's final perception of the freak Cockney *aérialiste* Fevvers:

> He saw, without surprise, she indeed appeared to possess no navel but was no longer in the mood to draw any definite conclusions from this fact. Her released feathers brushed against the walls; he recalled how nature had equipped her only for the 'woman on top' position and rustled on his straw mattress.[24]

Walser is in London to interview Fevvers as part of a series 'tentatively entitled: "Great Humbugs of the World"' (*Nights at the Circus*, p. 11). He possesses many of the successful journalist's attributes, such as a facility with words and an ability to travel lightly. A description of Fevvers' spectacular circus act is dovetailed into Walser's extensive interview with her in her dressing room, an episode that takes up the first third of the book. Fevvers as it were presents her credentials to Walser:

> 'And now,' she said, 'after my conquests on the continent' (which she pronounced, 'congtinong') 'here's the prodigal daughter home again to London, my lovely London that I love so much. London – as dear old Dan Leno calls it, "a little village on the Thames of which the principal industries are the music hall and the confidence trick".' (*Nights at the Circus*, p. 8)

---

[22]Angela Carter, *Wise Children*, p. 1.
[23]John Haffenden, *Novelists in Interview* (London: Methuen, 1985), p. 89.
[24]Angela Carter, *Nights at the Circus* (London: Chatto & Windus, 1984), p. 292. Further quotations in the text to this edition.

Fevvers, completely at home, offers Walser champagne (while drinking most herself), belches and farts, and – possessed of a gargantuan appetite – sends out for eel pie, bacon sandwiches and tea. Also taking part in the interview, and indeed frequently interrupting it, is Fevvers' dresser and adoptive mother Lizzie. What is conveyed during the interview is a history of Fevvers' life up until her recruitment in Colonel Kearney's circus.

This history begins with Fevvers' upbringing in Ma Nelson's brothel (an edifice she describes as a 'harmonious relic tucked away behind the howling of the Ratcliffe Highway' [*Nights at the Circus*, p. 26]), and includes an account of her stay in the monster museum of the ghastly if aptly named Madame Schreck, and of her ritual near-murder at the hands of the kinky Mr Rosencreutz. Containing as it does so much in the way of interpolation, this fertile, antiphonally presented narrative is also riddled with unspoken hints of another more sinister story that is *not* being related. That story is, however, hinted at by reference to the more crepuscular London visions represented in the work of Joseph Conrad and even Henry James (the James, that is, of works such as *The Princess Casamassima* [1886]), as well as in the London paintings of James Whistler (the Cremorne Gardens canvases, for instance). The narrative of Fevvers and Lizzie is rescued and set on course again just as it appears to be about to bifurcate down one of these darker paths. J. L. Borges seems the tutelary spirit as Walser feels 'more and more like [. . .] a sultan faced with not one but two Scheherazades, both intent on impacting a thousand stories into the single night' (*Nights at the Circus*, p. 40).

As the second and third parts of the narrative become more and more picaresque, so they offer less of the kind of narrative possibility with which the first part pulses. Perhaps it is significant that London is the setting of the first part, and Russia – and finally Siberia – the focus of the rest. There are references in these later sections that resonate when held beside the first: thus an injury to Walser's shoulder leads to his joining the clowns as the 'Human

Chicken' – the joke does *more* than merely remind the reader of Fevvers' identity, because Walser's predicament practically echoes one of the narratives of the first part of *Nights at the Circus* (that of the Wiltshire Wonder, one of Madame Schreck's freaks, who before her present employment had used to be served up in birthday cakes), as well as giving a *frisson* to Lizzie's sinister references to the *bombe surprise*. Indeed the very flamboyance of the presentation of the embedded narratives in the first part comes increasingly to look like the 'confidence trick' which is the metaphor for Fevvers' entire act. The interruptions of each of the tellers, Fevvers and Lizzie, when an unsavoury bifurcation is about to begin, are more than Borgesian, in fact: they conjure up an air of improvisational bravura in the face of a trick or an act that is about to go wrong.

In this way, such bravura interestingly pays tribute to that of Dan Leno himself as portrayed in Ackroyd's novel. Leno is faced with the fate of the hapless Aveline Mortimer, servant to Elizabeth Cree, who plays the murderess's part in the melodrama *The Crees of Misery Junction*, an act in which the hanging scene goes fatally wrong:

> And even as they travelled homeward, many of [the audience] remembered that wonderful moment when Dan Leno had risen from the trapdoor and appeared in front of them. 'Ladies and gentlemen,' he had announced in his best mammoth comique manner, 'here we are *again*!' (*Dan Leno*, p. 282)

The atmosphere of this aspect of *Nights at the Circus* contrasts with that of *Dan Leno and the Limehouse Golem*: if murder and inverted sexuality are characteristic of the latter, the former has its dark side too. The confidence-trick, whereby the character Mignon (rescued in the second part of *Nights at the Circus*) was employed by Herr M in an earlier phase of her career to dupe the recently bereaved parents of only daughters, is reminiscent of Madame Schreck's entire freak-show: 'she catered for those who were troubled in their . . . souls' (*Nights at the Circus*, p. 57, ellipses Carter's).

The association of London with fecundity is carried forward – even more joyously yet at the same time perhaps more profoundly – by Dora Chance's narration of *Wise Children*. On the termination of the interview that makes up the first part of *Nights at the Circus*, Walser has left Fevvers and Lizzie to go back to his lodgings in Clerkenwell, watching them return to London's bastard side as they 'set out for the smoky south over Westminster Bridge' (*Nights at the Circus*, p. 89) from the 'legitimate' part of a nineteenth-century London whose characteristic topographical trademark, the 'gilded [. . .] great dome of St Paul's', has already been gendered by Fevvers in terms of 'London, with the one breast, the Amazon queen' (*Nights at the Circus*, p. 36).

Spending most of their illegitimate lives on London's bastard side, to be precise, in Brixton's Bard Road, and equally precise (genealogically speaking), as the unacknowledged identical twin offspring of the thespian Shakespearian knight Sir Melchior Hazard and the foundling 'Pretty Kitty', Dora and Nora Chance (the 'wise children' of the title) are finally admitted to topographical legitimacy in the novel's fifth and last chapter (or act) when they attend the hundredth birthday celebrations of Sir Melchior in his Regent's Park house (the date happens also to be their own seventy-fifth birthday).

The denouement is provocatively complex, like Shakespeare's *Cymbeline*, that most outrageous example of London's best-known writer, and resists summary. But the fecundity extends to all kinds of narrative possibilities that remain open because of the imaginative profligacy featured in the celebratory attitude towards sexual procreation and indeed the nature of Dora Chance's telling of her own story ('There I go again! Can't keep a story going in a straight line, can I? Drunk in charge of a narrative' [*Wise Children*, p. 158]). In an excellent essay, Kate Webb shows how:

... *Wise Children* is like the proverbial Freudian nightmare – aided and abetted (as Freud was himself) by Shakespearian example. Dora's family story is crammed with incestuous love and Oedipal hatred: there are sexual relationships between parent and child (where this is not technically so, actor-parents marry their theatrical offspring – in two generations of Hazards, Lears marry Cordelias); and between sister and brother (Melchior's children Saskia and Imogen).[25]

The comic licence enhances the idea that illegitimacy opens the door to incest, since if the child, however wise, does not know its father, any sexual encounter (and by that token any narrative encounter) offers the potential for an unwanted recognition that can either be followed through or suppressed. Dora seems to negotiate these possibilities during the hundredth birthday revelry when she and the supposedly long-dead uncle-figure, Melchior's brother Peregrine, make love in the bedroom-cum-coat-room upstairs with such fervour that the chandelier starts to shake and Dora wonders if their act will really, finally, bring the house down. It turns out that this last sex of Dora's life with a man who may be (and is certainly old enough to be) her father replicates her first. The difference is that the 'progeny' are the twins – the first fraternal twins in the history of the Hazard–Chance dynasty – that Peregrine produces for Dora and Nora to take home to the bastard side of London and look after. In fact these baby twins, magicked lavishly from Peregrine's coat pockets like rabbits, turn out to be the abandoned offspring of Gareth Hazard, the Chances' half-brother, twin to Tristram. Dora and Nora thus replicate the pattern of receiving foundlings into their home and passing their remaining days as surrogate mothers. The clear suggestion is that this· kind of joyous fecundity is by definition spawned on the wrong side of the sheets, or

[25]Kate Webb, 'Seriously Funny: Wise Children', in Lorna Sage, ed., *Flesh and the Mirror*, p. 292.

tracks, in the purlieu of 'the side [of London that] the tourist rarely sees'.[26]

Resisting Dead Ends: Martin Amis

Martin Amis's three fictions, *Money: A Suicide Note* (1984), *London Fields* (1989) and *The Information* (1995), are all set in London (*Money* partly in New York too). In each case the metropolis plays such a role that it might even be considered another character. That role is topographical, to be sure, but also, and increasingly, sociological. The narrator of *Money* finds himself in an exhausted yet still streetwise 1980s London that is in as bad a state of health as he himself, and all its animate inhabitants, whether human or not:

> Driving home, as I sat in a jam on the Bayswater road, a frazzled wasp flew sideways through the window and twirled out of view between my legs. It was arguable who was in the worse shape, me or the wasp. My fist was on the horn as I hollered at the ugly gut of the tourist bus that had straddled the street ahead. I thrashed tubbily about – and the wasp stung me. I pulled into a sidestreet and dropped my pants. There was a little red dot on my thigh. It looked, and it felt, like the mildest cigarette burn. And I thought: is that the best you can do? You've lost the heft, you poor wound-down thing, raised on chops and pop, on car belch and gutter gook. As I zipped myself up, a pigeon clockworked past on the pavement, eating a chip. A *chip*. Like horseflies and other creatures who direct and star in their own tiny films, the pigeon lived in fast motion. It naturally preferred

[26]Carter, *Wise Children*, p. 1. Webb (Sage, ed., *Flesh and the Mirror*, pp. 339–40) has an interesting note on the implications of Carter's juxtaposition of real with fantasy topography in the Railton Road area of Brixton near where, for the last years of her life, she actually lived.

fast food. City life is happening everywhere. The wasp was dead. That sting was its last shot. Flies get dizzy spells and bees have booze problems. Robin redbreasts hit the deck with psychosomatic ulcers and cholesterol overload. In the alleys, dogs are coughing their hearts out on snout and dope. The stooped flowers in their sodden beds endure back-pinch and rug-loss, what with all the stress about. Even the microbes, the spores of the middle air, are finding all this a little hard on their nerves.[27]

(Even the microbes are given animate status here.)

Amis's profile among reviewers has always been high. Yet there is puzzlement in notices of these London novels, even though so many of their readers find in them a state-of-the-art distillation of the greed and yobbery of the Thatcherite era. The doubt is about whether the verbal virtuosity expressed in a self-conscious yet faultless ear for varieties of dialogue right across the social spectrum, the acute observation and the almost casual throwaway intelligence of the narration, have really been exercising themselves on subject-matter worthy of those gifts. Those doubts were largely removed when *Time's Arrow* appeared in 1991: that novel, presenting the life of a Nazi butcher spooled backwards so as to find a way of positively visualizing the images of that horror, moves away from a London canvas and seemed to usher in a new stage in Amis's career. On the other hand *The Information* (1995) has largely been received as a return to the city and its organic life as explored by Amis with characteristic stylishness in *Money* and *London Fields*: indeed, several commentators made the point that *The Information* appears to close a three-part London sequence begun with *Money*. Adam Mars-Jones's fine review articulates the atmosphere of *The Information* with real precision, concluding that it, like the rest of what

[27]Martin Amis, *Money: A Suicide Note* (London: Cape, 1984), pp. 250–51. Further references in the text are to this edition.

he terms the triptych, 'deserves to be read [. . .] for the ride, if not the view'.[28]

A typical response to *London Fields* was articulated by the late Julian Symons:

> Put aside, as nearly as one can, the nuclear or propaganda element, and the often enjoyable but self-indulgent jokes of the Mark Asprey kind, and how much is left? Enough to make this the most intellectually interesting fiction of the year, and a work beyond the reach of any British contemporary.[29]

Common denominators have been sought for Amis's London fictions, and Amis himself seems to feel that the doubles observed by so many readers illustrate warring aspects of his own personality, aspects magnified through grotesquerie and hyperbole into a characteristic blend that Amis has no hesitation in terming, generically speaking, comic, although most of his readers seem to see him as a satirist. Karl Miller, writing before the appearance of *London Fields*, made a persuasive case for regarding *Money*, along with its two immediate predecessors *Other People* (1981) and *Success* (1978), as 'turmoils, in which orphan and double meet',[30] stressing a Gothic element that might otherwise have lain hidden under the verbal pyrotechnics.

In those novels, Amis becomes increasingly obsessed with the different orders of reality to which orphan and double belong. The first of Miller's group of three novels catalogues the transfer of that elusive quality, success, from double to orphan and cunningly manipulates the reader's sympathies in

[28] Adam Mars-Jones, 'Looking on the blight side', *TLS*, 24 March 1995, pp. 19–20. Mars-Jones prefers 'triptych' to 'trilogy' on the grounds that the sequence is '[w]ithout continuous characters or overarching structure'.

[29] Julian Symons, 'Darts for art's sake', *LRB*, 28 September 1989, pp. 7–8. There is a strong nuclear (though not 'propaganda') element in Iain Sinclair's *Radon Daughters* (1994), which out-Amises Amis in this aspect of both *London Fields* and *The Information*.

[30] Karl Miller, *Doubles: Studies in Literary History* (London: OUP, 1985), p. 409.

doing so. *Other People* presents, in the awakening consciousness of the resonantly named Mary Lamb, what appears to be a nightmarish afterworld, a life-in-death,[31] in which she is a resurrected murder-victim, named Amy Hide in a previous existence. However, in a characteristic surprise ending Amis unsettles the reader's confidence as to whether what we have experienced in *Other People* is not so much an after-life as a time-warp, reversal or even hiccup, during which Amy has lost her reason and identity, and after which life begins as normal again. The problem is rendered still more complex by the presence of a clue-planting detective, John Prince, who may or may not have been related to Amy Hide, and by the presence of a voice which begins the narrative with the words: 'I didn't want to have to do it to her'.[32] In the Haffenden interview Amis confirms that the narrator's and Prince's are indeed the same voice.

In *Money*, *London Fields* and *The Information* Amis twists the screw further, and it does seem that one of his themes that has emerged in the 1980s and 1990s is a linking of 'doubleness' to narrative control. In *Money*, John Self, who describes himself as '200 pounds of yob genes, booze, snout and fast food' (*Money*, p. 35), finds at the novel's end that all the money he believes himself to have been making comprises a scam he has been tricked into financing himself. 'Martin Amis', introduced into *Money* as one of its characters, admits his complicity in this rip-off. Self has spent almost the entire novel commuting between London (where he has been making TV commercials that have had to be pulled on grounds of obscenity) and New York (where he is casting and scripting a high-earning feature film first entitled *Money*, then *Good Money*, then *Bad Money*). Self in fact meets two versions

[31]The phrase is used by Martin Amis himself in his explication of the *modus operandi* of *Other People* in interview with John Haffenden, *Novelists in Interview* (London: Methuen, 1985), p. 17. Within the very name of 'Mary Lamb' there are connotations of both nursery-rhyme innocence and the matricidal insanity of the twin sister of the historical Charles Lamb, the cockney Londoner 'Elia' (1775–1834).
[32]Martin Amis, *Other People: A Mystery Story* (1981; London: Penguin, 1982), p. 9.

of the double: in London he encounters Martin Amis the writer, whom he eventually coerces into rewriting the script of *Money* after the previous scriptwriter's failure to make it sufficiently attractive to the four leads, all of whom have refused their roles; in New York he is pursued by Martina Twain, who introduces the largely unread Self to works such as *Animal Farm* and *Nineteen Eighty-Four*, and takes him to see Verdi's *Otello* – meanwhile we discover that Martina's husband Ossie has been having an affair with Self's girlfriend Selina Street.

London Fields' Keith Talent, rightly described by Julian Symons as 'an outsize figure, the most complete portrait of a hooligan in modern fiction, born of the *Sun*, taught by the telly, worshipper of the dartboard', represents an extension of what Martin Amis in *Money* tells John Self:

> The further down the social scale [the hero] is, the more liberties you can take with him. You can do what the hell you like to him, really. This creates an appetite for punishment. The author is not free of sadistic impulses. (*Money*, p. 233)

Self is not, strictly speaking, an orphan, and one of the components of the rather complex denouement of *Money* concerns his discovery of his true paternity. On his own account Self believes he was born 'upstairs' in a London pub called the Shakespeare. Believing himself to be the son of Barry Self, he eventually discovers that his true father is Fat Vince, 'beer-crate operative and freelance bouncer at the Shakespeare', who has 'been in and out of this place every day for thirty-five years' (*Money*, p. 140). Martin Amis, who *in propria persona* was 35 at the time of the novel's publication (although of course younger in the year – 1981 – in which the novel is actually set) is introduced gradually into the narrative. The very first occasion on which Amis and Self meet shows how Amis is prepared to sacrifice credible characterization in the interests of his writing and obsessions. Self, not notably literate, asks Amis: 'Your dad, he's a writer too, isn't he? Bet that made it easier.' 'Oh sure.

It's just like taking over the family pub.' (*Money*, p. 87) This is what the 'real' Amis proceeds to do: and in his own person Amis has had much to say about the extraordinary freedoms available to and constraints limiting the fictional narrator. Interesting mishearings are dotted around the text of *Money*. Self's own interior consciousness is invaded and appropriated by other voices. Amy J. Elias has coined the term 'junk noise', which neatly relates Self's tinnitus to the other kinds of trash scattering Amis's cityscapes.[33] Self is often 'hearing things' and frequently blacking out because of powerful combinations of drink and drugs and not (as he discovers to his cost at the novel's end) hearing or recalling or being able to take in information that really matters. Importing his London life into a conversation with a girl called Moby in a Manhattan brothel, Self tells her that his name is Martin and that he is a writer; he is puzzled by her reply: 'John roar mainstream?', or at least by that part of it that doesn't refer to his own first name. This kind of wordplay is intensified in *London Fields*, where Keith Talent seems incapable of understanding the world around him in any way that does not use his own name, thereby demonstrating his own imaginative and lexical poverty. The virtually illiterate Talent reads Keats with Nicola Six: 'John Keith, thought Keith, as he drove away. Top wordsmith and big in pharmaceuticals. Books: one way to make a fast quid'.[34]

One particularly fascinating feature of both *Money* and *London Fields* is, indeed, the voice of the narrator: each is stylistically speaking virtuoso yet each contrives to make clear his failure as reader or writer.[35] The point is sharper in *London*

[33] Amy J. Elias, 'Meta-*mimesis*? The Problem of British Postmodern Realism', in Theo D'haen and Hans Bertens, eds., *British Postmodern Fiction* (Amsterdam & Atlanta, GA: Rodopi, 1993), p. 18.

[34] Martin Amis, *London Fields* (London: Cape, 1989), p. 356. Further references in the text are to this edition.

[35] *The Information*, in contrast, is narrated by a third-person figure who seems for the most part to represent the consciousness of the failed writer Richard Tull – yet the effect is paradoxically analogous to that of the earlier novels.

Fields where the speech-patterns of Keith Talent jar against and dominate those of Guy Clinch, Nicola Six and the narrator more acutely than those of Fat Paul do in *Money* ('Fat Paul, I would say, has few anxieties about his accent. [. . .] You could never do that voice justice, but here goes' [*Money*, p. 141]). This is Keith Talent on his own game:

> 'I've hit form just when I needed it . . . Come good at the right time. As long as I maintain my composure I don't fear no one, Tony, not throwing like I am. No way will I crap or bottle it on the night. I'd just like to thank you and the viewers for the superb support. The fans is what darts is all about.' (*London Fields*, pp. 110–11)

As if to underline the point that Keith Talent is entirely a construction of the rhetorical tricks by which tabloid media reporting covers up for its own imaginative sterility, he is at his most lucid in a conversation such as this:

> 'West Ham. Any good?'
> Some of the light went out in Keith's blue eyes as he said, 'During the first half the Hammers probed down the left flank. Revelling in the space, the speed of Sylvester Drayon was always going to pose problems for the home side's number two. With scant minutes remaining before the half-time whistle, the black winger cut in on the left back and delivered a searching cross, converted by Lee Fredge, the East London striker, with inch-perfect precision. After the interval Rangers' fortunes revived as they exploited their superiority in the air. Bobby Bonavich's men offered stout resistance and the question remained: could the Blues translate the pressure they were exerting into goals?' (*London Fields*, pp. 90–91)

London Fields is narrated by an American writer *manqué*, Samson Young, who is exchanging his New York apartment

with Mark Asprey.[36] Asprey's initials, like those of the pseudony-
mous Marius Appleby whom Asprey recommends to Samson,
offer a refinement on the self-reflexiveness of *Money* while
simultaneously insisting on the doubleness of the narration.
Samson Young finds himself walking into the Black Cross pub
in London, and being presented with a *donnée* that would be
beyond the reach, or perhaps beneath the dignity, of 'MA': the
denouement that succeeds nearly 500 pages of narrative relies on
a trick. The 'murderee' Nicola Six is murdered, not (obviously)
by 'the foil, the fool, the poor foal' (*London Fields*, p. 1) Guy
Clinch, nor (much less obviously) by the 'murderer' whom we
are constantly being invited to identify with Keith Talent, but
by Samson himself. At one level this can be read as Samson's
desperate twist out of a *cul-de-sac*: he must abruptly terminate
the story because he is too bored or incompetent to bring it
to the ending he has had his reader envisage. This is one way,
perhaps the only way, of justifying (in terms of the politics of
gender) the portrayal of Nicola. The criticisms that she is a male
rape fantasy are met, though not necessarily palliated, by seeing
her interest in anal sex as a metaphor both for the repeated
stress on the dead-end street location of her apartment and for
the dead end into which Samson's narration of the story that
awaits his telling finally leads him. Nicola's fantasy companion
Enola Gay and Enola's nuclear offspring Little Boy (the ultimate
black hole), together with Nicola's own abortions, all point to a
sterility that some of Amis's readers clearly felt was pushed to
an unacceptable degree.

Still, not all male rape fantasies are the same. The cheap
tabloid rhetoric – the most fluent language of which Keith
Talent is capable – operates, in *London Fields*, much as does
the bizarre hyperbolic grotesquerie of the book's portrayals of

---

[36]Patrick Wright has pointed out, in a brief essay, 'The Park that Lost its
Name', that the title *London Fields* is also that of 'a conventional fable of
working-class endeavour' published by John Milne in 1983 and finally eclipsed
on the appearance of Amis's novel; see Wright, *Journey Through Ruins*, p.
249. The eponymous London Fields is situated in Hackney, London E8.

Keith himself, or the destructive horror child Marmaduke Clinch, or the way the weather in *London Fields* constantly threatens apocalypse. These elements give us a way of accounting for the malleability of Nicola Six, even though her presentation may be felt to be as satirical as that of Keith Talent. That is to say, Nicola is constructed according to the male consciousness with whom she happens to make contact at any particular time. Amis would presumably maintain that this kind of malleability is primarily the essence of his fictional portrayal of Nicola, so that only in a secondary sense is it potentially offensive, but it is clearly difficult for many readers, men among them, to take this point without seeing Nicola in fantasy terms in which stylistic considerations are being used as a blind. It all seems to come down to the question of whether an honest portrayal of the inadequate aspects of male heterosexual consciousness can ever escape fantasies of domination and appropriation.

In this respect, the scornful, ridiculous, judging (and thus satirical) portrayal of Keith Talent's utter loutishness is another form of precisely that kind of honest inadequacy that affects, across the whole social stratum as figured in the range of London settings, every single male character in *London Fields*.

Perhaps Amis's manipulation of the excesses of London as metropolis, its unparalleled setting for fiction of fantasy both past and present, is not after all so different in kind from those of the other writers treated in this chapter. Amis's satires take his characters to the edge, offering them the choice between being pushed over it or persuaded back to safety.

It has been argued that the common ground between Ackroyd, Sinclair, Carter and Amis is that they have all responded to the London of the 1980s and 1990s. Ackroyd, Sinclair and Carter have realigned the city by reinventing it as a Gothic construct, whereas Amis deals with it direct. Yet both are extreme responses to an extreme situation in which London has become a monster again. Adam Mars-Jones fittingly reiterates a point that others have made:

Amis's originality as a stylist has been to separate verbal beauty from the cause that it has traditionally served, to detach lyrical language from the lyrical impulse. ('Looking on the blight side', p. 19)

What is certain is that none of the fictions discussed in this chapter, all of them in their different ways inspired by the Thatcher decade and its aftermath, would have been inspired, promoted, reviewed, sold and read a generation ago, because they could not even have been written.

6

Silenced Voices
and Hidden Histories

The previous two chapters dwelt on specific cities or regions that have, during the 1980s, become the subject of new kinds of treatment within the broader context of recent fiction in Britain. This chapter ranges more widely across two major areas of interest. Firstly, voices muted by and recovered from history, with particular emphasis on the history of both racial oppression as well as the sexual oppression that is so often a part of the racial. (By 'recovery', throughout this chapter, I mean that the novelist gives a voice to the dispossessed, but it shouldn't be forgotten that she or he is nevertheless inventing that voice.) Secondly, the inhibition and release of voices of sexual unorthodoxy – specifically, here, gay male writing in the mainstream of serious literary fiction. Each section concentrates on no more than a few books but each tries to broaden the debate through briefer discussions of other relevant novels.

Paradise Colonized – Historical Fictions of the Caribbean and the American South: Caryl Phillips, Fred D'Aguiar, Marina Warner, J. M. Coetzee, Barry Unsworth

The novelist Caryl Phillips was born on St Kitts in 1958 but relocated with his family to Britain in that year during the first wave of post-war immigration from the Caribbean. What is most notable about Phillips's work is the degree of complexity that his acts of narrative reclamation have achieved. As elsewhere in his work, for instance, throughout *The Final Passage* (1985), and in sections of *Higher Ground* (1989) and *Crossing the River* (1993), Phillips shows remarkable skill in reconstructing the voice of a female narrator.

The opening, and by far the longest, section of *Cambridge* (1991) consists of the journal of a young Englishwoman *en route* to supervising her father's Caribbean plantations (the first time she has left her native country) and relates her encounter with the realities of colonial life. Although ostensibly abolitionist, Emily Cartwright falls in love with the brutal overseer Arnold Brown shortly after her arrival, and indeed is discovered to be carrying his child at the novel's end. The major 'event' in the novel is Brown's murder, for which a slave named Cambridge is executed. Despite the novel's title, Cambridge's direct role in the narrative appears slight: a short passage towards the end, comprising about a sixth of the entire novel, is all we hear of his own voice. However, attention to this 'testament' Phillips gives him reveals the pervasiveness of his indirect presence, and also the inscrutability of his voice. A slave to various kinds of cultural conscription, a Protean figure, Cambridge does not really speak 'for' any single set of values in the postcolonial world. He takes on the voice of the oppressor, and in so doing it could be argued that he has sold out, but that voice is the only one that we, as modern English-speaking readers, can understand. The irony is poignant. Here is a brief sample:

> When I imagine myself to have been not yet fifteen years of age, I was apprehended by a band of brigands and bound by means of a chain to hand and foot. I must confess, to the shame of my fellow Guinea-men, that I was undoubtedly betrayed by those of my own hue. But it remains true that without instruction and encouragement my native people might never have hardened their hearts and tainted the generous customs of their simple country. Shackled unceremoniously to a fellow unfortunate at both stern and bow, we unhappy *blacks* formed a most miserable traffic, stumbling with jangling resignation

towards our doom. About my neck I sported a decoration of gold placed there by my own mother's *fair* hand, and from my ears hung larger and less delicate gold pieces of shape, though mercifully not size, resembling the orange fruit. These paragons of virtue who had possession of my body, if not my soul, soon divested me of these trappings, thus breaking off my tenderly formed links with my parents. In addition to this loss, I was forced to endure pain the like of which I had never suffered.[1]

What are we to make of the pointed opposition between '*blacks*' and '*fair*'? What can 'black' mean to a speaker who is using a word connoting 'otherness' or difference, borrowed from an alien culture, to identify himself? What of the juxtaposition with the figurative 'fair', a cliché borrowed from a language that turns colour into terms connoting moral extremes? What are we to make of the inscrutable punning on 'shackled', 'trappings' and 'links'?

The titular 'Cambridge' in fact represents the third renaming of this character, who had begun life as Olumide. Captured for a slave, he is renamed Thomas by his English owner, and educated and converted to Christianity, whereupon he becomes David Henderson. The reconstructed David Henderson plans to return to Africa as a missionary, but is recaptured by slave-traders who name him Cambridge. For all its disturbingly inscrutable ventriloquy, Cambridge's testament does reveal what Bénédicte Ledent has termed 'a very tragic self-alienation in so far as Cambridge has become convinced that Christianity . . . offers the only true spiritual salvation it claims'.[2]

The Guyanan-born poet Fred D'Aguiar published his first novel, *The Longest Memory*, to great acclaim in 1994. It won that year's Whitbread First Novel Award as well as the David Higham Prize

[1]Caryl Phillips, *Cambridge* (London: Bloomsbury, 1991), pp. 134–35.
[2]Bénédicte Ledent, 'Caryl Phillips', in *Postwar Literatures in English* 19 (March 1993), p. 9.

for Fiction, which is always awarded to a first novel. Whereas
Cambridge narrates only a small part of the story that bears
his name as title, the narrative of *The Longest Memory* is
related by different voices. But despite the presence of these
different voices, the novel *The Longest Memory* cannot be
regarded as a dialogue, since the various voices, while relating
a story that is comprehensible in its entirety, do not interact
with each other. The voices are those of the ancient and
senior slave Whitechapel, his (relatively) enlightened owner
Mr Whitechapel, the overseers Sanders Senior and Junior, a
slave girl employed as Cook, the young slave Chapel – the
son of Whitechapel and Cook (who becomes Whitechapel's
second wife) but has in reality been fathered by Sanders Senior
on the latter's rape of Cook, Lydia (Mr Whitechapel's youngest
daughter, who teaches Chapel to read – eventually making a poet
of him – and is reprimanded for doing so; the two subsequently
fall in love), a hostile chorus of oppressive and threatened
plantation owners (sounding like something out of a Greek
tragedy), a series of editorials from *The Virginian* newspaper
that offers moralistic commentary on the novel's events but
is unable to learn from them, and a great-granddaughter of
Whitechapel. The failure to communicate, despite (or rather
because of) Mr Whitechapel's progressive ways, is the real
tragedy of D'Aguiar's novel.

Whitechapel's very longevity through survival explains
D'Aguiar's title:

> I have buried two wives and most of my children. I am
> surrounded by grandchildren and great-grandchildren. They
> think I am a Judas and an old man who can make a great
> pepper stew when goaded to do so. They leave me alone most
> of the time, fuss over me from a suitable distance at meal times,
> check to see if I am still alive first thing in the morning with a
> tug or a prod, then disappear for the day into the fields.[3]

[3]Fred D'Aguiar, *The Longest Memory* (1994; London: Vintage, 1995), p. 8.

In fact the centenarian Whitechapel has so many descendants (he had twelve daughters by his first wife) that they outnumber the slaves who are not related to him by blood.

Where it could be argued that Cambridge has 'sold out' to the culture of the oppressor, but in so doing finds the only possible manner of communicating with us, his posterity, the longest memory of Whitechapel – 'pain trying to resurrect itself' (*The Longest Memory*, p. 138) – concerns an appallingly complex and painful act of betrayal, which explains the Judas reference in the quotation above. On the death of his mother, Cook, as a result of fever, Chapel runs away. Mr Whitechapel, who is about to escort some guests north, gives orders for Chapel to be recaptured but not harmed until he (Mr Whitechapel) returns. Chapel will be made an example of. But Sanders Junior prevails over the protocol established by Mr Whitechapel, assaults the privileged senior slave Whitechapel, and orders two hundred lashes for Chapel, as a result of which Chapel dies. (This punishment recalls a similar incident in the previous generation, and it is the repercussions of this event that have led to Mr Whitechapel's vowing to run the plantation more progressively than his father had done.)

The death of Chapel is complex and painful both because Whitechapel had, expecting his master's good faith, indicated to the trackers the direction Chapel had taken, and because Chapel is actually the half-brother of Sanders Junior, unbeknownst to the latter until it is too late. Whitechapel has to live with the consequences of his actions. Although Sanders Junior objectively comes to regret Chapel's death, he is seen to be too conditioned to white supremacy to consider himself related by blood to Chapel. So we have a paradox, wherein the true biological father, Sanders Senior, neglects the son whom his other son Sanders Junior kills; Whitechapel the foster-father has become the 'true' father but is powerless to prevent the death of the son. The various voices other than Whitechapel's, that all assert, or become persuaded of, Whitechapel's sheer goodness, are also powerless: D'Aguiar 'recovers' them so that they can speak to us. But we, the posterity of Whitechapel, cannot help, for the deed is done. Only by communicating with each other could the novel's characters have averted the tragedy.

Marina Warner's *Indigo* (1992) illustrates other ways in which novelists in Britain have responded to the triangular slave traffic between the British Isles, Africa and the Caribbean, and its legacy. This topic has become a major theme that is paralleled by the full-grown concern among African-American writers with the history of slavery in the United States. This history is seen, in contemporary American fiction, from the viewpoint of the oppressed rather than the oppressor – one thinks perhaps above all of Toni Morrison's *Beloved* (1987). We have seen examples of this in Caryl Phillips and Fred D'Aguiar, but entry into the tradition of writing about slavery by white writers is also characteristic of Booker-eligible fiction. Accordingly this section also contains briefer discussions of J. M. Coetzee's *Foe* and Barry Unsworth's joint Booker Prize winner *Sacred Hunger* (1992),[4] books that, like Phillips's and D'Aguiar's, extend the imaginative franchise by reclaiming histories and voices that have been hidden or silenced. In a recent essay, Marina Warner perhaps speaks not just for herself but for Coetzee and Unsworth as well in describing persuasively not just 'rewriting memory by revisiting familiar landmarks of culture' but of her anxiety, as a white writer, as to whether, in writing as she has done in *Indigo*, she is 'interloping' or 'ha[s] a title to this material'.[5]

Whereas Warner's *The Lost Father* (1988) engages with the culture within which her Italian mother grew up, and is dedicated both to her mother and to her mother's sisters, *Indigo* turns to the English-Caribbean background of her father's family, and the dedication of the later novel reflects this. Always an erudite

---

[4]Unsworth was shortlisted for the Booker again in 1995 for *Morality Play*. The prospect that Unsworth might create history by winning the prize twice was swamped in the speculation about Rushdie.

[5]Marina Warner, '*Indigo*: Mapping the Waters', *Etudes Britanniques contemporaines* 5 (December 1994), p. 11.

and original anthropologist whose earliest works included major studies of the Virgin Mary and Joan of Arc as constructions of female identity, Warner produced her third and fourth novels, more substantial works than her first two, after a period that saw her focusing her scholarly interests on fairy-tale and popular mythology. Indeed her more recent work has shared many of the interests of A. S. Byatt from *Possession* onwards. In these later novels Warner addresses more directly than before the theme of parental presence and absence. In addition, both *The Lost Father* and *Indigo* present lists of dramatis personae and reproduce quasi-mythical maps. *The Lost Father*, shortlisted for the 1988 Booker Prize, is prefaced with a map of 'Ninfania' that corresponds to Apulia on the real Italian peninsula: *Indigo* is prefaced by a map of the imaginary Caribbean island of Liamuiga. Liamuiga corresponds less explicitly to the St Kitts that has been inhabited by generations of Warner's paternal ancestors since the seventeenth century than Ninfania does to Apulia. Liamuiga is a fantasy island adorned with a feminized topography: there are oyster-beds at the mouth of its vaginally shaped 'The Creek';[6] salt ponds; and a 'stockade' consisting of pointed palings repels invaders by suggesting castration as well as perhaps recalling R. L. Stevenson's *Treasure Island*. The stockade is realistic, too: it is one of the marks left by the island's violation by the English colonizers in a fictional 1619.

In *Indigo* Warner also takes on board a debate that has fascinated many Shakespeare scholars: that of the 'lost' or 'absent' mother in so many of the plays, including *The Tempest* (1611). There are countless allusions to, but also displacements of, the plot of *The Tempest* in *Indigo*. Warner's is typical of a cluster of novels produced in Britain in recent years that take place in an historical period juxtaposed with the 'present', and write back into history (thus *augmenting* it) those voices, often but not exclusively those of women, that have been excluded

---

[6]Readers may be reminded of John Barth's use of the Chesapeake Bay as a vaginal figure in *Sabbatical* (1972) and elsewhere.

by patriarchal, societal and colonial tradition, literary tradition and interpretation. What is important about these rewritings is the way in which the presentation of the point of view gives us, as modern readers, fresh insight into the historical periods concerned. When dealing with Britain's imperial history, novels of this kind form part of a worldwide literature now widely known as the 'postcolonial'.[7]

It has been suggested that if any one single extended act of theoretical discussion initiated what has been termed '[c]olonial discourse analysis' in contemporary times, that text is Edward Said's *Orientalism* (1978),[8] a treatise that, as Homi K. Bhabha has argued, 'examin[es] the varied European discourses which constitute "the Orient" as a unified racial, geographical, political and cultural zone of the world'.[9]

Marina Warner is well aware of the theoretical position taken by Said and endorsed (not wholly uncritically) by commentators such as Bhabha. Her novel, as Patrick Parrinder notes in an enthusiastic and perceptive review:

> boldly enters such traditionally masculine domains as the imperial adventure tale, the 'first contact' narrative, and even, for a brief moment, the sporting epic (though in the latter case the heroine soon makes her excuses and leaves the stadium, and shortly afterwards the game is terminated by a riot).[10]

Warner specifically debates with recent feminist commentary that has noted the striking absence in Shakespeare of figures of motherhood. In Shakespeare's play, Prospero dispossesses

[7]For a fine recent survey of the field, see Elleke Boehmer, *Colonial and Postcolonial Literature* (Oxford: Oxford UP, 1995).
[8]By Robert Young; see his 'Colonialism and the Desiring-Machine', in Theo D'haen & Hans Bertens, eds., *Liminal Postmodernisms: The Postmodern, the (Post-)Colonial and the (Post-)Feminist* (Amsterdam & Atlanta, GA: Rodopi, 1994), p. 11. See Said's own retrospective essay, 'East isn't East', *TLS*, 3 February 1995, pp. 3–6, as well as his 1995 reissue of *Orientalism*.
[9]Homi K. Bhabha, *The Location of Culture* (London & New York: Routledge, 1993), p. 71.
[10]Patrick Parrinder, 'Sea Changes', *LRB*, 27 February 1992, p. 12.

Caliban of the island that is his by right through his absent
mother, the witch Sycorax. Part of the success of Warner's
recovering voices lies in her renaming of Caliban. This seems to
represent an attempt to 'decolonialize' his nomenclature (which
plays on 'Carib' and 'cannibal'): in *Indigo* he becomes Dulé,
an adoptive child. Another adoptive child to Sycorax is Ariel,
whose gender is frequently more problematic for Shakespearian
directors than is, say, Puck's: here Ariel is a daughter. Not only
are these relationships fleshed out in *Indigo*; in contrast to their
Shakespearian original Ariel becomes related to Caliban-Dulé
as his (adoptive) half-sister. In *The Tempest*, of course, Ariel is
a spirit, representing the 'airy' domain, who had been entrapped
by Sycorax and rescued by Prospero, although remaining for the
duration of the action the servant of Prospero's art until finally
given his freedom. Shakespeare's Caliban represents all that is
subordinate to the lower senses: his world is primarily one of
tasting, touching, and indeed being 'pinched' and suffering pain,
rather than seeing, although he does have a musical ear.

Sycorax, mother to Caliban-Dulé as well as to Ariel in *Indigo*,
is absent from, or exists only as a fossil and ultimately impotent
remnant in, *The Tempest*. For Warner, in contrast, Sycorax
becomes a benevolent life-giving character even after the death
she undergoes as a consequence of colonial invasion. In a
Shakespearian echo, Sycorax dies bent into a 'hooped' shape, a
disfigurement brought about by her broken back having 'healed'
in a hammock. Buried under the tree which has contained her
'cabin', out of which she had fallen after the Everard colonizers
attempt to set fire to it (Shakespeare's Ariel, in contrast, had
been imprisoned in a tree by Sycorax), 'Her long death has
barely begun [. . .] for she can still hear the prayers' of those
who come to ask her to intercede for them for a variety of
matters, nailing or tacking their prayers to the tree:

> The slaves pressing their tintacks into the tree whisper:
> – their love of a man, their love of a woman
> – their love of a child

– their hopes of reprieve from punishment
– their thanks for surviving punishment
– their fear of being burned alive on a barbecue like the young slave who ran away last week and was caught and tried and sentenced to death by this method
– their terror of having a foot chopped off for stealing (some of them have been stealing)
– their trust that their little boy will recover from the quartan fever.

Some women ask for:
– a fertile womb (they also ask for a barren womb sometimes).

Many pray, on the death of the master:
– that the new one may not be worse.

They imagine torments more atrocious for the bakkra (which is what the bosses are called) than they themselves received at the order of mistresses who wear bonnets and corsets and use the civilised manners of Liverpool or Birmingham or London –

They think of their children's warm squirming bodies and entreat that as they grow up they will not be hurt as they have been –

They beg to be protected against partings, disease, death and sorrow –[11]

Miranda, Prospero's motherless daughter in Shakespeare's original, is displaced into the twentieth-century part of the plot of *Indigo*, as a direct descendant of the Kit Everard who has led the seventeenth-century expeditionary force. Her grandfather's first, Creole, wife Estelle Desjours had died in a drowning accident in 1934. This plot detail resonates against the seventeenth-century native Caribbeans' belief in the sea-monster Manjiku, 'who swallows babies in his burning desire to be a woman' (*Indigo*, p. 85). In this way the death of Estelle not

[11]Marina Warner, *Indigo* (London: Chatto & Windus, 1992), pp. 211–12. Quotations in the text are to this edition.

only foreshadows that of Miranda's (younger) aunt Xanthe, but counterpoints Dulé's miraculous birth: Sycorax (a native Caribbean) manages to extract the living baby from the uterus of his drowned mother, mysteriously washed up along with the bodies of many other Africans one day in 1600.[12] We shall see that Warner thinks of her work typologically, and certainly the narrative of *Indigo* suggests that the lament uttered in 1700, eighty years after her death, by Sycorax ('Oh airs and winds, you bring me stories of the living [. . .] HEAR ME!') is as topical then as it is now. The retrieval of Sycorax's voice imbues the twentieth-century plot with richness, as the dye indigo does whatever it touches.

Miranda's grandfather, through his drowned first wife, is Sir Anthony Everard. Miranda's parents are the irresponsible and combative Kit and Astrid. At the opening of the twentieth-century part of the narrative, Sir Anthony has remarried an English society belle, Gillian. The twentieth-century narrative follows the rivalry between Miranda and her younger aunt Xanthe, daughter to Sir Anthony and Gillian, from Xanthe's fairy-tale christening party in 1948 to the 1980s. The opposition between the two girls is observed by the outside world in terms of dark (Miranda) and bright (Xanthe), and involves Miranda in choosing to identify with the black, diasporic element of her Creole ancestry: rejecting its white counterpart she embarks, at the novel's end, on a relationship with a radicalized African-American actor playing Caliban in a performance of *The Tempest*.[13] Significantly, in a rewriting of *The Tempest* that

[12]Parrinder, 'Sea Changes', p. 12, makes a fine observation: 'there are premonitions of the death of the old order even before Kit Everard's landfall. The island where there is so far (as in Gonzalo's ideal commonwealth) no use of metal has already a word for Europeans – "the tallow men" – and the corpses of manacled slaves have been washed up on its shore'.

[13]Warner has herself noted her childhood surprise when her (white) father returned from a visit to Trinidad in the 1960s photographed beside his (black) cousin Suzy: '(he had lost his heart to Cousin Suzy)' (Marina Warner, 'Rich Pickings', in Clare Boylan, ed., *The Agony and the Ego: The Art and Strategy of Fiction Writing Explored* [Harmondsworth: Penguin, 1993], p. 33. I am indebted to my colleague Christien Franken for the reference).

recovers the Shakespearian lost or absent mother, all three twentieth-century mothers 'fail' their children in *Indigo*, either through being silenced by death (Estelle) or through more specific inadequacies in communication (Astrid's alcoholism, Gillian's snobbery).

Sir Anthony Everard is an interesting distillation of a number of characteristics of the historical Sir Pelham Warner, whose son (Marina Warner's father) is one of the dedicatees of *Indigo*. The distinguished cricketer's sobriquet 'Plum' is echoed in the 'Ant' by which Everard senior is known. Sir Pelham Warner was even more highly regarded as a captain, strategist and writer of cricketing matters than as a player: one of Marina Warner's most remarkable achievements in *Indigo* is the invention of the game 'Flinders'. The London home of the game, much patronized by Ant, is Doggett's Fields, and it is worth recording that a special stand in Sir Pelham Warner's honour was built at Lord's cricket ground in St John's Wood, north-west London, in the late 1950s. St Kitts even has its 'Warner Park' cricket ground. The exact nature of Flinders is never specified, but it depends, as cricket is ideally supposed to, on style and judgement rather than solely on feats of physical strength or endurance.[14] Possession of these qualities – pre-eminent in the person of Sir 'Ant' – is termed *sangay*, which Parrinder ('Sea Changes', p. 12) terms 'preternatural insight and power'.

[14]Interviewed by Nicolas Tredell, in *Conversations with Critics* (Manchester: Carcanet, 1994), pp. 248–49, Warner made the following observations about her decision not to use cricket itself: 'I wanted the game – the Imperial game which did not cease to be an Imperial game but which became also the games of those who had been conquered and colonized and their successors – to be calqued exactly on the battle I describe between the indigenous inhabitants of the island and the first colonizers, because I wanted to show the irony that the most civilized sport is actually born out of conflict. And I wanted it to be the case not only that the nomenclature of the game should recall this forgotten battle – that all sorts of historical associations should have been decayed into the very names of the positions in the game and so forth – but also that the game should be more violent than cricket in the way it was played. So I put into it a little bit of the Sienese *palio*, the horse race which turns the town of Siena into a kind of ferocious civil war twice a year.'

Warner's distinguished cricketing forebear contributes to this novel in other, subtler, ways that suggest the many levels at which it works. Warner herself discovered, in researching the novel, how much Caribbean colonial history was 'mostly all driven by the hunger for sugar':

> I put something sweet into almost every chapter of the book – stealthily – just to hint at how pervasively sugar flows through our world. ('Rich Pickings', p. 30)

'Plum' is of course associated with fruit and sweetness, and part of the colonial impulse behind the Caribbean part of the novel is, as Warner discovered, the sugar trade and the human suffering that trade has caused. In addition, however, 'plum' (like 'indigo') is a colour. Indeed the book's sections contrive to 'radicalize' or 'retrieve' colour in a more sophisticated way than through a monolithic opposition between 'black' and 'white'. I suggest that, as with the blending of 'lilac' into 'pink', there is in 'plum' a specifically 'inner' sexualization of the Other: I take this hint from the clear suggestion of black labia in the title of Alice Walker's *The Color Purple* (1982). *Indigo*'s sections negotiate a kind of spectrum: the first is entitled 'Lilac/Pink', the second 'Indigo/Blue', and so on, until the last, 'Maroon/Black' is reached. *Indigo*, as Patrick Parrinder felicitously puts it, 'forcibly remind[s us that it comprises] both a narrative continuum and a changing spectrum' ('Sea Changes', p. 12). At the same time, Warner herself claims that it was not until after she had finished the book that she realized that, like all her other novels, it:

> shared a bipartite structure – that the past is recapitulated in the present with variations that I hope are telling. This [. . .] rises out of Catholic teaching: the New Covenant (the present day) fulfils the enigmatic prophecies of the Old (the past) in a typological pattern that seems to be etched into my mind. In *Indigo*, the Everard family attempt to repeat their colonial enterprise of the seventeenth century with tourist

development today, and Sycorax, who embodies the island, even though her voice is imprisoned and muffled, survives in an altered form to bring about the defeat of these plans and an almost happy ending – at least one filled with hope and reconciliation, a kind of salvation. ('Rich Pickings', p. 33)

Whether the choice of 'bipartite structure' in that description was conscious or not, it strikingly recalls one of the items listed at the beginning of 'Rich Pickings' (p. 29), which Warner 'kept around' her as talismans while she was writing *Indigo*: 'two oyster shells (fitting together) . . . the female sex symbolized as a sea-creature'.

Indigo is framed by the consciousness of the Caribbean nurse Serafine Killebree (b. 1892). She provides a chorus, commenting on Miranda's and Xanthe's growing up, and also functions as a kind of twentieth-century counterpart to Sycorax. Her night-time stories form yet another conversation whose survival depends on oral transmission from mother to daughter, much as Sycorax imparted her wisdom to Ariel. What is perhaps the most famous quotation from *The Tempest* – 'The isle is full of noises' – is transmuted into something Sycorax hears both in life and in death. Serafine, in her way equally ancient at the end of *Indigo*, is 'often too tired nowadays to unscramble the noises, but she's happy hearing them, to change into stories another time' (*Indigo*, p. 402). The voice of Serafine Killebree is clearly related to Warner's interest in fairy-tale mythology: Serafine's presumed illiteracy, oral skills and servant status are counterpointed in the English Princess who, as Warner herself has remarked, fulfils the role of fairy godmother to the ill-fated Xanthe. That voice reminds us of displacement: Serafine's stories are about where she has come from, and they sit exotically in the grey London world she inhabits in *Indigo*.

A novel that pushes the rewriting of colonial history even more problematically into areas of racial and gender confusion is J. M. Coetzee's *Foe*. Coetzee is a white-liberal South African with an Afrikaner background. Although he speaks Afrikaans and Dutch, and has translated a novel, *A Posthumous Confession*, by the nineteenth-century Dutch novelist Marcellus Emants, English is his first language. He achieved international recognition on winning the 1983 Booker Prize for *Life & Times of Michael K*. Coetzee's readers have experienced considerable difficulty in trying to define a relationship between *Foe* and its source – or indeed even in defining that source. Steven Connor has seen in *Foe* a diplomatic rewriting of Daniel Defoe's *Robinson Crusoe* (1719); John Thieme has seen in *Foe*'s lost daughter motif the ghostly presence of Defoe's *Roxana* (1724), and even, elsewhere in Coetzee's novel, other works of Defoe such as *Moll Flanders* (1722).[15]

This brief account of *Foe* stresses the indeterminacy surrounding the lost voice and history of Friday. Coetzee's rewriting is transgressive in a number of ways: the story is narrated, we later discover, to the character Foe by a woman, Susan Barton, who has been cast adrift after a mutiny on board ship returning to England from Brazil, and is washed ashore on Cruso's island; Cruso (the changed spelling is significant) is far from Defoe's resourceful castaway (he makes no attempt to escape from his island; he cultivates ground but has no crops to grow on it, holding that prospect open 'for those who come after us and have the foresight to bring seed';[16] he refuses Barton's repeated suggestions that he keep a journal). There is also considerable uncertainty as to whether Cruso himself has cut out Friday's tongue or whether, for instance, this mutilation had occurred at the hands of slave-dealers before Friday's and Cruso's paths crossed. The mutilation itself suggests to both Barton and (one would imagine) many of Coetzee's readers not perhaps so much castration as (and more disturbingly)

---

[15]Steven Connor, 'Rewriting Wrong: On the Ethics of Literary Reversion', and John Thieme, 'Passages to England'; both essays are collected in D'haen & Bertens, eds., *Liminal Postmodernisms*, pp. 79–97 and 55–78 respectively.

[16]J. M. Coetzee, *Foe* (1986; London: Penguin, 1987), p. 33. Further quotations from this edition in the text above.

clitoridectomy. I find it hard to resist this deduction from Barton's words:

> 'Hitherto I had found Friday a shadowy creature and paid him little more attention than I would have given any house-slave in Brazil. But now I began to look on him – I could not help myself – with the horror we reserve for the mutilated. It was no comfort that his mutilation was secret, closed behind his lips (as some other mutilations are hidden by clothing), that outwardly he was like any Negro. Indeed, it was the very secretness of his loss that caused me to shrink from him. *I could not speak, while he was about,* without being aware how lively were the movements of the tongue in my own mouth.' (*Foe,* p. 24, emphases added)

Friday is not just unmanned, I suggest: he is actually feminized. Barton's own voice is silenced in his presence because he reminds her of what she does not wish to be reminded. The suggestion of clitoridectomy is disturbing, not just because of the extreme repellence of the practice to Western minds, but more specifically because it prompts us to recall, with Edward Said, how the association of Orient and barbarism can be brought into uncomfortable juxtaposition in such a way that Otherness itself becomes demonized.

At any rate Friday has no tongue, in however many senses of the word we may choose to understand. Because he is dumb it is impossible to ascertain the extent to which he understands the English of Cruso and Barton, and we are to assume that he would be unable to convey his experiences anyway, because neither character troubles to ascertain his own language. The readerly uncertainty lies ultimately in the extent to which Coetzee's narrative, together with those of Foe and Barton, connive at the silencing of Friday's discourse. The novel might appear to 'end' at the conclusion of the third of its four sections, in an inscrutably bizarre scene in which Friday, dressed in Foe's wig and robes, is writing at Foe's desk. Foe addresses Barton:

'Is Friday learning to write?' asked Foe.

'He is writing, after a fashion,' I said. 'He is writing the letter *o*.'

'It is a beginning,' said Foe. 'Tomorrow you must teach him *a*.' (*Foe*, p. 152)

There is then a short fourth section that posits two further endings narrated by what John Thieme is surely right to call 'a Coetzee surrogate rather than a Defoe figure' (Thieme, p. 76). Each short episode reviews and indeed rewrites – in dreamlike fashion – episodes that have been part of the earlier narrative. In the first of these, Foe and Barton are lying in bed in a squalid room, apparently dead, while Friday lies apart, apparently only just alive. The 'I' figure lies next to Friday with his ear to Friday's mouth, and after a long while begins to discern 'the sounds of the island' (*Foe*, p. 154). In a stranger sequel still, that appears to begin similarly to its predecessor, the 'I' figure apparently enters or is consumed by the opening pages of Barton's narrative as told to Foe ('At last I could row no further . . .' [*Foe*, pp. 5, 155]), sinking underwater and discovering the wrecked ship from which Barton had apparently escaped, seeing Barton and the murdered captain submerged 'fat as pigs in their white nightclothes, their limbs extending stiffly from their trunks, their hands, puckered from long immersion, held out in blessing, float[ing] against the low roof', eventually discovering Friday, once again last of all. The narrator manages to get Friday's mouth open, and listens as before:

From inside him comes a slow stream, without breath, without interruption. It flows up through his body and out upon me; it passes through the cabin, through the wreck; washing the cliffs and shores of the island, it runs northward and southward to the ends of the earth. Soft and cold, dark and unending, it beats against my eyelids, against the skin of my face. (*Foe*, p. 157)

What seems to have happened is that the Coetzee surrogate comes to terms with his attempt to portray a Friday who has no tongue and no words. What streams out of Friday's mouth is not 'language' but significance unmediated by language. For the Coetzee surrogate to have realized Friday's otherness so fully as to be able to convey it as he does requires his own subjection to the attempts at ending that his fiction makes. Friday's voice has been muted and his history silenced, but it cannot be suppressed. The versions of Susan Barton as mediated by Foe were nothing more than failed attempts to tell us this; the precisely specified Otherness of Friday has silenced even the woman's voice conscripted by Coetzee to rewrite the desert-island fiction.

A perspective reminding us that recuperable voices include not just those of slaves but also colonizers and even hybrids is provided by Barry Unsworth's *Sacred Hunger* (1992). This may well be the novel that the blocked writer Clive Benson is trying to complete in Unsworth's earlier *Sugar and Rum* (1988).[17]

In *Sacred Hunger* Unsworth provides a wonderfully satisfying historical novel for the kind of reader who will be captivated by authentic registration – in this case of eighteenth-century locations (Liverpool, London, West Africa, southern Florida and the Keys) and customs (ranging from sartorial fashion through the most detailed nautical terminology and practice to the sheer physical brutality of life on board a slave ship).

However, there is more to *Sacred Hunger*. The novel is framed by the last days in the life of the mulatto ex-slave Luther Sawdust, who by 1832, aged approximately 80, has gravitated to New Orleans. The knowledge the reader gains as to Luther's 'place', his identity and origins, his construction of his identity through language, is presented, with arbitrary omniscience, as parallel to an act of reconstruction by the narrator from the fragmentary

---

[17]This possibility is also suggested by Peter Kemp in his 1993 Book Trust pamphlet on Unsworth produced for the British Council.

remains of the historical record. On the one hand, the detail of those parts of the events of 1752–3 and 1765 that are presented is staggering in its scope and range; on the other, the very fact that the book's two parts are devoted to those two periods ensures that the reader is (as it were) at the mercy of the narrator's selection process.

It is true that there is both flashback and anticipatory narrative in these main sections of the book, but their presence gives the reader the sense that the book is under tight yet arbitrary authorial control. This control is juxtaposed with episodes of unusually strong authorial omniscience. Perhaps it is meant to figure the vision of the monomaniacally driven Captain Thurso.

An example of Unsworth's narrative method is to be found in the treatment of the press-ganging of some 'scum' by Thurso, his first and second mates Barton and Simmonds and his bosun Haines, for the slave ship the *Liverpool Merchant*. Three such conscripts, Billy Blair, Daniel Calley and Jim Deakin, are found: Blair at least, we later discover, finally makes it to the strange paradise on the Florida Keys, where we glimpse a group of captives and ship's crew twelve years later living in a racial harmony whose lingua franca is pidgin. But that glimpse is 'controlled', in the sense that we perceive it through the eyes of Erasmus Kemp and through Kemp's obsessive mission to discover the fate of the *Liverpool Merchant* and bring to justice his cousin Matthew Paris, the ship's surgeon whom Kemp believes ultimately responsible for the death of Kemp's father and Paris's uncle, the ship's owner. Deakin, however, has been among a party that jumps ship on its first encounter with the West African coast. As readers we follow him through to the full specificity of a feverish and solitary death known to none of *Sacred Hunger*'s named dramatis personae:

No one on board ever knew what had become of Deakin.
He joined the company of those who have no official death.
For the Admiralty he remained a deserter in perpetuity. On

Thurso's crew-list he was entered as 'Run', and this was all his epitaph.[18]

Thurso's log-book, we later learn, is discovered by Erasmus Kemp, but by now it is only partly legible (and thus only partly recuperable). In this way the kind of anonymity usually considered the preserve of the slaves themselves becomes – one might almost say – a franchise extended to the slavers too. Still, unlike the majority of his captives, Thurso is a 'named' character, even though there are strong hints that he has been murdered in a final mutiny engineered by Paris, the alleged father of Kireku, who is later to become known as Luther Sawdust. This is only hearsay, however, and there is no unequivocal narrative endorsement of it.

The total effect is to complement those novels on the slave trade that stress that the hidden voices are those of slaves only. It is in turn neatly complemented in *Sacred Hunger* by the use made by a group of the characters of the rehearsals of a performance, not of Shakespeare's *The Tempest* but of Dryden and Davenant's Restoration rescripting of it, *The Enchanted Island*. Unsworth's actors make unwittingly comic attempts to profile more highly than their scripts allow the parts in which they have been cast. They also want to involve more women in their production of *The Enchanted Island* than even Dryden and Davenant allow for. Although part of the point is that women as actors only became a reality after the Restoration (so that original performances of *The Tempest* would have been acted by men), the desire Unsworth's characters reveal for an excess of speaking voices ironically contrasts with his attempts as a story-teller elsewhere to get blood out of stone, that is, inventively to recover voices that have been lost for ever. There is also a contrast with the 'absent mother' of the Shakespearian original. Authority is seen to be a force that shifts in unpredictable ways according to the culture and politics of a given age.

[18]Barry Unsworth, *Sacred Hunger* (1992; London: Penguin, 1992), p. 283.

Heterodoxies of Gender – The Suppression of Stories: Paul Bailey, Timothy Mo, Alan Hollinghurst

The last part of this chapter consists of a discussion of some male fictions of varying degrees of gay interest, the specific aim being to suggest ways in which given protagonists become displaced within their own fictions.

Paul Bailey's *Gabriel's Lament* (1986) is dominated by the voice of an elderly father Oswald, loudmouthed, deceitful and fraudulent, and haunted by the silence of a much younger mother, Amy, who disappears just before Gabriel's thirteenth birthday. Although Gabriel Harvey's life is charted into middle age, his voice throughout is that of a child who has been deformed by childhood experience.

That experience operates deformatively on both the psychological level (Gabriel finally discovers the truth about his mother in the papers of his father's bizarre 'bequest') and on the physical level (various characters in the novel comment in various ways on Gabriel's diminutive stature and sallow epicene beauty, characteristics we learn have arisen from a history of illness in young childhood including a near-fatal attack of diphtheria). Gabriel's father, like Dickens's Little Dorrit's, comes into an inheritance that changes his lifestyle for ever. Like Mr Dorrit, too, Gabriel's father is changed for the worse by this experience, which actually becomes the cause of Gabriel's lament. The novel also features the gay baroque (Gabriel discovers that he has a much older camp half-brother Tommy, and both contrive to keep this fact secret from Oswald until the latter is seriously ill).[19]

The narrative of *Gabriel's Lament* makes sense of Gabriel's life. A marginal character himself, Gabriel becomes intensely

[19]It may be noted in passing here that there is a music-hall turn in the lugubriously funny act of Stanley Vole that brings the world of *Gabriel's Lament* close to those of Peter Ackroyd and Angela Carter. Bailey's own memoirs, *An Immaculate Mistake* (1991), also capture a tone of thespian high camp. He has said that *Great Expectations* is his favourite book.

interested in the lives of the marginal. Among his discoveries is that of his illegitimacy, his mother having in fact become the *third* Mrs Oswald only several years after his birth. For many years Gabriel researches *Lords of Light*, a hagiography of Britain's sectarians, with a mixture of scholarship and serendipity. Some of these figures have historical reality, such as the Quakers' founding father George Fox; others come to a life predicated by the terms of the plot of *Gabriel's Lament*, such as Roger Kemp, an inhabitant of the former workhouse Jerusalem, later the old people's home where Gabriel has worked as a skivvy until its closure. Kemp is given to a bizarre syntax that attracts Gabriel:

> *I must to say that there fell upon my tongue in Liverpool such a wonder of speech that I stopped amazed; I must to remember that my mother cast me out in her white woman's fear; I must to tell how I was sore distressed when my illness flowered.*[20]

In a revealing moment, Gabriel's Aunt 'Swedie', herself a Swedenborgian (and contemptuously nicknamed by the intolerant Oswald), knowing she is about to die, writes a farewell letter to Gabriel in which she urges him not to remain 'a commentator rather than a participant' like his father (*Gabriel's Lament*, p. 134). Yet while Gabriel's role as commentator imbues Oswald with all Oswald's beguiling repulsiveness, it gives Gabriel a strange saintliness all his own. It is Bailey's remarkable achievement to portray this quality in Gabriel, in either the first person or as a centre of consciousness, without his ever becoming sanctimonious or pathetic: Gabriel remains, instead, inscrutable and the lament that is finally sparked by the late discoveries about his past becomes all the more poignant.

[20]Paul Bailey, *Gabriel's Lament* (1986; London: Penguin, 1987), p. 219. Further references to this edition in the text above.

Lecturing on *Lords of Light* in Minnesota, in the aptly named town of Sorg (Norwegian for 'grief' or 'sorrow'), Gabriel notices in George Fox's eccentricity a quality that his own father's is seen to lack. Gabriel is recounting how Fox believed himself commanded by God to pronounce doom on the town of Lichfield. Having cast off his shoes in a field, Fox entered the town crying 'Woe unto the bloody city of Lichfield!', whereupon 'some friends and friendly people came to me and said, "Alack, George! where are thy shoes?"' (*Gabriel's Lament*, pp. 300–301). Gabriel's account of this episode characterizes himself, Fox, and his attraction to Fox:

'Ladies and gentlemen, I like to think that I might have been one of those friendly people, worried about the condition of George Fox's feet. They represent the best of which we are capable, throughout history. And it says something for George's essential humanity that he should record what the friendly people said to him in the midst of his frantic "Woe"-ing. He noticed, and noted, their concern. George, in fact, can be counted our friend – with a small, as well as a capital, "f". I can't believe in his God, but I can admire his qualities as a believer.' (*Gabriel's Lament*, p. 301)

Gabriel's marginalism, figured in his capacity as a 'commentator rather than a participant', is not confined to this enlightened humanism: in its manifestation as a talent for mimicry (of, for example, queenly eccentrics in his boarding-house world such as the Countess Bolina; Sadie Jenkins, the luvvie who has seen better days; the dipsomaniac ex-barrister Matthew) it can give great joy and even comfort to his listeners, strange as this may sound to readers of a book crammed with dialogue and anecdote. Aunt 'Swedie"'s farewell letter, warning Gabriel away from 'becoming a collector of people (eccentric people)', nonetheless admits that he was 'diverting company this afternoon' (*Gabriel's Lament*, p. 134). Later, in Sorg, having read Oswald's 'bequest', Gabriel's Minnesotan hostess Barbara Pedersen articulates what has been a cathartic experience for him as well as for herself and her husband too (they have lost a son, Eric, in Vietnam):

> 'You were in hell when you made us laugh so much that evening in the restaurant. I call that honest-to-goodness goodness, the way you made us laugh. I call that real considerate. I know what hell's like, honey. Eric took us there.' (*Gabriel's Lament*, p. 315)

In the end, however, the kind of marginality Aunt 'Swedie' so much feared in Gabriel's tendency to collect eccentrics and never become a participant in life is seen to have burnt itself out. Gabriel's queerness may have been pathological in origin but it does not prevent him, once his lament is over, from emerging from his prolonged grieving adolescence.

Timothy Mo's earliest fiction dealt with the experiences of mixed communities in 1950s Hong Kong and China (*The Monkey King* [1978]) and in contemporary London (*Sour Sweet* [1982]). After this, Mo moved to larger canvases and – with *The Redundancy of Courage* (1991) – controversial historical themes, in this case a thinly disguised account of the invasion of East Timor by Indonesia in 1975 and the subsequent guerrilla war as seen through the eyes of its anti-hero, the gay, westernized, part-Chinese, part 'Danu'-ese Adolph Ng. Commentators have noted Mo's unsparing descriptions of acts of physical violence and even dismemberment; the controversial reception of *Brownout on Breadfruit Boulevard* (1995) was noted above.

Mo's first historical novel, *An Insular Possession* (1986), shortlisted for that year's Booker Prize, advances events by means of various kinds of documents – inserted press cuttings, letters, a theatre advertisement and an extract from Sheridan's *The Rivals* (1775). The narrative performance is relaxed, prolix and stylishly nineteenth century in tone. At nearly 600 pages, the action may seem a bit thin: it concerns the increasing disillusionment of the two young American clerks, Walter Eastman and Gideon Chase, at the cynical extent of the corruption within the European mercantile community in its support for the Cantonese opium trade of the late 1830s. The young men's response is to open their own newspaper, *The Lin Tin Bulletin and River Bee* as a competitor to the established *Cantonese Monitor*. Yet the moral ground claimed by Eastman and Chase themselves could hardly be described as 'high' as they fiddle their circulation figures and misrepresent the scale of donations to the *Bulletin*. The conflict between the young Americans and the European establishment extends to a more general one between the conservative values upheld by the European community and the more progressive, indigenous or ethnic values espoused by Eastman and Chase. In 1841 Eastman decides to leave Canton, a move that appears to signal the demise of *The Lin Tin Bulletin and River Bee*.

The experienced reader may come to observe, however, that the discussion between traditional European and traditional Chinese narrative technique is incorporated within the structure of Mo's novel itself. Thus the *Bulletin* of 22 May 1839 reports the mysterious disappearance (probably through drowning) of Thomas Veale, a Macao 'old hand'. Like Eastman and Chase themselves, Veale is portrayed as having assumed the values of the progressive colonialists:

> His conversation was energetic, animated often to the point of incoherence, his looks and gestures frequently wild to a degree, but those with the patience to listen to his anecdotes, usually delivered in a sequence not at all logical or chronological, found in him a valuable fund of the stories of the early trading days of the settlement.[21]

The conflict between East and West complexly played out in the tension between the novel's narrative mode and its narrative direction or indirection is itself undermined by the two Appendices with which *An Insular Possession* is provided.

[21]Timothy Mo, *An Insular Possession* (London: Chatto & Windus, 1986), p. 328. Further references in the text to this edition.

The first of these Appendices is a 'Gazetteer' dating from 1935 that is both geographical and biographical in nature. It gives a short account of Chase's life as an eminent philologist and sinologist who later settled in Rome, continuing to live there until his death in 1908. The second Appendix is an edited selection of Chase's unpublished memoirs. These apparently date from the beginning of the twentieth century. Although Chase treats any reference to his former partner with the utmost restraint, never actually mentioning him by name, it appears that the two have met once more, eighteen years after Eastman's departure from Canton in 1841. Eastman has died in 1870 but Chase apparently only discovers this two years later.

If at one level *An Insular Possession* can be read as a western version of a Cantonese history, these Appendices force us to consider further the veridical status of the historical novel. Each Appendix is itself an historical document. The bulk of Mo's historical narrative is undermined – or, perhaps better, suppressed and even censored – by the information presented in the Appendices. As far as Chase's memoirs are concerned, the reader must ponder whether their contents are not affected by a sense of homosexual attraction between the two young men that is never made explicit in the main part of the narrative. The effect of the first Appendix, the Gazetteer, from which Eastman is entirely missing, is still more puzzling, because it endorses, far more strongly than the Chase memoirs, the way in which Eastman has been completely written out of the story. To what forces can this act of censorship be attributed? One way of attempting to answer this kind of question is to suggest that the narrator of the main part of *An Insular Possession* has wrongly judged the historical significance of the events he describes. But this still leaves the puzzle presented by the sheer massive existence of the narrative that both Chase and Eastman inhabit.

There are other imaginable ways of writing a character out of a narrated action, and these would include such a character's discovery that the plot in which he thought himself to be playing a central part turns out to be another kind of plot altogether. The case of *An Insular Possession* illustrates this point in a very self-conscious manner, and one is tempted to link this aspect of its existence with the suggestion that Chase feels the need to suppress any suggestion of gay sexuality involving himself and Eastman. To try to shed more light on this kind of suppression, I conclude this chapter with an account of Alan Hollinghurst's *The Swimming Pool Library* (1988).

Alan Hollinghurst's language is poetic, by which I mean that it is more intricately punning and allusive than one expects in extended prose fiction. For instance, in *The Folding Star* (1994) there is an explicit play on the name of Luc Altidore, the pupil and – briefly but electrifyingly – sexual partner of the narrator Edward Manners. Manners' part-Dutch ancestry has led him to 'a mythical, silt-choked, fallen Flemish city', its identity mused on, in the gloriously celebratory review of *The Folding Star* by the American novelist Nicholson Baker from which that description is taken, as 'Ghentwerp? Brugeselles?',[22] but the self-conscious punning on the boy's name is not Flemish but French, as we learn (obsessionally) even from Manners' encounter with Flemish architecture:

> Note too the use of the fortified tower of St Vaast as a basis for the sketch of a castle which forms the *cul-de-lampe*: a word that disturbed me for a moment, Luc being a backward offering of cul, Luc's cul a dream palindrome – the two round cheeks of it and the lick of the s between: I was nonsensing and spoonerising it in my mouth all day long.[23]

Despite Manners' ancestry, Hollinghurst was apparently unaware of the joke provocatively floated on BBC2's 1994

[22]Nicholson Baker, 'Lost Youth' [review of *The Folding Star*], *LRB*, 9 June 1994, p. 6.
[23]Alan Hollinghurst, *The Folding Star* (London: Chatto & Windus, 1994), p. 178.

Booker Prize '*Late Show*' discussion by Germaine Greer: that the English-French 'Bruges' is 'Brugge' in Flemish, and thus that this naming of the Flemish town, unknown to most speakers of English, could be turned into an anagram as 'bugger'. Hollinghurst's unawareness of this pun[24] suggests that a surplus of anagrammatic or cryptic significance, such as is offered by this real-life example, may actually help us understand how his literary imagination works.

Visiting the elderly and eccentric but by no means dotty Charles Nantwich, the 'queer peer' whom the narrator of *The Swimming-pool Library* William Beckwith has earlier resuscitated from heart failure in the public lavatory of a London park, Beckwith finds Lord Nantwich completing a crossword:

> Charles was sitting in the library with *The Times*. He didn't get up but looked jolly, and chuckled to see me. I went over to him, and he slipped his arm round my waist, as parents shelter and draw to them a tired or evasive child. 'Can you think of anything to go in there?' he asked.
>
> There was one word of the crossword to do, and as I had filled the whole thing in quite quickly that morning I decided I would only pretend to think for a second or two before coming out with the answer. '"Hurry to start mischief in the women's quarters",' I quoted. 'Well, I should have thought it was "HAREM", but . . .' The three across answers, which gave the first, third and final letters of the word had been uncompromisingly filled in with 'SCREW', 'AZALEA' and 'PRESURIZE' (*sic*).
>
> 'C blank Z blank P,' Charles pondered. 'I'm dashed if I can think of anything. I seem to have boxed myself in.'
>
> 'I don't think some of those answers can be right,' I said kindly. '"I hear of a line in a bottle", for instance, must be "PHIAL".'

[24] Alan Hollinghurst, private communication.

Charles was pleased that I had fallen for it. 'Oh, I don't do the *clues*,' he said, in a tone of voice and with a little downward slap of the hand which conveyed tired contempt, an almost political feeling of disaffection. 'No, no, no,' he smiled; 'I do the *alternative* crossword, as they call things nowadays. You have to fill in words which aren't the answers. It's much more difficult. It's a kind of solitaire, you see, you have to make a clean sweep of it. And then, often, I'm afraid, you get buggered in the last corner.'[25]

This episode serves as an illustration in miniature not only of the hermeneutics of reading Hollinghurst's prose but of the unfolding of the plot of the entire novel itself. By 'hermeneutics' I mean what may be termed the philosophy of interpretation. 'PHIAL' can be explained cryptically as a homophone (clued in accordance with cryptic convention as 'I hear of') on 'file', glossed as 'a line'; 'phial' as 'bottle' is thus the entire word. This is not from a conventionally 'cryptic' point of view what many crossword *aficionados* would regard as the most satisfactorily elegant clue of its kind nor, strictly speaking, is it a homophone at all in what we may assume to be Charles's conservative Received Pronunciation (RP, or old-fashioned 'BBC English'). But Hollinghurst's poetic intelligence with language presses on the alert reader the idea that 'PHIAL' might well subconsciously represent, for William, a satisfyingly 'alternative' answer to his own unstated set of clues. For at this point in the narrative William is erotically obsessed with a boy named Phil: inserting 'A' into 'PHIL' would be acceptable cryptic convention for putting an 'article' in Phil, and if one recalls the scabrous *Private Eye* crosswords compiled by the late Tom Driberg MP in the 1970s, such insertion (the word is chosen with

[25]Alan Hollinghurst, *The Swimming-pool Library* (1988; Penguin, 1988), pp. 165–66. Further references in the text to this edition. For those readers who are not cryptic crossword enthusiasts, and at the risk of pedantry, 'HAREM' has been encrypted as 'HARE' (vb. [to] 'Hurry') followed by initial 'M' ('to start mischief'), the whole being glossed as: 'in the women's quarters'.

deliberate tastelessness) could legitimately – according to what one might term 'alternative' cryptic crossword convention – figure the letter 'A' as 'asshole' or 'arsehole' written into the body of 'PHIL'. Needless to add, 'Phil' is a homophone for 'fill'. We have seen from 'Luc' and 'cul' that Hollinghurst is alive to the erotic encrypting of names,[26] and whether or not he would endorse my little excursion on 'PHIAL' is in a way neither here nor there, since my point is precisely that I have just exercised myself in a way analogous to that of Germaine Greer and those others who would choose to read 'Bruges' = 'Brugge' = 'bugger' in *The Folding Star*.

Having pressed the idea that this little crossword episode illustrates the entire plot of *The Swimming-pool Library*, I must now defend it. The novel begins on a note of attractive guilelessness: the setting is London in 1983, 'the last summer of its kind there was ever to be' (*Swimming-pool Library*, p. 3). Hollinghurst simultaneously contrives to capture both a 'real-life' sense of the loss of that arcadian innocence that existed prior to Aids epidemically reaching London's gay bath-house, bar and disco subculture, as well as a 'literary' sense of glorious camp overripe burnished Mediterranean nostalgia for which the principal literary source is Ronald Firbank (1886–1926). At one point in the book Firbank, with whose work William's far less promiscuous friend James is obsessed, actually makes an appearance on some home-shot movie footage found in a Christie's auction lot. That opening lack of guile has been severely tested by the end of the novel on a number of plot-levels in ways that are beautifully decorated with countless carefully plotted arabesques.

What is signified by the crossword episode's self-mocking

[26]Although such poetic wordplay is not always full of erotic charge, there is one particularly interesting instance that refuses to divulge itself to Charles in the 'De Profundis' section of his journal, and is thus unable to rid itself of sinister obsessive undertones. In the prison library Charles finds 'a schools edition of Pope, with notes by A. M. Niven, MA – one of those frustrating near-palindromes with which life is strewn' (*Swimming-pool Library*, p. 256).

description by Charles as 'alternative', and the novel's own
darker reference to 'an almost political feeling of disaffection',
can (I ·suggest) be located at the level of a rites of passage
novel in which William as a Beckwith descendant is avenged,
vicariously and quite fortuitously, by Charles Nantwich the
solver of alternative crosswords, in his representative capacity
as a victim of a remarkably virulent climate of judicial British
homophobia in the 1940 and 1950s. Hollinghurst's dextrous
touch can be seen in a haunting passage in which William
responds to Firbank's prose for the first time in a way that
adds yet another layer of significance to what I take to be the
'unravelling' theme of *The Swimming-pool Library*:

> Much of the talk [of Firbank's characters] was a kind of
> highly inflected nonsense, but it gave the unnerving impression
> that on deeper acquaintance it would all turn out to be
> packed with fleeting and covert meaning. (*Swimming-pool
> Library*, p. 54)

Charles's commission to William to read and possibly edit for
publication a set of diaries kept intermittently from Charles's
own schooldays at Winchester (William is a fellow Wykehamist)
until the dark period of the 1950s allows William to uncover the
darkest secret imaginable. It is that, in contrast to the thoughtless,
careless lifestyle William is himself privileged to be able to lead
in 1983, his own grandfather's elevation to the peerage has
been nothing more nor less than an institutional expression of
gratitude for the fervour with which, as Sir Denis Beckwith, a
former high-ranking official to the British Director of Public
Prosecutions, he had pursued the pre-Wolfenden criminalization
of homosexual behaviour. And yet it is the Lord Beckwith of the
decriminalized 1983 who takes William and James to *Billy Budd*
at Covent Garden, and fascinates both boys with an account of an
occasion on which he had discussed the Forster–Crozier libretto
with Britten; the entire sense of the evening in Lord Beckwith's
box is distillingly characterized by a still innocent William:

> The three of us in our hot little box were trapped with this
> intensely British problem: the opera that was, but wasn't, gay,
> the two young gay friends on good behaviour, the mandarin
> patriarch giving nothing of his feelings away. (*Swimming-pool
> Library*, p. 120)

How inscrutable that 'mandarin patriarch' has really been, in
ways William could not know at the time, is revealed in William's
discovery that during Charles's period of imprisonment following Beckwith's '*crusade to eradicate male vice*' (*Swimming-pool
Library*, p. 260; emphases Charles's) during the 1950s, Charles's
Sudanese house companion and former lover Taha had been
murdered in a racial attack, leaving a widow and a four-year-old
son Abdul.

It turns out to be characteristic of Charles that he has contrived
with the utmost resourcefulness to use his social position in the
only way he can. Charles has crusadingly manoeuvred those
around him, who have been disadvantaged by the pre-Wolfenden
legislation, into positions that even long before 1983 have
compromised neither them nor him. Charles's achievements
in this field allow him, with the benign yet unpredictable
firmness of an elderly eccentric seen by the straight world as
having become 'an old wibbly-wobbly, as one, alas, now is'
(*Swimming-pool Library*, p. 36), to exercise the only revenge
he can. After making his discovery, William tries to intercept
Charles in his club, Wicks, only to find he has left for the
evening. In a comic-grotesque scene the normally dominant
William, 'slicked' from a 'catering-size drum of corn oil' is
complaisantly penetrated on the chopping table in the Wicks
club kitchens by the seductive and slightly sinister Abdul, now in
his forties and revealed to be the club's chef who has so fascinated
William on an earlier encounter, before being ignominiously
ejected ('Fuck off out of here, man') (*Swimming-pool Library*,
p. 262).

One cannot help feeling that, if in no other realms than those of
the politics of sexual orthodoxy and racial equality, a composite

wrong has been symbolically righted, an oppressive history or (as Marina Warner might say) racial memory rewritten. William Beckwith, simultaneously a privileged Englishman and a scion of the new nobility, is displaced from the centre of his story and indeed world by the fortuitous machinations of the queer peer Charles, the 'alternative' representative of the old – and in the nature of things the last of his line.[27] William, in a final twist, is perhaps ultimately too superficial a figure to appreciate the full extent of his humiliation. On the contrary Hollinghurst himself, precisely in the manner in which he contrives to distance himself from this aspect of William's character, shows great technical skill in deftly suggesting how, in this aspect of 1980s Britain at least, the old order has triumphed over the new, albeit at a poignant cost.

[27]There is no space to develop this aspect of the argument further, but it is worth noting, if we are not too proud to seek it there, that in a more 'popular-intellectual' comedy such as Stephen Fry's *The Liar* (1991), the hero Adrian Healey is not dissimilarly displaced.

III

PERFORMANCE

7

Performance, Trickery, History and Narrative

Although the previous section dealt with cities, regions and preoccupations that I discussed under the heading of 'Margin and Privilege', it will be evident that many of the novels that fell into this category also had a strongly experimental, performative aspect. In this section I shall focus on the theme of performance, ending with a discussion of Salman Rushdie, the writer who has done more than any other single author to define the spirit of fiction in Britain during the 1980s and 1990s.

First comes a chapter treating three novels that draw attention to particular regions (Britain's East Anglia) or nations (Australia, Canada) within the Booker-eligible world that have not yet been discussed in this book. The regionalism or nationalism in question will be approached from the perspective of performance much more explicitly than in the previous section. What underlies each discussion is the appetite the Booker has helped create for adventurous non-realistic fiction. There follows, secondly, a discussion of the work of Julian Barnes. This is intended to show that while 'fiction as performance' involves tackling big themes it can nevertheless do so on a domestic scale: the aim will be to demonstrate Barnes's extraordinary high-wire achievement in exploring the limits of fiction as a form while at the same time exercising himself on material that many writers would not be capable of lifting above banality. Thirdly, follows the discussion of Rushdie the great entertainer, the writer who in many respects breached the seawall of English fiction, consolidated a bridgehead and has since transformed the land he took by storm in 1981. A brief conclusion recapitulates the impact of the Booker Prize since the early 1980s, attempting to bring the argument of this book full circle. It reviews the development fiction in Britain has undergone during the past fifteen years, and suggests with reference to Pat Barker's 1995 Booker success how vital and robust English fiction has once more become. English fiction has been invigorated by the pluralism that the Booker Prize pre-eminently (but inextricably supported by the other entrepreneurial developments outlined in the first section above) has encouraged since the early 1980s.

The three novels discussed in this chapter are: Graham Swift's *Waterland* (1983), whose narrator's professional function as a history schoolteacher allows him to manipulate his narrative's chronology, bringing it into confrontation with his own personal dynastic history as the most diffident of all three narrators; Peter Carey's *Illywhacker* (1985), whose narrator performs the most ostensibly linear rendering of his national history but is quite explicitly the least trustworthy of all three; and Mordecai Richler's *Solomon Gursky Was Here* (1989), whose narrator discloses a trickery performed by the very object of his historical quest, so that that narrator's own existential presence in his narrative is challenged, fragmented and reflected.

Firstly, though, a brief word is in place on the international context of this discussion. Novelists such as Swift, Carey and Richler (and, as we shall see, Rushdie) have joined a pantheon consisting of writers as diverse as the Argentinian Jorge Luis Borges, the Mexican Carlos Fuentes and the North American Toni Morrison. All these writers (and many others) employ 'magical realism', a term that has recently and usefully been defined as:

> [the] self-conscious depart[ure] from the conventions of narrative realism [in order] to enter and amplify other (diverted) currents of Western literature that flow from the marvellous Greek pastoral and epic traditions to medieval

dream visions to the romance and Gothic fictions of the past century.[1]

Borges, Fuentes and Morrison have all departed self-consciously from the conventions of narrative realism by rewriting history so as to transgress its 'given facts'. They have done so in a variety of ways: the master-fabulist Borges explores various kinds of 'possible worlds' in his most famous stories such as those collected in *Labyrinths* (1956, etc., English translation 1964); Fuentes rewrites sixteenth-century Iberian colonial history (Columbus has yet to discover the Americas; meanwhile Philip II of Spain marries Elizabeth I of England) in *Terra Nostra* (1975, English translation 1976); and Morrison has the post-Civil War characters of *Beloved* (1987) 'rememory' the suppressed history of slavery in a story in which the ghosts of dead children and grandmothers are realistic presences.

Graham Swift, Peter Carey, Mordecai Richler

Graham Swift's remarkable achievement in *Waterland* is to have produced a story to stand beside the 'magical realism' of Borges, Fuentes, Morrison and others not by the use of 'exoticism' that characterizes international writing of this sort, but rather by implanting various kinds of history into a vividly evoked regional English setting. The region is the East Anglian Fenlands, and its portrayal of a part of England as a locality, with a strong sense of identity, is rare enough and worth remarking on.

Swift's strategy in *Waterland* is to allow alternative performances of history to stand beside what might be thought of as the public and available regional and national histories of the Fens and England respectively. One could list at least five kinds of narrative historical performance evident in this novel. In doing so, one notices that the five kinds tend to flow into and out of each

[1]By Lois Parkinson Zamora and Wendy B. Faris, eds., *Magical Realism: Theory, History, Community* (Durham & London: Duke UP, 1995), p. 2.

other, an aspect of *Waterland* clearly related to the unusually interesting tone of voice of the narrator, the history teacher Tom Crick. Publicly available documented political events such as the French Revolution and Napoleonic conquests (1789–1815), the Coronation of George V (1911), and the 1914–18 and 1939–45 Wars, run alongside the dynastic history of the narrator Tom Crick's own family. We shall see that only intermittently is public history actually made to offer an explanation for the private dynastic history: Tom's shell-shocked father is nursed back to health by his future bride; the teenage Crick himself enters a relationship with the equally youthful Mary Metcalf, the course of which is certainly affected, though in no way decisively, by his being posted to Germany in the mid 1940s. What does affect the course of that relationship will be seen to belong to another realm altogether.

Running beside these two narratives, the publicly national and the privately dynastic, is a third. This is a fantasy cast by the historical period to which it relates, and among its constituents are Crick's description of the events leading up to the catatonia of his great-great-grandmother Sarah Atkinson, her living death – following an assault by her husband – covering the period 1820 to 1874, her portentous cries of 'Smoke!' 'Fire!' 'Burning!', the ghostly apparitions allegedly seen after her flood-ridden funeral in October 1874, and the fire that consumes the Atkinson brewery after a frenzied communal celebration by the town of Gildsey of the Coronation of George V in 1911. All this belongs to a recognizable tradition of English Gothic.

A fourth narrative is the topography of the unique Fen landscape of East Anglia. Reading this involves understanding how that landscape has shifted, advanced and retreated over the years; how rivers alter their courses, and coastlines change; how man has attempted to control the landscape. (It is not surprising that *Waterland* was a bestseller in The Netherlands.) A significant theme is thus drainage, and it is preposterously brought into confrontation with aspects of other narratives, notably bloodshed (that of a manslaughter victim in civilian life, that of the victims of the French Revolution).[2] Christopher Driver, reviewing *Waterland* when it first appeared, related this aspect of the novel to its narrative mode most felicitously:

> [Swift's] very narrative method [is] preoccupied with ebbs and flows, backings and fillings. It floats hither and thither, and under critical pressure floods at an irresistible pace, but it avoids any sense of steady current. Crick's story is an apologia for history . . .[3]

A fifth narrative is the life-cycle of the eel, *Anguilla anguilla*. Its mysteriousness seems incommensurate with or disproportionate to the seemingly primitive nature of the animal that undergoes it, yet a chapter is devoted to the patient quest of the Danish ichthyologist Johannes Schmidt, who from 1904 until the 1920s traced the tiny larvae of *Anguilla anguilla* as far away as the Sargasso Sea. At the same time, Europe is documented as teetering towards, then collapsing into, cataclysm ('this four-year intermission').[4]

Early on in the fiction, we are given instances of Fenland superstition:

> When you see the new moon, turn your money in your pocket; help someone to salt and help them to sorrow; never put new shoes on a table or cut your nails on a Sunday. An eel-skin cures rheumatism; a roast mouse cures whooping cough; and a live fish in a woman's lap will make her barren. (*Waterland*, pp. 15–16)

These superstitions coexist arbitrarily for a while until during an adolescent game of sexual daring, the future manslaughter

---

[2]This aspect of *Waterland* is similar to parts of Rushdie's *Midnight's Children*.
[3]Christopher Driver, 'Floating', *LRB*, 6–19 October 1983, p. 20.
[4]Graham Swift, *Waterland* (London: Heinemann, 1983), p. 174. Further references to this edition in the text above.

victim, sixteen-year-old Freddie Parr, drops a live eel, a 'good three-quarter-pounder', into Mary Metcalf's 'school-regulation knickers' (*Waterland*, p. 166). Because of a botched abortion carried out by the village wise-woman Martha Crick, and possibly also because of Mary's prior attempts to effect the abortion herself, she becomes infertile. That fact is to affect the postmenopausal Mary's judgement, and she snatches a child from a supermarket.[5] The episode threatens to terminate Crick's career, jeopardized as it already is by a combination of his own subversive history classes and the headmaster Lewis Scott's desire for retrenchment. Fenland folklore – or one aspect of it – comes disastrously true, and we have here perhaps the most outrageous instance in *Waterland* of a kind of osmosis between rival narrative histories as they merge into each other.

The botched abortion cannot be isolated from the stories that surround it, and the reader must wonder at Swift's superb structural control of the multiple interrelated strands of the narrative Tom Crick relates.[6] The adolescent Mary Metcalf and Tom Crick have embarked on a sexual relationship; but Mary has also experimented sexually with Tom's mentally handicapped elder brother, named (with apt inscrutability) Dick, and flirted with Freddie. Dick is the product of an incestuous union between Tom's mother, Helen Atkinson, and her own father, Ernest. Ernest has been born during the portentous 1874 floods that cause the funeral ceremony for his grandmother, the 92-year-old Sarah Atkinson, to pass effortlessly into folk memory. Although possessing the mental age of a young child, Dick is endowed with extraordinary physical strength and legendary genitalia: he wins a swimming contest that is the pretext for the game of sexual bravado, and is thus entitled to a 'show' from Mary. He desists, but Mary keeps both Tom and Freddie Parr on a string

---

[5]Where the outcome here is a happy one for the child and its parents, the more gruesome possibilities of this contemporary urban nightmare form the *donnée* of Ian McEwan's *The Child in Time* (1987).

[6]Alan Hollinghurst, 'Of time and the river', *TLS*, 7 October 1983, p. 1073, plausibly saw a source in George Eliot's *The Mill on the Floss* (1860).

by intimating that she has tried to have sex with Dick but that the latter is 'too big'. Dick knows, obscurely, that he himself is 'a bungle [. . .] [s]omething that shouldn't be' (*Waterland*, p. 279), the result of a union that in the human world is socially taboo, and that he must not attempt to reproduce himself. The counterpoint between Dick and *Anguilla anguilla* is maintained to the end, with Dick's apparent suicide by drowning, or rather, perhaps, his affirmative reception into his true element, the real event to which his entire life has been leading and for which the swimming triumph has been a mere rehearsal:

> He turns. [. . .] He clambers onto the rail, stands shoeless, upon it, disdaining the handhold of the adjacent derrick stanchions. Stretches to full height. For a moment he perches, poises, teeters on the rail, the dull glow of the western sky behind him. And then he plunges. In a long, reaching, powerful arc. Sufficiently long and reaching to quite discount the later theory that he must have become entangled in the anchor-chain or the sling-lines; sufficiently reaching and powerful for us to observe his body, in its flight through the air, form a single, taut and seemingly limbless continuum, so that an expert on diving might have judged that here indeed was a natural, here indeed was a fish of a man. (*Waterland*, p. 309)

The play on 'natural'[7] suggests that Dick has plunged not just from one element into another, but from the realistic narrative into the magically realistic world that has always been flowing through Crick's story.

This story moves forward very little in time to culminate in the child-snatching episode (another 'miscarriage') involving Crick's increasingly disturbed wife Mary. That the narrative does not return, after Dick's suicide, to the naturalist mode is significant. Yet what actually drives Dick to his watery

---

[7]In addition to the primary sense of 'one in or returning to his natural element', we may cite *OED* 14a: 'one who is by nature deficient in intelligence'.

apotheosis is contained in an episode that belongs fully to the realistic world. Tom Crick the narrator discovers that Freddie Parr has been killed by Dick, owing to Dick's confusion concerning the paternity of Mary's child. Freddie has told Dick the child is Dick's; yet even she seems uncertain which of the Crick brothers is actually the father. The possibility that the father might, after all, be Dick, perhaps at one level motivates Mary's inducing the abortion that Martha Clay, 'the witch', performs. Tom must discard the foetus into the Ouse without looking (since that is supposed to be unlucky), but he does so all the same. Is this another instance of Fenland superstition only engaging occasionally and by pure chance with the reality it purports to predict? Although the story gives no decisive answer, it creates an appropriate atmosphere.

The post-mortem has shown Freddie's blood-alcohol to be of a level consistent with death by drowning while in a stupor (his father has been bootlegging whisky from the American air force pilots stationed in the area in the early 1940s); we have learnt from the narrative that Freddie cannot swim; in trying to fish Freddie's corpse out of the river (the episode with which Tom Crick's narrative begins), Tom's lock-keeper father Henry damages it with a hook. In so doing, Henry Crick obscures what turns out to be the mark inflicted by his 'half-son' Dick, who has struck Freddie with a beer bottle from a collection bequeathed to him by his (and Tom's) late mother. Dick, having once tried this potent and potional beer and having suffered the consequences unusually severely, has superstitiously hoarded the rest. Now, prepared for his apotheosis, he swallows a final bottle (one liquid element comprising his and Tom's shared dynastic identity) and commits himself to the Ouse (another liquid element comprising his and Tom's shared regional identity).

The novel ends with the arresting image of a human, who has never been in his true element, instinctively and atavistically finding his natural one, as do the eels with which this extraordinary narrative wriggles and threshes.

*   *   *

If *Waterland* is suffused with instances of regional and national narratives constantly being elbowed out of the limelight by an obsessive dynastic preoccupation with pedigree, the national story running alongside Herbert Badgery's performance as the narrator of Peter Carey's *Illywhacker* is constantly upstaged by the characters making up the diaspora that has brought about twentieth-century Australian society. The entire effect, I suggest, is a vast chronicle in which the national gene pool is dynamically stirred up and displaced.

This vision of Australian society in search of a self is, as elsewhere in Carey's work, counterpointed by the belief that Australia consistently presents itself as an exploited colony. As its history has progressed, the colonizing power has changed: from the British through the nineteenth century, the colonial reins pass to American hands in the period of the 1939–45 war, before finally being surrendered to Japan, as the Pacific rim is constructed to conform to its late twentieth-century post-industrial contours.[8] In this way Australia's national story differs from Canada's, but both consider themselves defensively, with respect to the financial and popular-cultural power of the United States. The comparison with Scotland, whose assertion of an identity within the British Isles is as I have argued above similarly defensive, is worth noting.

I have already observed that *Illywhacker* is the most linear narrative of the three under discussion here, but I must make two qualifications at the outset. Certainly the entire 600-page novel is one enormous flashback from the point at which the bandy-legged Herbert Badgery claims to be 139 years old, and apparently in some way an exhibit. However, there are, firstly, smaller movements back and forth within the larger framework of the flashback. Secondly, and more significantly, despite Badgery's admission that he is a 'terrible liar', his age, he tells us, is:

[8]Carey subsequently turns his attention to the nineteenth-century period – in *Oscar and Lucinda* (1988) – and a postcolonial imaginative future – in *The Unusual Life of Tristram Smith* (1994).

the one fact you can rely on, and not because I say so, but because it has been publicly authenticated. Independent experts have poked me and prodded me and scraped around my foul-smelling mouth. They have measured my ankles and looked at my legs. [. . .] When they photographed me I did not care that my dick looked as scabby and scaly as a horse's, even though there was a time when I was a vain man and would not have permitted the type of photographs they chose to take.[9]

This linear narrative of Badgery's affects a trustworthiness that is free of the evasions and chronological manipulations of Swift's and Richler's novels. Yet there is a problem at the outset, for Carey flaunts the dubiousness of his whole enterprise from the very start: the flashbacks are episodic, but Badgery (who has promised that he is not lying about his age even though he may lie about anything else) begins with an episode that takes place in 1919 when he is himself 33. If this is so, we must accept that he was born in 1886, and has reached the age of 139 in 2025.[10] The reader may be able to accept the magical realist convention of excessive longevity (think, for example, of the 200-year-old Francisco the Man in Gabriel García Márquez's *One Hundred Years of Solitude* [1967; English translation 1970],

[9]Peter Carey, *Illywhacker* (1985: London & Boston: Faber & Faber, 1986), p. 11. Further references to this edition in the text above.

[10]The point is noticed but not developed in Nicholas Spice's perceptive review, 'Phattbookia Stupenda', *London Review of Books*, 18 April 1985, p. 20. Luc Herman has put the paradox well: Badgery 'is evidently lying when he goes on to say that his age is the one thing the reader can rely on. If so, this means that he is lying about everything, including the lying itself, so that as a confidence man, he is beaten at his own game'; see Herman, 'Peter Carey', *Postwar Literatures in English* 14 (December 1991), p. 6. While recognizing the paradox I prefer to express it differently. Herman usefully points out that the Australian historian M. V. Anderson the gaoled Badgery cites ('Our forefathers were all great liars' [*Illywhacker*, p. 456]) is or was himself fictitious. On his release from gaol in 1949, Badgery undergoes a 'transformation . . . model[ling him]self on M. V. Anderson' (*Illywhacker*, p. 488). In this light the status of purloined letters and notebooks commented on by others in this novel is fascinating.

but she or he is then faced with a need to accommodate to the status of such a fiction narrated, apparently, some forty years after the novel's historical publication in 1985.[11] Even by 'standard' magical-realist criteria this opening obliges the reader to go a long way towards imaginatively accommodating the confidence trickery of the narrator of *Illywhacker*, especially as the novel's second epigraph is one of philological pedantry: it uses a dictionary of Australian colloquialisms to trace the term 'illywhacker' as 'A professional trickster, esp. operating at country shows' (*Illywhacker*, p. 9. The first epigraph cites Mark Twain on the lying truthfulness of Australian history.) Later, Leah Goldstein will curtly echo the dictionary: 'A spieler, [. . .] A trickster. A quandong. A ripperty man. A con-man' (*Illywhacker*, p. 246).

Three major periods in Badgery's life conform to the novel's division into three Books. Through these Books *Illywhacker* contrives to rewrite the larger historical narrative of twentieth-century Australia. Immigration leads to cultural pluralism, that is, the idea that many coexisting cultures are subsumed into a single monolithic (and dominant if not frequently oppressive) culture. Britain and its former colonial possessions may be 'Christian' countries with a national Church, but the very dominance of that culture is able to accommodate a great deal of other systems of belief and practice.

Carey's pluralism takes the form of a particular kind of hybridity: legitimacy and thus genetic descent undergo various blips, as we shall see; and for Carey, pluralism extends beyond the human race to the animal kingdom and to the realm of machinery. What emerges from the narrative is that the magical-realist fiction can present genetics and heredity that are simultaneously literal and figurative, or – to put it another way – that operate in a literal and/or figurative sense at more

---

[11]The point may be illustrated by contrasting the way in which Angela Carter's *Nights at the Circus* (1984) may be full of magical-realist trickery, but never extends its carefully plotted time-scheme into a period 'outside' its own history.

than one level simultaneously, as the straightforward realist fiction cannot. The literal and the figurative coexist, in this particular magical-realist fiction, through the displacing agency of trickery.

Reducing the many riches of Carey's novel to barest essentials in order to sketch out patterns of dynastic displacement, then, we discover that the novel's first Book opens in 1919. Badgery, a model T Ford sales agent and amateur air pilot, encounters the McGrath family: Jack (who suffers from deafness), Molly (née Rourke, who may have inherited a trait of insanity from her own mother), and their daughter Phoebe, whom he will marry. Not until towards the end of the Book do we discover that the marriage is (on Badgery's part) bigamous: indeed Badgery has not only suppressed his first wife from his story, but largely written his own parents out of it as well. Jack and Molly McGrath thus come to fulfil the parental role, giving the illicit relationship with the bisexual Phoebe a further, quasi-incestuous, twist.[12]

There are two children of Badgery's marriage to Phoebe, Charles and Sonia. The elder, Charles, apparently conceived on Phoebe's and Badgery's wedding night, survives Phoebe's attempt to abort him after she has fallen in love with an epileptic poet. For a while before Charles's birth Badgery repeatedly sees a ghost he takes to be that of Jack (who has been mortally bitten by one of Badgery's collection of snakes) and Badgery begins obsessively to connect this ghost, writhing with snakes, to the impending event.

The second Book advances Badgery's narrative to 1931 and beyond. In this most picaresque section of *Illywhacker*, Badgery and his two children encounter the dancer Leah Goldstein, whose relationship with her estranged husband Izzie Kaletsky and his left-wing parents Rosa and Lenny is presented as analogous to that between Badgery and the McGrath household in the first Book. Badgery and Leah set up a peripatetic circus act (Badgery & Goldstein). Here is an instance of pluralism being forced to

---

[12]In this way, Carey echoes a theme from his earliest novel, *Bliss* (1981).

defer to the dominant culture: the Badgery & Goldstein act is constantly harassed and made to move on. The pretexts may be various but the subtext is quite clearly anti-communist and anti-Semitic. Badgery & Goldstein is rescued by Charles's emerging affinity for snakes, which become a part of the act, Badgery's own contribution being his disappearing act.

Leah reminds Badgery of what she at any rate sees as the reason for their picaresque lifestyle:

> '[This] is not a country where you can rest. It is a black man's country: sharp stones, rocks, sticks, bull ants, flies. We can only move around it like tourists. The blackfeller can rest but we must keep moving. That is why I can't return with my husband as he wishes,' she announced, seeking rest in a simple theory, 'because I am selfish, addicted to movement.'
> (*Illywhacker*, p. 323)[13]

The second Book is terminated by two tragedies. Leah returns to Izzie after he has lost both legs under a train while trying to escape from police thugs. In addition the train, 'like some Corsican bandit who wishes to leave a sign, cut[s] the top of an index finger with a neat razor slice' (*Illywhacker*, p. 362).

Charles and Sonia have both been intrigued by the possibility of the disappearing trick, and each have tried it, repeatedly and unsuccessfully. For each it represents something different: for the physically gauche and unprepossessing Charles, truly his father's son, it is an escape from a hostile world that he is fortunately too doggedly unselfconscious to see as such (in this sense, if no other, he can make himself disappear). Sonia, in contrast, has developed into a pious little girl who dreams of a Blessed Assumption, and performs the disappearing trick conclusively and spectacularly when she vanishes down a disused mine shaft.

Badgery, blaming Charles for the fatal disappearance of Sonia,

---

[13]The late Bruce Chatwin's extraordinary novel *The Songlines* (1987) explores this aspect of the Australian outback.

hits him so hard over the head as to deafen him. Badgery's narrative sleight of hand, and his bizarre stirring up of the national gene pool, allow him to portray Charles as having 'inherited' from his grandfather Jack McGrath his deafness and his affinity for snakes. Charles has also inherited his bandy legs from Badgery himself. Manipulation of Charles's hearing aid will enhance his ability to 'disappear'.

The third Book finds Charles in 1938 – having missed an opportunity to fight against Franco in Spain, and having left what he sees as the threatening sophistication of Sydney (where he has been briefly reconciled with Phoebe) – riding his motorbike into the Victorian outback to cure a mouse plague with his bag of pythons. This Book will take us up to the 'present' – whenever that is – from which Badgery is relating his flashback.

Stranded near Jeparit, Victoria, when (the mouse plague in the Chaffey household having been eradicated) his host Les Chaffey obsessively dismembers Charles's motorbike and puts off its reassembly, Charles begins to amass the fauna that will form the basis for The Best Pet Shop in the World. He makes his mark on the community of Jeparit when he rescues the young schoolteacher Emma Underhill, whom a six-foot goanna has mounted thinking her to be a tree. Only Charles has sufficient affinity with the animal kingdom to capture the goanna and free Emma, whom he subsequently marries.

On the outbreak of war and Australia's mobilization on 11 September 1939, the goanna, attacked by a fox terrier it manages to disembowel, nonetheless parts with a foreleg. Izzy's earlier dismemberment now becomes part of a cluster of comparable episodes in the novel: there are at least two torn-off fingers, one of which is preserved in a jar of formaldehyde; and at one stage Badgery tears the head off a parrot when it refuses to leave its cage (*Illywhacker*, p. 331).

Emma loses her reason (much as Molly McGrath née Rourke had earlier lost hers – another instance of repetition that hints at heredity before as it were reminding us that it can't be), and confines herself and her baby Henry to a cage. Emma has two more children, George (a little younger than Henry) and Hissao (much younger, whom Charles had thought to be named Michael). There is a question mark concerning the paternity of Hissao, whose looks are Japanese. Badgery sees in Hissao his lost daughter Sonia, and in a marvellously ironic passage Badgery tells us that Hissao:

> had somehow slipped through the genetic minefields his progenitors had laid for him. Not only were his legs straight but he avoided the lonely excesses of masculinity represented by his bull-necked, jut-jawed Easter Island father. He had curling black hair, smooth olive skin, and red cherubic lips which suggested, strongly at some times, weakly at others, an oriental parent who did not exist. (*Illywhacker*, p. 557)

Not only is Hissao bisexual, apparently losing his virginity in both orientations on consecutive days at the age of eighteen: he is capable of appearing feminine rather than masculine, Italian rather than Japanese, according to the beholder and/or the circumstances.

It is Hissao who is particularly fascinated by the goanna's double penis, and Charles who is revolted by the way Emma likes to stroke it (or them) into arousal. Eventually Emma discloses that the contents of the formaldehyde jar have turned into a half-human, half-goanna foetus, claiming this to be Hissao's half-brother; perhaps the goanna's mistaking Emma for a tree is to be regarded wilfully as some kind of delayed reptilian impregnation. Charles has Hissao take him and the by now twenty-four-year-old goanna to a patch of waste land and shoots it before turning his rifle on himself. Later, back in Badgery's possession, the contents of the formaldehyde bottle reveal themselves to him as 'a dragon, a solid being, two inches tall. [. . .] It reared up on its hind legs and scratched at the glass with its long black claws while its whole body pulsed with rage, changing from a deep black green to a bloated pearlescent grey' (*Illywhacker*, pp. 578–79).

Charles's suicide occurs on the day The Best Pet Shop in the World comes under American management. Hissao's fascination with the goanna's double penis is mysteriously connected with the wanton puzzles Badgery proffers and withholds concerning what Emma may or may not have known about his parentage. In this way the genetic pool is stirred still further. Eventually Hissao secures a deal from the Mitsubishi company that enables a Japanese take-over of The Best Pet Shop in the World, and Badgery the illywhacker and Leah Goldstein (advertised as 'Melbourne Jew') are revealed to be among the exhibits.

The distinct communities that my reading of *Illywhacker* has served to highlight in its portrayal of Australia's national story are profiled more sharply still in Mordecai Richler's chronologically chaotic portrayal of the Canadian cultural mosaic. In *Solomon Gursky Was Here*, communal myths are examined quite explicitly as they come into conflict with each other, dissolving at the novel's end into a profoundly unanswerable icon: the black raven comes to represent some kind of statement as to where Canada's cultural identity can be said to lie.

I can only highlight some of the many ways in which Eskimo myths of creation, Judaic myths of diaspora, and WASP myths of colonization combine and intermingle to place legitimacy and bastardy in a delicate balance. Here there is no 'either/or' between dynastic claims made through close blood relations (as in *Waterland*) neither are there dynamic stirrings-up of the national gene pool (as in *Illywhacker*). What faces the reader of *Gursky* before the narrative even begins is a genealogical tree (complete with a list of 'begats') asserting the centrality of the hot-eyed Ephraim Gursky (1817–1910), the sage whose 'anointed one'[14] is his second grandson Solomon (1899–1934 [*sic*]). The perception of Solomon's special status is that of

---

[14]Mordecai Richler, *Solomon Gursky Was Here* (London: Vintage, 1990), p. 422. Further references to this edition in the text above.

the eldest grandson Bernard (1898–1973). Yet the novel does not hide their grandfather Ephraim's promiscuousness: indeed it explicitly records the fact or legend that Ephraim 'never [. . .] laid eyes on his son [by a Mrs Nicholson in the early 1830s], the first of what would become twenty-seven unacknowledged offspring, not all of them the same colour' (*Gursky*, p. 220). In fact *Gursky* confronts the Canadian community with various forms of inheritance.

At the realist level, the narrative relates the rise of the whisky empire headed by Bernard Gursky, a deliciously drawn, larger than life caricature apparently modelled on the historical Samuel Bronfman of Seagrams, at once God in his own empire yet powerless to break into Canada's WASP establishment. As with the historical Bronfman, Bernard Gursky's greatest yearning is for public acclaim expressed in terms of a Senate seat and an OBE, and these things are denied him. It later transpires as a matter of some significance that Canadian citizens, though subjects of the same head of state as the United Kingdom, are ineligible for British knighthoods. Bernard's deathbed is phlegmatically recalled by his cryptic youngest brother Morrie (b. 1901):

> Mr Bernard tried to scratch [his wife Libby], intent on drawing blood, but he no longer had the strength. 'No, no' was all he could manage.
>   'Bernie, Bernie,' she sobbed, 'do you believe in God?'
>   'How can you talk such crap at a time like this?'
>   'It's not crap, sweetie pie.'
>   'It's not crap, she says. Don't you understand? Don't you understand anything? If God exists, I'm fucked.'
>   And then, Mr Morrie said, he was gone. (*Gursky*, p. 496)

This episode is related to Morris Berger, himself caught in a variety of ways in the Gursky web. Moses' father, L.B., an intense but quixotic literary hack, finally begins to achieve some

worldly success, and in consequence finds himself losing touch
with the Jewish bohemians of his younger days before being
actually lionized by gentile Canadian high society.

> Then came the summons from Sinai. L.B. was invited to an
> audience at Mr Bernard's opulent redoubt cut high into the
> Montreal mountainside and he descended from those heights,
> his head spinning, pledged to unheard-of abundance, an
> annual retainer of ten thousand dollars to serve as speech
> writer and cultural adviser to the legendary liquor baron.
>   'And this,' Mr Bernard had said, leading him into a long
> room with empty oak shelves running from ceiling to floor,
> 'will be my library. Furnish it with the best. I want first
> editions. The finest morocco bindings. You have a blank
> check, L.B.'
>   Then Libby was heard from. 'But nothing secondhand.'
>   'I beg your pardon, Mrs Gursky?'
>   'Germs. That's all I need. We have three children, God
> bless them.' (*Gursky*, p. 18)

Characteristically, Richler has the hitherto taciturn Shloime
Bishinsky surprisingly speak out, in a way Moses will later recall
more than once:

> 'What I'm trying to say, forgive me, is that such princes
> in America are entitled to their mansions, a Rolls-Royce,
> chinchilla coats, yachts, young cuties out of burlesque shows.
> But a poet they should never be able to afford. It has to do
> with what? Human dignity. The dead. The sanctity of the
> word. I'm explaining it badly. But the man I took you for,
> L.B., you are not. Forgive me, Bessie, but I can't come here
> any more'. (*Gursky*, p. 19)

This reproach exercises Moses in profound and complex ways.
It begins to alienate him from his father, and leads him to seek
identification with another such figure. Moses becomes obsessed

with the Gursky family, and in particular with Solomon's mysterious disappearance during the 1934 prosecution brought by the Royal Canadian Mounted Police for tax evasion consequent on the family's pursuing a lucrative bootlegging trade during the United States Prohibition years (1919–33). It is on this trade that the bulk of the Gursky fortune has been built, although it should be pointed out that the initial capital is actually raised by Solomon's spectacularly successful poker gamble with the minute Gursky holdings as they had been in 1916.

Like the historical Bronfman, who was tried under similar circumstances, the surviving Gursky brothers are acquitted. A later encounter with an anglicized European exile, Sir Hyman Kaplansky, appears finally to result in Moses having once more found his lost father figure. Not only does L.B.'s becoming lapdog to Bernard Gursky result in Moses first encountering Lionel, the outrageous Gursky heir-presumptive; Moses also meets Lionel's cousins, the late Solomon's children Henry and Lucy, both severely disturbed psychologically and emotionally. Moses keeps up with both into later life: with Lucy as she declines into an eccentric and increasingly drug-ridden existence as a theatrical impresario; with Henry as he grows into even more eccentric retreat into the Arctic north (from where Ephraim first appears in the narrative's opening in 1851), and into marriage with the Eskimo Canadian Nialie, who bears the first legitimate son to a Gursky by a member of the local ethnic community.[15]

This son, Isaac, is paradoxically (in view of his maternal inheritance) brought up into orthodox Jewry at Henry's behest and with Nialie's compliance. Henry's childhood stammer and enuresis disappear, and he becomes as adept as his father and great-grandfather at survival north of 'sixty degrees'.

Moses becomes additionally intertwined in the Gursky history

---

[15]Cf. the way in which 'a roving band of natives out of King William Island', granted surnames instead of numbered identification disks by the Ottawa government in 1969 along with the rest of the Eskimo community, chose 'Gursky or variations thereof, including Gor-ski, Girskee, Gur-ski, and Goorsky' (*Gursky*, p. 55).

through his alcoholism: he is seriously addicted to the liquor through which the grandsons of Ephraim Gursky have made their millions. (In this way, incidentally, the entire narrative self-consciously defies a stereotype of Judaism and alcoholic temperance.) It is perhaps helpful to relate this subversion to the way in which Moses' own Judaic inheritance is something he comes to feel deeply ambivalent about: indeed in this respect his plight illustrates the dilemma of any member of the Canadian 'mosaic'. This is a community unlike any other: in being in a position to offer immense subsidies to preserve one's ethnic identity within a pluralist community, the Canadian establishment has traditionally presented its minorities with a troubling dilemma. Accepting such subsidy can be a gesture of affirmation on the part of the ethnic minority; on the other hand it can be seen as permitting one's minority to become marginalized or even ghettoized, since the more it is permitted to lay claim to its own identity the more it is denied purchase on that of the host culture. This dilemma, which Moses never manages to solve, both gives the narrative great poignancy and at the same time motivates his quest for what really happened to Solomon Gursky when he took off into a whiteout in his Gypsy Moth during the 1934 tax-evasion proceedings.

That disappearance is the mirror image of Ephraim Gursky's irruption into the narrative, a narrative whose authorship remains unclear but at any rate changes irreversibly on a second and subsequent reading. Much but by no means all of what appears to be omniscience from a voice outside the story turns out on a second or subsequent reading to be Moses' reconstruction and rewriting of Solomon's diaries, which come into Moses' hands thanks to Sir Hyman Kaplansky. The chaotic nature of the entire narrative serves simultaneously to refract Moses' alcoholism, which takes the form of binges alternating with clinic treatment, and the extended mirror relationship binding Ephraim and Solomon Gursky. For, just as the factual realist aspect of the story is constituted out of the narrative of the Gursky whisky empire, so the magical realist aspect is compounded of the events preceding Ephraim Gursky's appearance in southern Quebec in the record cold winter of 1851 and those subsequent to Solomon Gursky's disappearance in 1934.

Ephraim's arrival in Canada itself is presented as a piece of transgressive history-making. *Gursky's* reader is invited to believe that Ephraim is the illegitimate progeny of an affair between his father Gideon (1773–1828) and an opera singer that brings Gideon's career as cantor in a Minsk synagogue to an end. The Gurskys move to Liverpool, and when orphaned at the age of eleven, Ephraim makes his picaresque way to London. During the course of this journey Ephraim learns Latin and penmanship from a pederastic schoolteacher named Mr Nicholson, a training that enables Ephraim to forge documents. After a brief exotic youth of crime, Ephraim is sentenced to transportation to Van Diemen's Land in 1835 on forgery charges. He manages to escape this fate and he and his companion Izzy Garber instate themselves as bone-setters. In the Orkneys they illicitly join the doomed Franklin expedition in search of the Northwest Passage in 1845, with Ephraim as surgeon to HMS *Erebus*. History tells us that there were no survivors of this expedition: *Solomon Gursky* tells us otherwise.

Izzy Garber apparently dies shortly after the pair's arrival in Canada in 1846. Meanwhile Ephraim sets himself up as a shamanic rabbi and brings his bizarre Judaeo-Eskimo millenarianism to the local population, contriving to discredit the local shaman by trickery. Included in the millenarian credo is a version of Yom Kippur, a law 'laid down [by Ephraim] in a foolish and absent-minded moment, overlooking the fact that his faith provided for all contingencies save that of the Arctic adherent' (*Gursky*, p. 403). It is Ephraim's great-grandson, the Dostoevskian holy fool, Henry, who takes it on himself to ensure no errant members of the sect be consigned to spend Yom Kippur in the four-month Arctic night.

One indication of the complexity with which the magical realist elements intermingle with the realist family chronicle of the Gursky whisky empire may be briefly given here. In one of his aliases, that of the Reverend Isaac Horn, it can be said that it is Ephraim Gursky who actually sows the seeds of the 1934 prosecution. Horn charismatically engineers a fraudulent campaign of disaffected English emigrants in 1901, offering them the Promised Land in northern Saskatchewan. After a nightmare voyage, the emigrants arrive to discover the ghastly truth of their barren destination. A descriptive sample of the surreal nature of that voyage will show how skilfully Richler can control the tone of the various forms of realism he employs:

> In two weeks at sea the Reverend Horn, secure in his cabin, was seen below decks only twice. On the fourth day out a miner had his arm broken in a drunken brawl, and it was the Reverend Horn who set the bone and fixed it with a splint. He was seen again after another fight, this one with knives, come to stitch the men's wounds. But a certain Mrs Bishop swore she had seen him striding up and down the bridge the night of the gale, the puny *Excelsior* scaling twenty-foot waves before plunging into a trough, sliding trunks smashing into walls, splinters flying, the ship's fracturing surely imminent. Bare-chested he was, drunken, howling into the lashing wind and rain. 'Face-to-face. I want to see you face-to-face just once.' (*Gursky*, p. 77)

Among the ship's emigrants are a hapless couple named Archie and Nancy Smith. Their son Bert, born in 1903, receives a strictly fundamentalist upbringing. He forms a counterpart to Bernard Gursky. Where Gursky's deliciously captured caricature allows us to forgive much of the repulsiveness in his character, Bert lacks that charisma. He is plagued with halitosis and abnormally crooked teeth, and he is obdurate to the point of obsessiveness. Yet these qualities finally secure, against the better judgement of those establishment parties with vested interests, the 1934 prosecution.

The 'elusive, obscenely rich' Sir Hyman Kaplansky emerges in wartime London as a philanthropist, receiving his knighthood for services to the Conservative party. He too transgresses authorized historiography: in his iconic guise as an elderly man sitting with his chin propped on his malacca cane, he is seen in a July 1962 photograph in Moses' possession of John F. Kennedy and Marilyn Monroe. (Other photos picture Solomon with George Bernard Shaw and H. L. Mencken.) Among his Monroe autopsy material Moses also possesses an unsigned telegram sent from Madrid: I KNOW WHAT YOU ARE THINKING BUT THE LAST PHONE CALL WAS NOT FROM ME (*Gursky*, p. 71). At the novel's denouement Moses discovers in Kaplansky's possession in England the striking portrait of Solomon Gursky's abandoned *femme fatale* Diana McClure, one eye blue and one eye brown, a portrait that had disappeared from the Gursky mansion shortly after Solomon himself did.[16] Kaplansky deftly rescues the occasion by pointing to another picture:

> A raven perched on a half-open seashell, human beings struggling to emerge from it.
> 'This is the raven that stole the light of the world from an old man and then scattered it throughout the skies. After the great flood had receded, he flew to a beach to gorge himself on the delicacies left behind by the water. However, he wasn't hungry for once.' Looking directly at Moses, a stricken Moses, [Kaplansky] went on to say, 'But his other appetites – lust, curiosity, and the unquenchable itch to meddle and provoke things, to play tricks on the world and its creatures – these remained unsatisfied.' (*Gursky*, p. 455)

Kaplansky then sends Moses on a wild-goose chase to Paris, and while Moses is away he learns that Kaplansky has 'apparently

[16]In a way Diana McClure functions in Solomon's life much as the 'raven-haired beauty [Beatrice Wade], with breasts too rudely full for such a trim figure and coal-black eyes that shone with too much appetite' (*Gursky*, p. 49) does in Moses' – and both relationships are doomed.

drowned in stormy seas' (*Gursky*, p. 456) while taking his pre-breakfast swim, despite warnings about the weather. Opening the package with which he has been entrusted, Moses not only finds three more volumes of Solomon Gursky's journals but discovers that his further investigations into the Gursky myth will be financed by Corvus Investment Trust, Zürich. This is the legacy of which at various points earlier in *Gursky* Moses has been unwilling to speak.

Perusal of earlier instalments of Solomon's journals have confirmed Moses' belief, against all probability, that the 1934 disappearance was faked: there is, for instance, an account of Mao's Long March of 1935, with Solomon and the remnants he accompanies being saved after the mysterious appearance of a raven Solomon has apparently summoned, as both Ephraim and Solomon have done elsewhere. Later, Kaplansky resurfaces in various increasingly preposterous guises, as Mr Cuervo, Mr Corbeau, or retrospectively in wartime aliases such as the Swiss financier Herr Dr Otto Raven. The etymologies supply the links at which the narrative hints.[17]

Both Ephraim and Solomon are connected by their multiple aliases, protean identities, and by their impossible presences (by realistic criteria) in authorized historical events. They are also linked by such things as the social poise and sexual charisma that exercise universal appeal and destabilize the social and sexual identities of those around them; astonishing powers of survival in hostile environments whether air, land or water; and the ability constantly to wrong-foot their opponents.

Is all this merely the raven's 'unquenchable itch to meddle

---

[17]The forms 'Gor-ski' and 'Goorski' are particularly interesting in that they suggest not a Russian but a Germanic etymology: a 'gorcrow' is an English dialect form referring both to the raven and its greed. *Gursky* is filled with episodes of gastronomic and sexual excess of which the most memorable is probably Kaplansky's revenge on the anti-Semitic elements in the British establishment in the 'infamous dinner party in his Cumberland Terrace flat [, a] Passover seder, of all things' (*Gursky*, p. 458). The Eskimos called Ephraim 'Tulugaq, which means raven in their lingo' (*Gursky*, p. 176). The 'lingo' is elsewhere (*Gursky*, p. 45) identified as Inuktituk.

and provoke things'? Not entirely: Solomon's disappearance is linked with the quarrel among the Gursky brothers at the time of the 1934 prosecution as to whether or not Bernard should be the majority shareholder. Solomon threatens to return from the grave if necessary to prevent his own children Henry and Lucy from being disadvantaged – a feat he manages to achieve, perhaps even desecrating the tomb of Bernard Gursky with '[a] raven skewered and harpooned to the grave' (*Gursky*, p. 234). Is the mark on the harpoon a Gimel, the third letter of the Hebrew alphabet, or the 'maker's sign' (*Gursky*, p. 236)?

As things turn out the Gursky empire is inherited by Isaac and Barney (son to Mr Morrie), and Bernard's line is cut out. Isaac has been rehabilitated by the family following the accident in which Henry had been killed on his last Arctic journey and Isaac had had to cannibalize his father's corpse to survive, just as Ephraim and Izzy had survived by cannibalism in 1846. Mr Bernard's portrait is removed from the Fifth Avenue office in New York and replaced by that of Ephraim. The inheritance has been reclaimed. Solomon, who has been quoted in the novel's epigraph as saying 'Living twice, three times maybe, is the best revenge', has sent Moses a perplexing note that voices a doubt the reader must feel too:

> I once told you that you were no more than a figment of my imagination. Therefore, if you continued to exist, so must I.
> (*Gursky*, p. 507)

In *Waterland* Graham Swift presents us with a magical realist fiction embedded within the recall that constitutes the subversive history lessons of Tom Crick. Crick's own contemporaneous narrative is impoverished, sterile and reduced. What gives Swift's text the magic it possesses is the way in which Crick's alternative narratives, Gothic, topographical and atavistic, bleed into each other through various kinds of trickery in performance. All are suffused with a suffocatingly intense feeling for the English regionalism of East Anglia, and for pedigree, dynasty, legitimacy and its opposite.

In *Illywhacker* Peter Carey allows Herbert Badgery's narrated genealogies to exercise a displacing effect so that genetic transfer can actually be figured metaphorically as well (as in the narrative trickery whereby deafness and madness pass down the generations). Herein lies the magic of this text. *Illywhacker's* unorthodox histories displace dynastic inheritance: the national gene pool is stirred up so that Australia's national story is punctuated by individual dynastic subversions.

Communal narrative in *Illywhacker* is in total contrast to that of *Waterland*: Carey's is made up of unbelonging, it is nomadic and picaresque; and it is so strongly counterpointed by illicitness and collusion in performance that in the end the book gives no distinct answer as to whether Badgery is indeed to be seen as the trickster or the tricked. In *Solomon Gursky Was Here*, the trickery of Solomon increases in the magical-realist sections of the narrative set in the period after his disappearance from Canada in 1934, and in so doing it mirrors that of his grandfather Ephraim prior to the latter's mythical arrival in southern Quebec in 1851. Moses Berger, the assembler and chronicler of these lives, is magically animated as he performs his discovery of how Ephraim's heritage is passed on through the trickery of his 'anointed one', Solomon. Moses' appreciation of a magic dimension to the accepted story of Canadian history requires him to discard a failed myth of Canada (as represented in the sheer materialism of the Bernard Gursky family): here is that myth, as drunkenly expounded to Solomon by Tim Callaghan, a former bootlegging confederate of Solomon's:

'Let me put it this way. Canada is not so much a country as a holding tank filled with the disgruntled progeny of defeated peoples. French Canadians consumed by self-pity; the descendants of Scots who fled the Duke of Cumberland; Irish the famine; and Jews the Black Hundreds. Then there are the peasants from the Ukraine, Poland, Italy, and Greece, convenient to grow wheat and dig the ore and swing the hammers and run the restaurants, but otherwise to be kept in their place. Most of us are still huddled tight to the border, looking into the candy-store window, scared by the Americans on one side and the bush on the other. And now that we are here, prospering, we do our damn best to exclude more ill-bred newcomers, because they remind us of our own mean origins in the draper's shop in Inverness or the *shtetl* or the bog. What was I talking about?' (*Gursky*, p. 367)

Perhaps nothing in all three novels discussed in this chapter puts the sense of the here and now so uncompromisingly. But it is through narrative performance that the here and now is transformed: in their various ways each novel discussed in this chapter crosses a boundary into a communal domain in which past, present and future are united in multiple and exciting ways.

8

Domestic Performance: Julian Barnes and the Love Triangle

One of the most versatile novelists writing in Britain today, Julian Barnes belongs to a select group of writers (Jim Crace in the 1990s, Ian McEwan and Rose Tremain since about 1980, and the William Golding of the period up till the end of the 1970s spring to mind) who appear provocatively to set out to do something absolutely different with each new novel. Nevertheless, certain underlying themes such as obsession, and its particular expression in the love triangle involving two men and one woman, can be identified in Barnes's fiction. Some readers have related this obsession to Barnes's interest in François Truffaut's film *Jules et Jim*. Further reading shows that, different on the surface as all Barnes's books are, there are a number of recurring motifs.

The aim of this chapter is to show how performance, the theme of this last section of my book, can encompass domestic concerns, lifting what might at first seem to be banality into an arena in which much larger issues of human existence and behaviour are faced and tackled.

Barnes's career prior to his debut as novelist in 1980 was as varied as any. Apparently considering then abandoning a career in philosophy, he trained as a barrister before working for the *Oxford English Dictionary* as a lexicographer. His subsequent career as a journalist displayed a fondness for the *nom de plume*. As Basil Seal he was restaurant critic for the *Tatler* and as Edward Pygge wrote the 'Greek Street' column for the *New Review* in the late 1970s. Barnes also wrote for the *Sunday Times*, and for a while acted as that newspaper's deputy literary editor. From 1982 to 1986 he was best known to readers in Britain as TV critic of the *Observer*. He also wrote for the *New Statesman*, during a period in which he acted as deputy to Martin Amis, then literary editor of that magazine. Admitting in the mid 1980s that he had probably written a quarter to half a million words of TV criticism, Barnes gave up regular journalism for a while. He was tempted back to it in late 1989 by an invitation from Bob Gottlieb, editor of the *New Yorker*, to act as the magazine's London correspondent, a post he held for the next five years. A collection of Barnes's *New Yorker* essays, *Letters from London*, was published to warm acclaim in 1995.

Julian Barnes's first novel, *Metroland* (1980), won the Somerset Maugham Award, but it was with *Flaubert's Parrot* (1984), included in that year's controversial Booker shortlist, that his international reputation was secured. Frank Kermode's substantial notice in the *New York Review of Books* in April 1985, which also contained an account of *Metroland* and *Before She Met Me* (1982), brought Barnes to the attention of a wide American readership for the first time.[1] Barnes now sells increasingly healthily in paperback in the United States. He has captured a more significant segment of the international market (as expressed in numbers of translations) than the peers (Martin Amis, Ian McEwan) with whom he has been associated since the early 1980s.

A chapter from *Flaubert's Parrot*, 'Emma Bovary's Eyes', appeared in the 1983 'Best of Young British Novelists' issue of *Granta*. The chosen novelists were introduced by short blurbs, often tongue-in-cheek, that for Barnes including the following passage:

> It is possible that under other pseudonyms [than that of Edward Pygge], he may have written a novel or three . . . He is the certified author of two novels, *Metroland* and *Before She Met Me* (witnesses were present).[2]

---

[1]Frank Kermode, 'Obsessed with Obsession', *NYRB*, 25 April 1985, pp. 15–16. Collected in Frank Kermode, *The Uses of Error* (Cambridge, MA: Harvard UP, 1991), p. 362–68.
[2]*Granta* 7 (1983), p. 60.

As a novelist Barnes managed to lead a double writing life quite successfully during the 1980s. He appears to have allowed the mask to drop towards the end of the decade, despite a leak in the *Bookseller* in 1980 on the publication of *Duffy*, the first of the now complete series of four stylish thrillers. The 15 October 1987 issue of the *London Review of Books* carried as its headnote the caption 'Spot the Author'. A moustached figure with sleeked-down hair is photographed on the front cover walking past some railings. The cover is captioned as:

a rare photograph [. . .] of the novelist Dan Kavanagh [. . .]. *Going to the Dogs* [1987] is [the] fourth thriller [featuring] Duffy, the bisexual security consultant and former policeman. The earlier books dealt in their informative way with Soho, Heathrow Airport and professional football: this one treats dogs, snooker and moneyed misbehaviour on the Buckinghamshire/Berkshire borders. It is unique in Mr Kavanagh's *oeuvre* that at one point a character is discovered reading a book. Dan Kavanagh is a pen-name . . .

The alias carries the last name of the dedicatee of most of the novels Barnes has published under his own name, his agent Pat Kavanagh, to whom he is married. The Duffy blurbs, too, are engagingly tongue-in-cheek:

Dan Kavanagh was born in County Sligo in 1946. Having devoted his adolescence to truancy, venery and petty theft, he left home at seventeen and signed on as a deckhand on a Liberian tanker. After jumping ship at Montevideo, he roamed across the Americas taking a variety of jobs: he was a steer-wrestler, a waiter-on-roller-skates at a drive-in eaterie in Tucson and a bouncer in a gay bar in San Francisco. He is currently working in London at jobs he declines to specify, and lives in North Islington. (From *Fiddle City* [1981]; 1988 Penguin reprint)

Barnes (but not Dan Kavanagh) has been honoured in various ways, so continuing to gain international visibility, and entering the academic postmodernist canon from the late 1980s onwards. As well as being shortlisted for the 1984 Booker Prize, *Flaubert's Parrot* was awarded the French Prix Médicis in 1986, Barnes (surely the most Francophile British novelist at least since John Fowles) being the first Englishman to have been honoured in this way. In 1988 Barnes became a Chevalier de l'Ordre des Arts et des Lettres.

Barnes's commercial breakthrough, which can be dated to the late 1980s with the titles *Staring at the Sun* (1986), *A History of the World in 10½ Chapters* (1989) and *Talking It Over* (1992), was undoubtedly helped by the energy with which he was promoted after the acclaim received by *Flaubert's Parrot*, and offers a good example of what was discussed in Chapter 3 above: that is, the way in which a publisher (in this case Jonathan Cape) has to feel passionately about and show confidence in a novelist's work in order for the books to become lead titles.

At least three of the four books from *Flaubert's Parrot* onwards raised among several reviewers the question whether they really were, in any conventional sense, novels at all. Most of *Flaubert's Parrot*, which is as much a series of essays as a story, is narrated by a retired doctor, Geoffrey Braithwaite; *Staring at the Sun* is in three distinct parts, one set in the 1930s and 1940s, one roughly contemporary, and one at some time in the early twenty-first century; *A History of the World in 10½ Chapters* is (perhaps even less than *Flaubert's Parrot*), not so much a story as a series of stories or even essays laminated or layered over each other, inviting and challenging the reader to make connections but withholding authorial judgement on those connections; the formal uniqueness of *Talking It Over* is discussed below. A typical pronouncement in *A History* reads:

Where Amanda discovered in the world divine intent, benevolent order and rigorous justice, her father had seen only chaos, hazard and malice. Yet they were both examining the same world.[3]

These brief accounts make Barnes sound like an experimental novelist. They also make his enviable position as a writer who appeals to both a general and an academic readership seem rather surprising. In focusing on Barnes's work so as to emphasize its performative aspect in the domestic arena, I'll concentrate on the frequent absence of a single authoritative voice from the page, and its replacement by an orchestration of voices that compete for the reader's attention and even belief. This competition is most evident when the rival claims of the participants in the various love triangles vie for their readers' or listeners' esteem, as in *Talking It Over* – with its celebrated epigraph (apparently a Russian saying) 'He lies like an eye-witness' – although the presence of rival voices is not restricted to this aspect of human experience, and it is more diffused in *A History of the World in 10½ Chapters*. (*The Porcupine* [1992] is written in a more journalistic spirit than any of Barnes's other fiction and cast [as it were] as a barrister's imaginative reconstruction of the trial of one of the more interesting leaders of former Warsaw Pact Eastern Europe, Todor Zhivkov. It must be unique among the fiction discussed in this book in having first appeared in Bulgarian, with the English 'original' following shortly afterwards.)

Although Barnes is held in high regard amongst a wide readership, it is possible to find notices that – while conceding that his is one of the most interesting talents to be observed from his generation of English novelists – still assume his talents to be 'exercising' themselves rather than triumphing decisively.[4] I do not share this view; on the contrary, I believe Barnes to be one of the most fascinating novelists writing today. If there is a

[3]Julian Barnes, *A History of the World in 10½ Chapters* (London: Cape, 1989), p. 148. Further quotations from this edition in the text above.

[4]See, for instance, Mick Imlah's review of *Talking It Over*, 'Giving the Authorized Version', *Times Literary Supplement*, 12 July 1991, p. 19.

tendency to underestimate his work, it is because the intelligence his domestic performances display is far less demonstrative than the bravura voices of – say – Salman Rushdie's characters. In drawing attention in this chapter to the undemonstrativeness of Barnes's performances, I hope to create space to do justice in the next to Rushdie's very different talents.

A typical reviewer's response to *Metroland* was that a *Bildungsroman* narrated in the first person formed a curiously downbeat debut from a writer of Barnes's speculative intelligence and unquestionable capacity to enter imaginations very different from his own.[5] Writing in 1985, Frank Kermode saw Barnes as 'obsessed with obsession', constraining his readers to see and hear his characters chronicling their fixations. For others, Barnes's training as a barrister seems to account for the forensic nature of much in the novels, including the questions repeatedly posed in *Staring at the Sun*, which (according to Ian Hamilton) contains over three hundred interrogation marks in just under 200 pages.[6] Still others have been puzzled by the Kavanagh pseudonymy because it seems (in John Sutherland's words) not to be performing the usual 'prudential' role of masked authorship.[7]

Reviewers, writing on the hoof, are not granted the benefits of hindsight: more attention might otherwise have been paid to the debate *Metroland* conducts with Gustave Flaubert (1821–81), above all with *L'Education sentimentale*, but to some extent too with the unfinished *Bouvard et Pécuchet* (published posthumously in 1881). In *L'Education sentimentale* Flaubert's third-person narration treats Frédéric Moreau's obsession with Madame Arnoux. Flaubert minutely nuances the social effects of the financial vicissitudes suffered by Frédéric and his widowed mother.

In *Metroland* Barnes uses a first-person narrative. The Paris

---

[5]Paul Bailey, 'Settling for Suburbia', *TLS*, 28 March 1980, p. 345.
[6]Ian Hamilton, 'Real Questions', *LRB*, 6 September 1986, p. 7.
[7]John Sutherland, 'Pseud's Corner', *LRB*, 17 July–6 August 1980, pp. 14–16.

portrayed by Flaubert in the run-up to the 1848 revolutions is just as Bohemian as the pre-revolutionary city of 1968. Yet Barnes's narrator Christopher Lloyd, favoured with an intellectually precocious upbringing in Metroland (the area of outer north-west London served by the Metropolitan line), ironically experiences '*les événements*' indirectly. Sexually initiated while in Paris by a Breton girl, Annick, of approximately his own age, Christopher remains blissfully unaware of the wider political context. Flaubert's Madame Arnoux, on the other hand, is older, married, and the mother of a young daughter when Frédéric first becomes obsessed with her. The *deus ex machina* role of Frédéric's uncle – the hope of release from the constraints of provincial confinement unexpectedly fulfilled by an intestate death enabling Frédéric to inherit the estate – is counterpointed in the eccentric and stingy lifestyle of Christopher's Uncle Arthur, one of several such figures in the Barnes *oeuvre*. The love triangle involving two men and a woman is prefigured rather than explored in *Metroland*. In later manifestations this situation leads to unsettling portrayals of disturbingly obsessive behaviour among the men concerned.

The last part of *Metroland* returns to the suburban setting in 1977, and to the troubling conflict of interests that Christopher feels when together with his wife Marion and Toni his former schoolfriend and intellectual sparring-partner from the Metroland days of 1963. Has Christopher sold out into marriage, child-rearing and the bourgeoisie, as Toni, provocatively arriving for lunch without his partner ('we believe in having separate friends'), clearly believes? Or is Toni's having replaced the flip mutual 'épat'-ing of 1963 with his own committed (albeit cynical and coarsely expressed) left-wing radicalism now an option Christopher must reject out of genuine respect for Marion's feelings and his relationship with her?

Challenged by Toni as to whether he has been unfaithful to Marion in the six years they have been married, Christopher admits he has not, and *Metroland* delivers, in what is a remarkable technical achievement, an affirmation of the value of sexual manners and tact. Forced by Toni to broach the thought of infidelity to Marion, Christopher is struck by her disconcerting blend of candour and diplomacy ('Yes I did once, and Yes it was only once, and No it didn't make any difference to us at the time as we weren't getting on perfectly anyway, and No I don't particularly regret it, and No you haven't met or heard of him [. . .] and it's all right, Chris, it's really all right').[8] The delicate parrying of unasked questions will resurface later in Barnes's work. *Before She Met Me*, in complete contrast, narrates the retrospective sexual obsession of Graham Hendrick, pathologically incapable of the mutual trust of a Christopher and a Marion. Indeed, this intriguing novel shows how the Barnes and Kavanagh output might indeed be thought of as the product of a single imagination, for, like Peter Ackroyd, Barnes is capable of stunning acts of ventriloquy, and considering those acts in the context of performance may suggest affinities with Ackroyd's work that might otherwise go unremarked.

Before She Met Me documents madness so horrifyingly because its tone is so reasonable. Criticisms that all the characterizations except Graham's own are thin and two-dimensional fail to take on board the imposing technical task the novel sets itself of revealing the breakdown of a single consciousness while moving skilfully in and out of it. Can we believe Graham's completely plausible version of his first wife Barbara's repeatedly planting the bedclothes on him in order to reproach him the next morning, once we have seen his second wife Ann experiencing Graham's nightmares during which 'his side of the bed had come completely untucked'?[9] To realize that questions of this level of domestic banality need attending to with the seriousness we give the text's more melodramatic unfoldings is to realize with a shock how we are being coerced unawares into viewing Barbara through Graham's eyes as a nagging stereotype. Ann concedes privately that Graham seems pleasant enough to

[8]Julian Barnes, *Metroland* (1980; London: Robin Clark, 1981), p. 163.
[9]Julian Barnes, *Before She Met Me* (1982; London: Picador, 1983), pp. 100, 122. Further quotations from this edition in the text above.

her friends, and the achievement of this novel lies in the way the reader, against all the evidence to which those friends are not privy, can still make sense of Ann's concession.

Graham, introduced to Ann by the bantering, farting macho novelist Jack Lupton, abandons Barbara and their daughter Alice for her. Graham becomes obsessed with Ann's past as an actress in a series of somewhat salacious B-movies, and this obsession spills over into all the sexual experiences Ann may or may not have had before meeting him. Given the bald outlines of the plot, it is remarkable how little mendacity there actually is: the fatal lie turns out to be Ann's, who persuades Jack to write their past affair out of existence.

One of the virtuoso touches in *Before She Met Me* is a series of couch sessions in which Graham and Ann variously confess the disintegration of Graham's psyche to Jack, who becomes a kind of surrogate novelist. Jack, however, is unable to cope with the forces unleashed by that disintegration, and becomes a victim of the plot. Jack's cheery infidelity to his own second wife Sue contrasts with Graham's obsessiveness and Ann's distress.

Within the novel as a whole there is a continuo of sexual disgust that takes the form of a series of half-humorous, half-sinister references to the butcher's trade. Graham and Ann attempt to patch things up by going on holiday to France. Barnes's fondness for the Franglais absurdity leads to a little disquisition on bulls' balls in which a 'very precise French butcher' informs the couple that '*Ce sont des frivolités, Madame*' (*Before She Met Me*, p. 120); yet a few pages later Ann, back in England, experiences a disquieting epiphany in her local butcher's as she is struck by the disjunction between the boater and apron that are the uniform of the trade:

> Looking at this man was like looking at a schizophrenic: civility and brutishness hustled together into a pretence of normality. And people *did* think it was normal; they weren't astonished that this man, just by standing there, could be

announcing two incompatible things. (*Before She Met Me*, p. 123)

Before She Met Me brings 'two incompatible things' together into a gruesome because plausible ending.

The novel that projected Barnes to international recognition, *Flaubert's Parrot*, has been extensively discussed. I shall give a very brief account here in order to stress how the way it suspends authorial judgements, instead allowing various voices to compete for authority, does (despite the extraordinarily variegated nature of Barnes's work) characterize not just *Metroland* and *Before She Met Me*, but *Staring at the Sun* as well, and (above all) the two novels *A History of the World in 10½ Chapters* and *Talking It Over*. It is illuminating to think of *Flaubert's Parrot* as a series of episodes, meditations, and approaches to the subject that are obsessively written over each other.

The book's title is richly allusive: at the literal level it refers to the stuffed parrot Flaubert is supposed to have kept on his desk while at work on *Un Coeur simple*, and to Braithwaite's painstaking detective work in deciding which of several extant claimants is the true talisman, an object mysteriously and even miraculously capable not just of bringing good fortune, but of being identified with, even symbolizing, artistic creativity. Braithwaite regards the parrot as it features in *Un Coeur simple* as a perfectly controlled instance of the Flaubertian grotesque; in the heart of its simple owner, Félicité, it comes at the end of her emotionally impoverished life to stand for the Holy Ghost:

'There was a smile on her lips. The movements of her heart slowed down beat by beat, each time more distant, like a fountain running dry or an echo disappearing: and as she breathed her final breath she thought she saw, as the heavens opened for her, a gigantic parrot hovering over her head.'[10]

[10]Quoted in Julian Barnes, *Flaubert's Parrot* (London: Cape, 1984), p. 17. Further references to this edition in the text above.

To Geoffrey Braithwaite, by the end of his quest, the parrot has become 'a fluttering, elusive emblem of the writer's voice' (pp. 182–83). We cannot even rule out the possibility that Braithwaite himself may be Flaubert's parrot, uncomprehendingly repeating all he hears his own talisman, his idol, say.

Yet there are some teasing similarities between Braithwaite and Barnes. Barnes is a generation or so younger than his narrator, but a number of attitudes, particularly Francophilia and judgements on literature, must be considered as shared, and there seems to have been no strenuous attempt on Barnes's part to detach himself from, or create a strikingly different self in, Braithwaite. During the sixth chapter (the one that originally appeared in *Granta*), which consists of a rebuttal of Dr Enid Starkie's view that Flaubert was too careless of detail to be a truly realistic writer, we listen to Braithwaite meditating on whether mistakes in literature matter:

> What, though, about 'internal mistakes', when the writer claims two incompatible things within his own creation? Emma's eyes are brown, Emma's eyes are blue. Alas, this can be put down only to incompetence, to sloppy literary habits. I read the other day a well-praised first novel in which the narrator – who is both sexually inexperienced and an amateur of French literature – comically rehearses to himself the best way to kiss a girl without being rebuffed: 'With a slow, sensual, irresistible strength, draw her gradually towards you while gazing into her eyes as if you had just been given a copy of the first, suppressed edition of *Madame Bovary*.'
>
> I thought this was quite neatly put, indeed rather amusing. The only trouble is, there's no such thing as a 'first, suppressed edition of *Madame Bovary*'. The novel, as I should have thought was tolerably well known, first appeared serially in the *Revue de Paris*; then came the prosecution for obscenity; and only after the acquittal was the work published in book form. I expect the young novelist (it seems unfair to give his name) was thinking of the 'first, suppressed edition' of *Les*

Fleurs du mal. No doubt he'll get it right in time for his second edition, if there is one. (*Flaubert's Parrot*, p. 78)

The simile comes from the 1980 Cape edition (p. 93) of *Metroland* – and it is not 'corrected' in the paperback reprints. Braithwaite here shows himself unwilling to distinguish between his own knowledge of Flaubert and the fictive knowledge (which may include error) that a narrator can assume. If Braithwaite had been playing completely fair he would have found, in a letter to Christopher from Toni four pages later in *Metroland*, a reference to 'the grown-up' edition of *Les Fleurs du mal*, for which Toni now deems Christopher fit, after his sexual initiation, to read. The first chapter of *Flaubert's Parrot* remarkably demonstrates how a writer may assume a self and yet blend that self with his own experience: isolated paragraphs describing the Flaubert mausoleum, the Croisset pavilion, could be read as Barnes's own journalism, but at the same time are flawlessly incorporated into the surrounding texture of Braithwaite's literary detective work. A similar deduction must be made in the case of the Dr Enid Starkie chapter.

Staring at the Sun – according to an interview given in 1989 Barnes's own favourite among his novels[11] – begins with an astonishing opening image, of the sun rising twice as the RAF pilot Prosser drops 10,000 feet in his Hurricane over the English Channel one night in June 1941. This little episode captures a note of authority that is assiduously avoided elsewhere in the narrative. The opening words of *Staring at the Sun* are: 'This is what happened.'[12] In this way the rest of the novel represents an ontological flipside to its introduction.

Towards the end the ageing Jean Serjeant asks whether one of the (imagined) relationships in the novel might have been 'a photographic negative' of the one she has experienced with

[11]Interview with Amanda Smith, *Publishers Weekly*, 3 November 1989, pp. 73–74.
[12]Julian Barnes, *Staring at the Sun* (London: Cape, 1986), p. 1. Further references in the text are to this edition.

her former husband (*Staring at the Sun*, p. 181). The metaphor
seems appropriate in any attempt to determine the relationship
the main part of the text bears to the introduction. Although
Prosser's experience as he relates it to the 20-year-old Jean while
he is being billeted with the Serjeant family never captures the
authority of the narrator's initial description of it, it haunts
Jean all her life, which continues throughout almost a century
to beyond 2020. Its corollary is an ascent towards the sun in
a leaky aircraft cockpit and the attendant euphoria caused by
oxygen deprivation. Staring at the sun can mean crashing to
earth but does not exclude the need to aspire.

In the book's first section, Jean (apparently born in 1922)
seems almost abnormally retarded yet at the same time persistently inquisitive[13] as she tries, for instance, to understand
the enigmatic pronouncements and practices of another Barnes
uncle, Leslie (who 'seemed to consider money a very primitive
form of exchange' [*Staring at the Sun*, p. 82]). The second
section projects us into roughly contemporary time, with Jean
as the (by now more intelligent) single mother of Gregory. After
twenty sterile years of marriage to Michael, a policeman, whom
she leaves, she almost miraculously gives birth at 40. The last
section projects us further, into the early twenty-first century.
Here Jean fades into the background: the emphasis is primarily
on the 60-year-old Gregory's search for answers to questions of
being similar to those his mother had earlier posed, this time on
the General Purposes Computer (GPC) and its refinement TAT
(The Absolute Truth). One of the lessons of *Staring at the Sun*
is learnt by Gregory: 'A careful question is, after all, a sort of
answer' (*Staring at the Sun*, p. 177). There is a revealing passage
in the third section when Gregory's sessions with GPC and TAT,
related by him to Jean, are contextualized by Jean's, as it were
superimposing on to them her recollections of her apparently
inconsequential games with Uncle Leslie.

---

[13]In this respect she has much in common with Rose Tremain's Mary Ward
in *Sacred Country* (1992).

The reader of *A History of the World in 10½ Chapters*, like that of *Flaubert's Parrot*, is likely to feel that the order of the chapters could be changed without the story suffering undue damage. Otherwise, each of these novels appears (like *Staring at the Sun* and *Talking It Over*) to be generically at the edge of what is usually thought of as 'fiction'. The chapters of *A History* contrive to suggest that they *are* distinct and selected episodes in a cosmic history, but at the same time they reject attempts to detach them from each other entirely: various motifs recur, as in other Barnes novels provocatively drawing attention to the presence of an authorial god in a world whose history seems anarchically devoid of any guiding principle.

However, it would be incorrect to argue that the sense of formlessness in *A History* is total: after all, the first chapter – an iconoclastic account of Noah's Ark by a stowaway woodworm – is historically speaking set in the earliest time the book documents, and the last ('The Dream') ends in a kind of secularized heaven whose inhabitants 'are stuck with [. . .] millennia after millennia of being themselves'[14] – certainly it is concerned with a sense of the end of a life. The penultimate chapters are set in our own times. But elsewhere there is considerable moving back and forth within these set historical limits. How is this process enhanced by the various motifs? And is the role they perform sufficiently weighty to rescue the novel from charges of frivolousness?

A recurrent motif is the closed community, usually a ship at sea and/or a group of outsiders within a hostile environment, suffering because of their identity, although whether in a justified or paranoid manner is not always made wholly clear. Perhaps each such episode is presented as a distinct historical epoch of which the lesson is that all history's 'ships' are distinct only in degree and not in kind, despite the irresistible interpretative drive to see uniqueness in one's own historical moment.

[14]Julian Barnes, *A History of the World in 10½ Chapters* (London: Cape, 1989), p. 306.

Thus, apart from the first chapter about Noah's Ark, there are others presenting the Arab hijack of a cruise ship with an international clientele, the memoirs of the survivor of a nuclear disaster, an account of the shipwreck of the *Medusa* in 1816 (the book actually reproduces Géricault's painting along with thoughts on the inadequacy of representational art in the face of unimaginable reality). Another chapter, in fact consisting discretely of 'Three Simple Stories', provides accounts of a (possibly fictitious) episode from the *Titanic* disaster and the infamous voyage of the German liner the *St Louis* with its cargo of Jewish refugees vainly hoping for sanctuary in Cuba. Inserted between these stories is an account of how one James Bartley was swallowed by a whale in 1891 and (like Jonah) survived. The theme of Noah's Ark is recurrent: a pious nineteenth-century explorer, Miss Fergusson, perishes on Mount Ararat in an attempt to find the site of Noah's Ark; a hundred years later a fundamentalist astronaut from North Carolina (modelled, it would seem, on the late James Irwin [1930–91]), his mind turned by the experience of having seen the earth from the moon (a motif touched on elsewhere in the novel), stumbles on Miss Fergusson's skeleton during his own slightly mad quest for the Ark and believes he has found Noah's remains.

Perhaps the problem concerning the seriousness or otherwise of these motifs is actually part of a more substantial enquiry into the distinction between various categories of episode. Some are factual and documented (the wreck of the *Medusa*, the plight of the *St Louis*), some purely fictional (an epistolary narrative of a film actor's psychic breakdown while journeying on location up what is presumably the Amazon). Some negotiate between these two areas as cunningly constructed historical pastiche (the quest of Miss Fergusson, a series of clerical depositions in medieval France). A fourth and perhaps most significant category, as Frank Kermode saw in his review of the novel, might be described as typologically mythical.[15] These are episodes which, according

15Frank Kermode, 'Stowaway Worm', *LRB*, 22 June 1989, p. 20.

to who it is that reads them, can fall into any of the other categories. But they would most likely be taken – certainly in Western culture – as providing a mythic framework that does not simply permit but actually authenticates given ways of reading the other episodes.

Talking It Over seems to return to more domestic ground. It is one of Barnes's most accessible narratives, yet in it he manages to contrive a formally unique mode of narration. The status of the narrative in fact hovers uneasily between fiction and drama, though a drama from which all stage-directions have been removed. Indeed, there is no authorial or indeed authoritative voice at all; the text is constructed entirely as dialogue, often the kind in which the main characters come uncomfortably close to, and even obsessively buttonhole, the reader, who is frequently directly addressed by them, unable to escape. Within individual accounts there are accounts of conversations held, and something approaching conventional narrative; but at the 'narrative about narrative' level each character exists for the reader alone in total isolation, so that a 'metanarrative' of a completely different order undercuts these miniature narratives.

In *Talking It Over* Barnes returns to the obsessive triangular relationship between two men and a woman that he had explored in *Before She Met Me*. We are to assume that the time-span of a few years belongs entirely to the 1980s. The three main characters are Stuart Hughes, a banker; his wife Gillian Wyatt, a restorer of paintings; and Oliver Russell, a supply English teacher who has been Stuart's best man. The briefest account of the plot would be that Stuart is abandoned by Gillian for Oliver, or that Oliver takes Gillian away from Stuart: even the difficulty in deciding which version to formulate shows how deceptive the plot's apparent simplicity is. Others' voices are heard from time to time: these include Gillian's French mother, Madame Wyatt, whose own husband had deserted her for a much younger woman several years previously; Michelle, a 16-year-old florist's assistant; Val, a militantly feminist contemporary and former acquaintance of both Stuart and Oliver; and a brace of landladies, a Mrs Dyer and a Madame Rives, who are positioned with symmetrical elegance in relation to Oliver and Stuart respectively.

Again, as in *Before She Met Me*, Barnes lifts domestically banal differences of opinion into questions that compel attention. Only a selective account is possible here. There is one rare direct confrontation between the two men in a drama in which for much of its course observation, or rather voyeurism (even listening to the telephone), seems the norm. Does Stuart head-butt Oliver or is Oliver's later admission into Harringay Hospital's casualty ward occasioned by a clumsy accident at the conclusion of a man-to-man whisky session? This question gains seriousness when juxtaposed with a strange episode that is all too easily set aside because it disturbs the smoother ripples of the yuppie world of *Talking It Over*: Val is literally bundled out, and thus written out, of the story in an act of some violence. Both men in their different way suggest that Val obscurely represents 'trouble' – indeed this is practically the only thing they are united on; her subversiveness lies in her suggestion that Stuart and Oliver have entered a triangular relationship because Oliver is attracted to Stuart. (But Val has apparently been to bed with Stuart and apparently been rejected by Oliver.) Because there is no authoritative voice to be believed or disbelieved, Val's expulsion from the story becomes an act in which one particular feminine voice or discourse is effectively silenced. In a similar way, what Michelle interprets as Oliver's making a pass at her in the flower shop is given another context by Stuart's entry and our discovery that the flowers are for Gillian. Madame Wyatt's version, too, registered with fine idiomatic control, forms an interesting alternative continuo. Do the suppression of Val, the sexual vanity of Michelle, or the unfathomable (perhaps even Gallic-stereotypical) sagacity of Madame Wyatt lead to Gillian's thus becoming an object of desire and nothing more, incapable of sustaining the politics of her gender? Does a male discourse of desire ultimately triumph? (Yet Gordon Wyatt, Gillian's father, gets a brief chance to put his version too.)

We learn not only that Gillian's father has abandoned her, but that Oliver's has violently abused him. A distinct register is used for each voice. That of Stuart is no-nonsense ('I remember everything')[16] and ostensibly the most reliable; he assures us that his is the only name that won't change, yet towards the end, as he obsessively tries to observe or spy on his ex-wife's and Oliver's apparent felicity in a French village, he shelters in Madame Rives' neighbouring *pension* under a pseudonym and transparently false (Canadian) nationality. Gillian's register is also matter-of-fact at the start, yet despite her initial claim ('I'm an ordinary, private person') (*Talking It Over*, p. 7), it affords us the most sexually explicit moment in the book as she describes how she is aroused to lubricity on hearing both Oliver's voice on the telephone and Stuart's key being inserted in the front door; at this point Oliver has moved into nearby lodgings at Mrs Dyer's. Gillian's name alters from Wyatt to Hughes to Russell, yet (on her account) actually remains her own throughout. It is Gillian's voice that examines the phenomenon of 'Greengrocer's Apostrophe' with more compassion than anyone else in the novel would be capable of:

Gillian [. . .] The man who runs [the shop] does these price labels which he hand-letters in sort of italic capitals. And very carefully, without ever missing, he puts an apostrophe into everything he sells. *APPLE'S PEAR'S CARROT'S LEEK'S* – you can buy them all there – *SWEDE'S TURNIP'S* and *SWEET POTATO'S*. Stuart and I used to find this funny and a bit touching, this chap doggedly getting it wrong all the time, every single time. I walked past the shop today and suddenly I didn't find it at all funny any more. *CAULI'S COX'S SPROUT'S*. I just found it so sad that it went right through me. Not sad because he couldn't spell, not that. Sad because he got it wrong, and then he went on to the next

[16]Julian Barnes, *Talking It Over* (London: Cape, 1991), p. 1. Further references to this edition in the text above.

label and got that wrong, and then he went on to the next
one and got that wrong too. (*Talking It Over*, p. 152).[17]

Oliver's is the most characteristic voice in *Talking It Over*,
and the one that echoes most once the book has been laid down.
He is fond of Barnes's own coinages such as 'crepuscular'; he
frequently refers to Stuart's less prepossessing physique as
'steatopygous' (Graham Hendrick in *Before She Met Me* is
also favoured with what Oliver would offensively term 'the
Hottentot *derrière*' [*Talking It Over*, p. 23]); he attracted several
reviewers with a flamboyant expression of disgust ('Hie me to
the vomitorium *pronto*') (*Talking It Over*, p. 43); and he is
engagingly fond of 'rumpy pumpy' as a euphemism for sex.
Oliver was Nigel Oliver Russell when he and Stuart attended
school together. Despite the attractiveness of 'Oliver's riffs', as
they become known, no voice can be privileged because each
'lies like an eyewitness', to quote the epigraph once more.

In the absence of an authoritative voice, the reader is compelled
to accept or reject, or more likely suspend judgement on, the
various versions. However, it must be said that there are other
glimmers than the expulsion of Val that suggest, without
asserting, that 'control' of this drama is in ambivalent or even
inscrutable hands. In addition to the coincidence of Stuart's
meeting Oliver in the florist's, there is the bizarre presence of
Oliver on the ferry back from Boulogne which Stuart and Gillian
have apparently fortuitously decided to take on their return from
a weekend in northern France, yet of this episode we are forced

[17]This compassionate examination might be contrasted with the virtuoso
outburst by the educated, but unfortunately temporarily jailed, Alec Llewellyn
to John Self in Martin Amis's *Money*, a text that at one of its countless
frenetic levels throbs with all kinds of jokes about punctuation: 'Listen. It
says "Light's Out At Nine". L-i-g-h-t-apostrophe-s. *Apostrophe*-s! It says
"One Cup of Tea or 'Coffee'" – coffee in inverted commas. Why? Why?
In the library, the library, it says "You can NOT Spit" – cannot two
words and the not in capitals. It's a mistake, a mistake ... It's not me,
it's you! It's a literal, it's a fucking typo!' Martin Amis, *Money: A Suicide
Note* (London: Cape, 1984), p. 239.

to ask: have Oliver and Gillian (despite her insisting that it was a spontaneous and amicable agreement with Stuart not to continue on to Calais, Stuart's version offering no help) arranged a tryst, or should we believe Oliver's almost ritualistic pronouncement ('I got them home safely. I got her home safely')? (*Talking It Over*, p. 108) Again, it is profundity masquerading as banality that seems Barnes's hallmark.

Be all this as it may, it is Oliver who senses in Gillian's profession as restorer of paintings an insight that may serve as an emblem for the reader's experience of this remarkable novel – and indeed, in its various forms, something that might be thought to characterize the essence of a great deal of Barnes's fictional output (whether or not in *propria persona*):

> **Oliver** [. . .] 'But there must be a point . . . when you've hosed off all the muck and the glaze and the bits of overpainting and your musks of Araby have done their work and you get to the point when you *know* that what you see before you is what the chap would have seen before him when he stopped painting all those centuries ago. The colours just as he left them.'
> 'No.'
> 'No?'
> 'No. You're bound to go a little bit too far or not far enough. There's no way of knowing *exactly*.' [. . .]. Isn't that wonderful? Oh effulgent relativity! *There is no 'real' picture under there waiting to be revealed.* What I've always said about life itself [. . .]. It's just my word against everybody else's! (*Talking It Over*, p. 120)

Barnes's performances, understated as they are, take on big issues (this is perhaps seen more clearly in *A History of the World in 10½ Chapters* than anywhere else). They include: the nature of love; altruism versus the selfish need to survive; definitions of authority as expressed (for instance) in the various pecking orders of communities both human and non-human, or in the question of who is telling the truth (whatever that may be); how observed phenomena are to be interpreted, and on the many ways of doing so:

> Miss Fergusson had maintained [. . .] there were two expla-
> nations of everything, that each required the exercise of faith,
> and that we had been given free will in order that we might
> choose between them. This dilemma was to preoccupy Miss
> Logan for years to come. (*A History of the World*, p. 168)

Julian Barnes's moral universe is characterized by his downbeat yet profoundly examined way of articulating it.

We turn finally, and in contrast, to a novelist whose rhetorical performances are far fuller of public and political conviction, and whose expression of those performances is one of bravura.

9

Bravura Performance:
Salman Rushdie and
the 'Privileged Arena'

The novel is the privileged arena where languages in conflict
can meet, bringing together, in tension and dialogue, not only
opposing characters, but also different historical ages, social
levels, civilisation and other, dawning realities of human life.
In the novel, realities that are normally separated can meet
[. . .]. [This] encounter [. . .] reveals [. . .] that, in dialogue,
no one is absolutely right; neither speaker [. . .] has an
absolute hold over history. Myself and the other, as well
as the history that both of us are making, still are not. Both
are unfinished and so can only continue to be. By its very
nature, the novel indicates that we are becoming. There is
no final solution. There is no last word. [. . .] Fiction is a
harbinger of a multipolar and multicultural world, where
no single philosophy, no single belief, no single solution,
can shunt aside the extreme wealth of mankind's cultural
heritage.[1]

If the 1980s in Britain were marked by the career of one single
novelist, that novelist was Salman Rushdie. At the beginning of
the decade he was unknown; by its end he was in hiding and
under the protection of British security agents.

To recapitulate: in 1981 Rushdie won the Booker Prize with
Midnight's Children and changed for ever the way a British
readership looked back on its colonial past. Rushdie's next

---

[1]Carlos Fuentes, 'Words Apart', *Guardian*, 24 February 1989; reprinted
in Lisa Appignanesi and Sara Maitland, eds., *The Rushdie File* (London:
ICA/Fourth Estate, 1989), pp. 245–48.

two novels, *Shame* (1983) and *The Satanic Verses* (1988) were shortlisted for the prize, and *The Satanic Verses* went on to win the Best Novel category of the 1988 Whitbread Award, although not the overall prize. To mark the twenty-fifth anniversary of the Booker Prize in 1993, *Midnight's Children* was selected as the 'Booker of Bookers'. Rushdie's success had been created by the prize-winning culture of the 1980s more completely than was the case for any other novelist under discussion in this book.

During the closing months of 1988, it was becoming evident that *The Satanic Verses* was arousing controversy within the Moslem world both inside Britain and beyond. There were – on an increasingly global scale – riots, book-burnings and even deaths. And, as the world now knows, on 14 February 1989, just before *The Satanic Verses* was scheduled for publication in the United States, Iran's Ayatollah Khomeini pronounced a fatwa, a decree sentencing the book's author to death for blasphemy.

The fatwa could, and still can, be carried out by devout Moslems worldwide. It was irrevocable, and in theory extended to anyone promoting the book in any way. In the ensuing months, two liberal imams were shot in Belgium, Rushdie's Japanese translator was stabbed to death, and his Italian translator seriously wounded; and bookstores around the world were fire-bombed for stocking the novel. After a long and bitter controversy, *The Satanic Verses* did finally appear in paperback under various imprints, but bookstores have stocked it with restraint. Rushdie himself has led a beleaguered life from that day on, although more recently he has come out of complete hiding.[2] With the launch of *The Moor's Last Sigh* (1995) Rushdie made his first announced appearance since the fatwa. Security on this and subsequent such occasions has been strict.

The epigraph to this chapter comes from the author of *Terra Nostra* (1975), that extraordinarily transgressive rewriting of

[2]In a *Face to Face* interview with Jeremy Isaacs, broadcast on BBC2 on 10 October 1994 to mark the publication of the short-story collection *East, West* (London: Cape, 1994), Rushdie confirmed that he no longer actually considered himself to be 'in hiding'.

the history of the Iberian colonization of the Americas in the sixteenth century. I chose it not only because it is crucial to the argument of the last section of this book, but also because it offers one of the clearest insights into the nature of the Rushdie controversy, an event that spawned a great deal of print.[3] As Fuentes saw, and as Rushdie himself correctly claimed in his brilliant defence 'In Good Faith', the impasse between two different cultures completely obscured the artistic process of 'how newness enters the world'.[4] The purpose of this chapter is to identify and abstract what seem to be the principal elements in that defence, and use them to trace what I shall argue has really been a consistent development in Rushdie's fiction from the time of *Grimus* (1975), an unheralded and commercially unsuccessful beginning, through Booker Prize exposure and lionization by the British literary establishment to *The Moor's Last Sigh* twenty years later.

Grimus won't be read as anything other than an interesting prelude to the historically politicized, culturally hybrid fictions of the 1980s and 1990s. Rushdie now regards its publication as his 'worst mistake'.[5] Still, the point is worth making that *Grimus* begins, as does his most notorious, with a piece of bravura: what (in one of the many interviews given on the appearance of *The Satanic Verses*) its author was later to describe as a 'drastic act of immigration'.[6]

[3]Initial reactions are usefully assembled in *The Rushdie File*. The most balanced and informative analysis I have come across is Malise Ruthven's *A Satanic Affair: Salman Rushdie and the Wrath of Islam* (1990; London: The Hogarth Press, 1991).

[4]Salman Rushdie, 'In Good Faith', *Independent on Sunday*, 4 February 1990, pp. 18–20. Rpt. in *Imaginary Homelands* (London: Granta, 1991), pp. 393–414.

[5]Interview with Jeremy Isaacs, *Face to Face*, BBC2, 10 October 1994. Rushdie revealed that *Grimus* sold only 800 copies in hardback before being pulped. However, his later successes have ensured retrospective paperback reprints.

[6]Quoted by Sean French in interview with Rushdie, *Observer*, 25 September 1988, and reprinted in *The Rushdie File*, p. 8. One of the few reviews of *The Satanic Verses* to attempt to see it in the context of the other fictions is Patrick Parrinder, 'Let's get the hell out of here', *LRB*, 29 September 1988, pp. 11–13.

Flapping Eagle's arrival into the narrative of *Grimus* takes place in terms whose fantasy strains the credibility even more than does that of the celebrated fall of Gibreel Farishta and Saladin Chamcha from the doomed jumbo jet Bostan:

> Sometimes, people trying to commit suicide manage it in a manner that leaves them breathless with astonishment. Flapping Eagle, coming in fast now on the crest of a wave, was about to discover this fact. At present he was unconscious; he had just fallen through a hole in the sea. The sea had been the Mediterranean. It wasn't now; or not quite.[7]

The worlds of science fiction are possible worlds, worlds apart from our own. We judge sophisticated practitioners of the genre by their ability to render those possible worlds so that we can apprehend them in terms of the one we think we know.

It seems consistent with Rushdie's own reflections on being forced into hiding – here I am thinking not only of 'In Good Faith' but of the 1990 Herbert Read Memorial lecture, 'Is Nothing Sacred?', too – to focus on the astonishingly fecund allusiveness of *Grimus*.[8] To be sure, that fecundity can become wearying, but what it illustrates can now be seen, if we are to heed Rushdie's post-fatwa thoughts, as issues of major aesthetic, and indeed ultimately historio-political, concern.

Among these issues are Flapping Eagle's hermaphroditic status, and the narrative's use of anagrams and palindromes. For these elements, thematically prefigured in Flapping Eagle's immigration into the text 'through a hole in the sea', serve as likenesses of each other: they force the reader of *Grimus* to ask which is the mirror and which the reality it is mirroring. To regard *Grimus* as 'failed' because it fails adequately to place and thus politicize its subject-matter (this isn't to say it may not legitimately be thought to have failed for other

---

[7]Salman Rushdie, *Grimus* (1975; London: Panther, 1977), p. 14.
[8]These reflections are reprinted in *Imaginary Homelands*, pp. 415–29.

reasons) is to run the very serious danger of wishing it to be a finished history, or a final solution: in short, it is to deprive *Grimus* of its characteristic space, what Fuentes would call its privileged arena.

Let us briefly consider the claims for his art that Rushdie makes in 'In Good Faith', a defence that must surely one day take its place among the most lucid and humane essays in the English language – a worthy companion to Sir Philip Sidney's posthumous 1595 *Apology* – to concern the relationship between the work of art and the world we perceive. Here are some extracts that form its opening proposition:

> I am not trying to say that *The Satanic Verses* is 'only a novel' [. . .]. I do not believe that novels are trivial matters. The ones I care most about are those which attempt radical reformulations of language, form, and ideas, those that attempt to do what the word *novel* seems to insist upon: to see the world anew. [. . .] Those who oppose the novel most vociferously today are of the opinion that intermingling with a different culture will inevitably weaken and ruin their own. I am of the opposite opinion. *The Satanic Verses* celebrates hybridity, impurity, intermingling [. . .]. It rejoices in mongrelization and fears the absolutism of the Pure. ('In Good Faith', p. 18)

Yet this opening point is not an end in itself for Rushdie, however combatively formulated. Referring to himself as 'a bastard child of history' (elsewhere he has said: 'I am not who I was supposed to be'),[9] Rushdie significantly adds, almost as an aside: 'Perhaps we all are, black and brown and white, leaking into one another, as a character of mine once said, *like flavours when you cook*' [emphases Rushdie's].[10]

Although Rushdie does not, in 'In Good Faith', make the

---

[9]Sean French interview, *The Rushdie File*, p. 9.
[10]The reference is to the narrator Saleem Sinai's explanation to Padma, in *Midnight's Children* (London: Cape, 1981), p. 39, for his telling his story in the way he does. Further references in the text above.

point explicitly, the reference to metamorphosis is nevertheless one of great importance to his performative aesthetic, and in this way integrally bound up with the politics of his major fiction. The big novels of the 1980s, *Midnight's Children, Shame,* and *The Satanic Verses,* allow us to understand the ways in which what Rushdie terms artistic 'reclamation' can 'teach us who we are'. (Not for nothing was Rushdie politically active, prior to 1989, in promoting healthy race relations within Britain's various pluralist communities.) To reiterate, it is (after all) the novels rather than political discussion in the abstract that create the 'privileged arena' in which such understanding can be reached.

Reviewing *Midnight's Children,* Robert Taubman saw 'the book's predominant image' as seepage or leakage.[11] In a collection of retrospectives marking the twenty-first anniversary of the inception of the Booker Prize and published in 1989, Rushdie himself seemed to connect this predominant image to the particular nature of the chosen narrative mode. Admitting some unintended errors of factual history in his novel, Rushdie at the same time contrived to aim back at the pedants the challenge: can mistakes exist in literature, and if so, do they matter? Rushdie thereby provides a context for his assertion that 'history is ambiguous'.[12]

Midnight's Children is an act of virtuoso narrative recall. The narrator, Saleem Sinai, has been born on the dot of the magic hour of India's independence in August 1947, and like all the survivors among the thousand-and-one children to share this fate, Saleem is blessed or cursed with supernatural powers, powers whose effectiveness decreases the further from midnight itself the birth took place. Keith Wilson has pointed out that these

[11]Robert Taubman, 'Experiments with truth', *LRB,* 7–20 May 1981, pp. 3, 5–6.
[12]Salman Rushdie, 'Errata: or, Unreliable Narration in *Midnight's Children'*, in Martyn Goff, ed. & intro., *Prize Writing* (London: Sceptre, 1989), pp. 165–68. Rpt. in *Imaginary Homelands,* pp. 22–25.

babies become 'both tellers and, like their Arabian analogues, tales':[13] the *Tales* have exerted a constant fascination on Rushdie. Saleem is – at the time of writing – a pathetic figure. Physically disintegrating as a consequence of his having been 'mysteriously handcuffed to history' (*Midnight's Children*, p. 11), he appears to be writing in the first instance for a readership of one, Padma, his 'dung-lotus' and second wife-to-be; and the isolation in which he is suspended throughout the telling is as assistant in a pickling factory in Bombay run by Mary Pereira, his former amah or wet-nurse. Taubman (p. 5) describes Saleem as 'only the most porous, the most fissured' of all the book's characters. Mary's guilty secret is that it is she who has been responsible for an action whereby Saleem has been brought up as 'not who [he] was supposed to be' (to adapt Rushdie's own words cited above): she has swapped Saleem immediately after his birth. His alter ego, Shiva, is thus the true child of Saleem's parents – and will ironically father Saleem's child by his (Saleem's) first wife, Parvati-the-witch.

It is appropriate that Mary Pereira should, under an assumed identity (that of a Mrs Braganza: the name recalls that of the princess through whom Britain inherited the Bombay area in the seventeenth century), be running the pickle factory for which Saleem in his premature dotage is reduced to working. Saleem (like Rushdie throughout his fictions) is replete with the figurative potential of every imaginable aspect of his story:

Symbolic value of the pickling process: all the six hundred million eggs which gave birth to the population of India could fit inside a standard-sized pickle-jar; six hundred million spermatozoa could be lifted on a single spoon. Every pickle-jar (you will forgive me if I become florid for a moment) contains, therefore, the most exalted of possibilities: the feasibility of the chutnification of history; the grand hope of the pickling of

[13]Keith Wilson, '*Midnight's Children* and Reader Responsibility', *Critical Quarterly* 26/3 (1984), pp. 23–37.

time! I, however, have pickled chapters. (*Midnight's Children*, p. 442)

The pickling process provides an apt metaphor for the persistent narrative leakage, and operates on many levels. In pickling, what is perishable is preserved by means of a chemical process whereby it is simultaneously steeped in and absorbs its surroundings. Yet seeing the book's chapters as a series of jars of pickles – as Saleem does – is paradoxically a way of mounting a formal attack on the idea of seepage, for the chapters are discrete entities that remain so. At the end of the book, Saleem thus seems to intimate – in the third-person form he often uses – that there are other ways in which he could have told his story:

> Sometimes, in the pickles' version of history, Saleem appears to have known too little; at other times too much . . . yes, I should revise and revise, improve and improve but there is neither the time nor the energy. (*Midnight's Children*, p. 443)

Accordingly, some of the pickling is conceived of as having been mixed wrongly, unsatisfyingly, unduly ambiguously (perhaps – as he admits – Saleem has 'invented the whole story of the baby-swap to justify an incestuous love'). As will be made quite explicit in *Shame*, the very fecundity of the story-telling impulse can lead to a sense of loss, of what cannot be told – here, bravura performance is pushed to its limits.

In *Midnight's Children*, however, the emphasis is more on the kind of narrative unreliability with which we are faced in the person and story of Saleem. Among the many fictional models towards which Rushdie deliberately gestures is Laurence Sterne's *Tristram Shandy* (1760–66): a third of the narrative is taken up with the preliminaries to Saleem's actual entry into it. Rushdie thus forestalls any doubts as to the momentous nature of Saleem's existence. The 'mysterious' way in which Saleem is 'handcuffed to history' raises many questions of narrative form, questions one could range along a spectrum running from (a) the fairly superficial (by which I mean the irrepressible allusions embodying a kind of osmosis, so that a significant word or concept seeps from one set of associations into another, to which it is thereby seen to be related), through to (b) a profound ontological uncertainty lying at the heart of Saleem's (or Rushdie's) use of the figurative potential of language. In this way the reader is forced to ask what is the signifier and what is being signified, or to see 'signifier' and 'signified' as reflections of each other. The disconcerting result is that one does not serve a priori to make sense of the other, as we normally expect of metaphorical language.

Examples of the more 'superficial' kind of expression of momentousness include the confusion between blood and mercurochrome with which Aadam Aziz's involvement in both the riots that serve as a prelude to the Amritsar massacre of April 1919, and then the massacre itself, confronts Naseem (*Midnight's Children*, pp. 35–37). Examples of the profounder kind of mutual reflection (what is signifier? what is signified?) include Saleem's descriptions of two crucial 'mutilations' closely related in time (the sadistic teacher Zagallo's tearing out of a clump of Saleem's hair, Saleem's loss of part of a middle finger in a fracas with Glandy Keith and Fat Perce occasioned by precocious sexual rivalry for Masha Miovic, one of several *femmes fatales* in Saleem's life [*Midnight's Children*, pp. 224–29]):

> Uncork the body, and God knows what you permit to come tumbling out. Suddenly you are forever other than you were; and the world becomes such that parents can cease to be parents, and love can turn to hate. And these, mark you, are only the effects on private life. The consequences for the sphere of public action, as will be shown, are – were – will be no less profound. (*Midnight's Children*, pp. 231)

Seepage, from inside to outside, from the homogeneity of the 'body' to the heterogeneity of the 'human being', from the private to the public sphere – all these are surveyed in what Saleem at one point terms 'his desperation for meaning' (*Midnight's Children*, p. 345). So in answer to the question whether historical mistakes matter, Rushdie, in his 1989 retrospective view of his novel, argues:

> When I began the novel [. . .] I hoped that if I could only imagine vividly enough it might be possible to see beyond those filters [of time and migration], to write as if the years had not passed, as if I had never left India for the West. But as I worked I found that what interested me was the process of filtration itself. [. . .] [Saleem] is no dispassionate, disinterested chronicler. He wants so to shape his material that the reader will be forced to concede his central role. He is cutting up history to suit himself, just as he did when he cut up newspapers to compose his earlier text, the anonymous note to Commander Sabarmati.[14]

Elsewhere, Rushdie has remarked (admitting the remark as a simplification): 'In England people read *Midnight's Children* as a fantasy, in India people read it as a history book'.[15] To affirm with Carlos Fuentes that the novel is a 'privileged arena' is thus precisely not to affirm cultural homogeneity between West and East. If sharing Fuentes' affirmation is to realize how far these worlds are apart, though, it is also to suggest at least the possibility of reconciliation.

The narrator in *Shame* is not one of the characters: indeed, this novel raises for serious scrutiny the question who is actually the central character. The reader of *Shame* is offered a conception of the 'hero' Omar Khayyam Shakil's selfhood that is constantly referred to as 'peripheral' to a narrative invested with a largely

---

[14]Quoted in Goff, *Prize Writing*, p. 167, and *Imaginary Homelands*, pp. 23–24. The cutting-up episode to which Rushdie refers occurs in *Midnight's Children*, pp. 252ff. Saleem calls it 'my first attempt at rearranging history'.
[15]Quoted in interview with Sean French, *The Rushdie File*, p. 9.

untold multiplicity of tales. Yet *Shame* shares much of the characteristic fecundity of *Grimus* and *Midnight's Children*: the countless patterns, parallels, echoes and other kinds of word-play are once more typically proffered then withheld or rejected. Narrative unity is undermined by frequent digressions, pauses, and changes of scene. The narrator is apparently unable to control the passage of time, so that among ancillary instances of seepage must be counted that from future into present: this characteristic also recalls *Midnight's Children*, although it is more integral to *Shame*. Lack of control extends to the puzzled tone of the narrator's periodic reviews of the character of his peripheral hero; the narrative omissions resulting from a sense of what cannot be told reflect the existence of taboos that convey some of the many nuances of the vernacular form of the book's title.[16] The narrator poses as omniscient, offering various kinds of pattern and motif, and even setting himself up as interpreter of his own text, yet admits the existence of arbitrary limits and controls to both his knowledge and indeed his ability.

During the course of the novel the tensions sharpen into an opposition between 'reality' and 'fairy-tale': the narrative requires its readers to see it in terms of its allegorical relationship to historical reality, yet that narrative conducts the process of allegorization with such ostentatious bravura that it becomes impossible to think in the conventional terms whereby allegory is considered to offer an obscure figuring of a given reality. The reader is drawn into collusion concerning the arbitrariness, even frivolity, of the narrator's connections between the levels at which his tale is subject to interpretation.

Omar is mysteriously sired after a scandalous party given, instead of a wake for their father, by three sisters all of whom subsequently exhibit symptoms of pregnancy. His name alludes to the twelfth-century author of the *Rubáiyát* translated into English in the mid nineteenth century by Edward FitzGerald

---

[16]Salman Rushdie, *Shame* (London: Cape, 1983), pp. 38–39. Further references in the text above.

(1809–1883) and thus made accessible to a dominant imperial culture as a new kind of work from the original text. Nishapur, the historical Omar's birthplace, is the name of the fantastic mansion inhabited by the fictional Omar and his mothers. Omar's desire to escape from Nishapur at the onset of puberty is related to his discovery of a telescope that fuels the voyeuristic instincts that are to remain with him throughout his life: these are 'the bitter-sweet delights of living through other human beings' (*Shame*, p. 45). As a doctor, following (like Aadam Aziz in *Midnight's Children*) the profession described as that of 'legitimized voyeur' (*Shame*, p. 49), Omar pursues an acquaintance with the brain-damaged Sufiya Zinobia, the elder daughter of Raza and Bilquìs Hyder.

Here it becomes difficult to maintain Omar's 'centrality' to his story much further, since his destiny seeps into – yet cannot but affect – the 'duel' between *Shame*'s two conflicting types of epic hero. The destinies of Raza Hyder and Iskander Harappa, a pair who in many ways foreshadow Gibreel Farishta and Saladin Chamcha, are inexorably intertwined. Harappa's political triumph precedes a fall that in turn precedes Hyder's own political ascendancy, itself to be followed by a nemesis that predates by several years the sudden death in an air crash of the historical Zia ul-Haq, who seems figured by Hyder just as the historical Zulfikar Ali Bhutto is figured by Harappa. Harappa does not meet his death by hanging – that was merely the 'official' version of events – and in this subversive allegorization of history he leaves an Amazonian daughter, Arjumand, the 'virgin Ironpants', to pick up his political mantle.

Such a necessarily brief account of *Shame* must at least indicate how the female offspring of the epic heroes Hyder and Iskander move into centre stage. There are actually three women: the younger daughter of Raza and Bilquìs, Naveed ('Good News'), is the only one to bear further progeny. Sterility (or the real) and fertility (or the fictional) are two of the opposing states of being that are constantly held before the reader: the 'wrong miracle', the birth of unintended progeny, is the motif linking seepage of one into the other. This motif suggests a host of tales that cannot be told, and supports the narrator's claim that in rejecting the temptation to write a realistic novel about Pakistan ('Just think what else I might have to put in' [*Shame*, p. 69]), he is nevertheless forced to allude to what he cannot directly relate any further: 'Every story one chooses to tell is a kind of censorship, it prevents the telling of other tales'. The narrative offers us a distilling reflection of this assertion in the fate of Naveed. She marries Talvar ul-Haq (here as elsewhere Rushdie's daring play with 'real' names is noticeable), and hangs herself during her seventh pregnancy, having borne twenty-seven children in the previous six (starting with twins and ending with septuplets).

The seepage of fiction into reality (and vice versa) is figured in many ways, as must now be clear, but one of the most interesting is an 'untranslatable' cultural concept, *takallouf*, already referred to in *Midnight's Children* but elaborated on here, and defined as a law obliging one to believe that another's words 'meant no more than they said' (*Shame*, p. 104). Worlds apart – such seems to be the claim – from Western custom, this extraordinary cultural phenomenon (whose working out is far more elaborate than any bald formulation can suggest) informs a later comment on his own fiction by this intrusive narrator:

I had thought, before I began, that what I had on my hands was an almost excessively masculine tale [. . .]. But the women seem to have taken over; they have marched in from the peripheries of the story to demand the inclusion of their own tragedies, histories and comedies, obliging me to couch my narrative in all manner of sinuous complexities, to see my 'male' plot refracted, so to speak, through the prisms of its reverse and 'female' side. [. . . . The women's] stories explain, and even subsume, the men's. Repression is a seamless garment [. . .] it turns out that my 'male' and 'female' plots are the same story, after all. [. . .]
If you hold down one thing you hold down the adjoining.

In the end, though, it all blows up in your face. (*Shame*, p. 173) [emphases Rushdie's].[17]

The apocalypse duly takes place. Omar finally returns from the periphery of narrative (as indeed does the initial setting Q., the 'mother country' from which Omar has 'escaped') to be caught up in the prospect of both a private 'consummation' of his marriage to Sufiya and the superhuman ('Beastly') strength within her, and a public political nemesis involving his parents-in-law the Hyders. Son and parents-in-law are all humiliated by the *takallouf* exhibited by Omar's mothers: later Omar, having woken from a nightmare vision in which Talvar subjects him to a bizarre trial for many of the violent crimes (often of dismemberment) that the narrative has detailed, is discovered by an excited crowd in the empty house. Deserted first by his mothers and then by the crowd as Sufiya closes in upon him in the fantastic 'womb' of Nishapur, Omar is left to await her arrival 'like a bridegroom on his wedding night'. Then she strikes:

> His body was falling away from her, a headless trunk, and after that the Beast faded in her once again, she stood there blinking stupidly, unsteady on her feet, as if she didn't know that all the stories had to end together . . . (*Shame*, p. 286).[18]

Omar's encounter with Sufiya brings about the final, irrevocable draining out of his selfhood. We recall one of the narrator's earlier declamations:

> This is a novel about Sufiya Zinobia [. . .]. Or perhaps it would be more accurate, if also more opaque, to say that Sufiya Zinobia is about this novel. (*Shame*, p. 59)

[17]The strategy of inversion is characteristic of Rushdie's non-fictional polemic, too, as the title and theme of 'Outside the Whale', *Granta* 11 (1984), pp. 123–38 (rpt. *Imaginary Homelands*, pp. 87–101), amply indicates.
[18]I have emended 'drunk'.

In the London ('Ellowen Deeowen') of the Thatcher decade, the actor of 'theologicals' Gibreel Farishta, in *The Satanic Verses*, dreams recurrently, in alternating chapters, of worlds apart in time and place. These proved the parts of the book that gave the most offence. At the same time, the 'Brown Uncle Tom' Saladin Chamcha faces problems of assimilation; in the last chapter he returns to Bombay. The city worlds of *The Satanic Verses* are even more pluralist than those of its predecessors, although Rushdie maintains his use – established in *Midnight's Children* and *Shame* – of 'double' protagonists representing opposing sets of values. Unlike Saleem's dominance over Shiva through narration in *Midnight's Children*, or the way *Shame*'s 'duelists' Hyder and Harappa contribute to the marginalization of the peripheral hero Omar, Gibreel and Saladin wrestle for supremacy over each other throughout the book, a struggle figured in the way they become entangled during their dramatic act of immigration, and metamorphose into each other once arrived in London.

The central section of *The Satanic Verses* is also its most substantial piece of narrative: 'A City Visible but Unseen'. It falls into two halves. In the first, the grotesquely metamorphosed Saladin Chamcha – formerly the immigrant Indian who aspires to become more British than the British – escapes the clutches of the police. To them he appears as a literal form of the stereotype of prejudice. Harboured by the family of Muhammad Sufyan in the rooming-house above the Shaandaar Café he eventually recovers from the goatish, diabolic proportions he has assumed on the descent from Bostan, when he and Gibreel appeared to have exchanged identities.

The two Sufyan daughters, Mishal and Anahita, are themselves symptomatic of the dilemmas of acclimatization facing Chamcha and so many of the book's other characters: the girls' response is principally one of rebellion against the parental culture rather than Chamcha's more positive gesture towards the host culture. In turn, the conflict between these teenagers and their parents' values reflects that of the two sisters Ally and Elena Cone. In each case, an elder sister's rebelliousness is outdone by a younger's promiscuity. At the time of the narrative Elena, Ally's elder and adulated sister, has died of a drug overdose; and Ally, sought after by Gibreel, is now a retired mountaineer whose fallen arches cause her at one point to be compared to the mermaid in the Hans Christian Andersen fairy-tale (a figure Rushdie has used elsewhere):

> [Gibreel] had read a Bumper Book of fairy-tales in which he found the story of the sea-woman who left the ocean and took on human form for the sake of the man she loved. She had feet instead of fins, but every step she took was an agony, as if she were walking over broken glass; yet she went on walking, forward, away from the sea and over land. You did it for a bloody mountain, he said. Would you do it for a man?[19]

As this example amply indicates, once any kind of account of the narrative of *The Satanic Verses* is begun, the strands become impossible to separate: the narrative metamorphoses, it fractures and fissures. Should one go on to mention Allie's recurrent hallucination of Maurice Wilson, the climber who had perished on Everest in 1934, contrasting him, as the narrative itself does ('There were still closed doors between them for all their physical intimacy: each kept secret a dangerous ghost' [*The Satanic Verses*, p. 304]), with Rekha Merchant, the suicide who has destroyed her children as well as herself for love of the film star Gibreel (*The Satanic Verses*, p. 15), haunting him recurrently? Or should one instead (or in addition) be reminded of Mahound climbing Everest/Mount Cone for revelation from the 'real' Gibreel? Or should one dwell on the particular manner of the suicides of Otto Cone, Allie's father, and Rekha: each has jumped to death – and then recall the book's beginning ('To be

[19]Salman Rushdie, *The Satanic Verses* (London: Viking, 1988), p. 197. Further references to this edition in the text above.

born again [. . .] first you have to die'), in which Gibreel and Chamcha have defied the odds (if indeed they have) in falling from the height of Everest and apparently surviving? It turns out that there are many ways of telling the same story: in the words of the recurrent formula: 'It was so, it was not, in a time long forgot' (*The Satanic Verses*, pp. 143, 544 and the various reflections in which this formula occurs elsewhere).

In the multiple narratives making up *The Satanic Verses* the concept of an infinite recession of reflections is pushed as far, surely, as it can be, for the limits of human existence itself are probed. Who are the dead and who the living in this book? There are ghosts who are just as alive as those they haunt. One might have in mind the cities of Provan and Unthank in Alasdair Gray's *Lanark* in asking whether 'Ellowen Deeowen' or the 'City Visible but Unseen' are more or less 'real' than Jahilia, the city made of sand, in which the subversive actions and roles are to wash or to be a water-carrier.[20] Or, another way of asking the same question, who is the dreamer and who the dream? Does Gibreel dream Mahound or does Mahound dream Gibreel?

> But when he has rested he enters a different sort of sleep, a sort of not-sleep, the condition that he calls his *listening*, and he feels a dragging pain in the gut, like something trying to be born, and now Gibreel, who has been hovering-above-looking-down, feels a confusion, *who am I*, in these moments it begins to seem that the archangel is actually *inside the Prophet*, I am the dragging in the gut, I am the angel being extruded from the sleeper's navel, I emerge, Gibreel Farishta, while my other self, Mahound, lies *listening*, entranced, I am bound to him, navel to navel, by a shining cord of light, not possible to say which of us is dreaming the other. We flow in both directions along the umbilical cord. (*The Satanic Verses*, p. 110; emphases Rushdie's)

[20]For discussion of the 'fundamentalist' senses of the place-name 'Jahilia', see Ruthven, *Satanic Affair*, pp. 40–41.

To perceive these mirror images of each other, to perceive, too, the structure of *The Satanic Verses* as a series of bravura performances – the odd-numbered chapters offer a frame-story whose 'now' is inserted into the 'then' of the even-numbered dream chapters – allows us to see in those dovetailed narratives countless echoes ranging from turns of phrase to quite complex structural motifs, echoes that we pick up from the framing, odd-numbered chapters. Here, unlike the case in *Midnight's Children*, the chapters are not pickled apart but flow into and out of each other: the formal onslaught discernible in the earlier book cannot be detected here. The amorphous sand of Jahilia consists, like all sand, of a silicon compound; its potential is and is not picked up in the name ('Mount Cone') given to Everest, as well as the anglicization of the Polish Cohen (Cone) in Allie's family (contrast the way Chamcha has anglicized his name so that it ironically comes to mean a 'spoony' or 'toady');[21] silicon, a component of glass, reminds us not only of the allusion in Allie's fallen arches to the sea-woman who appears to walk on glass, but to Saladin's recurrent nightmare of a woman whose skin has turned to glass: there is persistent allusion to the djinn or genie emerging from the glass lamp once rubbed. The motif of the sea-woman walking on land that feels like glass is itself inverted in the narrative of the Parting of the Arabian Sea,[22] in which, in one of the most stunning cadences in the entire book, the theme of revelation (true or false? it was so, it was not so) is held before us: '[o]n the last night of his life' (*The Satanic Verses*, p. 506) Ayesha the butterfly girl fails to win the doubting, sceptic, Westernized Mirza Saeed (he is closed) but yet succeeds (he is opened). It is thus actually Mirza's own body that becomes the 'privileged arena' for what we must assume is the revelation itself, a revelation that simultaneously brings life and death:

[21]Ruthven, *Satanic Affair*, pp. 16ff., is informative on this aspect of the novel, as well as on some of its sources in recent history.
[22]According to Ruthven, *Satanic Affair*, this passage reworks an historical episode that took place in Karachi in February 1983 (pp. 45–46).

He was a fortress with clanging gates. – He was drowning. – She was drowning too. He saw the water fill her mouth, heard it begin to gurgle into her lungs. Then something within him refused that, made a different choice, and at the instant that his heart broke, he opened.

His body split apart from his adam's-apple to his groin, so that she could reach deep within him, and now she was open, they all were, and at the moment of their opening the waters parted, and they walked to Mecca across the bed of the Arabian Sea. (*The Satanic Verses*, p. 507)

And so on: insomnia and nightmare, dream and reality, continually metamorphose into and out of each other. In this way, what happens to Gibreel and Chamcha is not an isolated spectacle (however spectacular the book's opening) but absolutely integral to those many ways of telling that comprise *The Satanic Verses*' way of telling. The lives of Gibreel and Chamcha, in all their experiential and dreamlike richness, show us, as ours teach us, who they and we are: the book cannot be read as an insult to Islam because, in being the 'privileged arena' that it is, it does not assert offence to any orthodoxy, which is to say with Carlos Fuentes that 'no one is absolutely right'.[23]

Haroun and the Sea of Stories (1990) has been read as a children's tale, and as an allegory of the fate to which Rushdie himself has been subjected. I would like to consider it briefly on the level of a story about telling stories, in the light of what I have been trying to argue about the ways in which the literal and the figurative can be subject to seepage.

I'll concentrate briefly on one distilling episode, that of Mudra the Warrior and his Shadow. Haroun and his father Rashid the Story-Teller, the Ocean of Notions, the Shah of Blah (as he is known to his friends and enemies respectively) have arrived on

[23]This said, the reader is once more referred to Malise Ruthven, *Satanic Affair*, for sensitive and informed commentary that sheds the kind of light the Western reader needs on the opposite view.

the imaginary moon Kahani ('Story') on a quest to clean up the pollution by Khattam-Shud ('Silence') of the Sea of Stories. The people of Gup ('chatter') are at war with those of Chup ('suppression'). Mudra is a 'good' Chupwala, a virtuous and selfless member of the realm of silence:

> As he watched the Shadow Warrior's martial dance, Haroun thought about this strange adventure in which he had become involved. 'How many opposites are at war in this battle between Gup and Chup!' he marvelled. 'Gup is bright and Chup is dark. Gup is warm and Chup is freezing cold. Gup is all chattering and noise, whereas Chup is silent as a shadow. Guppees love the Ocean, Chupwalas try to poison it. Guppees love Stories, and Speech; Chupwalas, it seems, hate these things just as strongly. [. . .] But it's not as simple as that,' he told himself, because the dance of the Shadow Warrior showed him that silence had its own grace and beauty (just as speech could be graceless and ugly); and that Action could be as noble as Words . . .[24]

Rashid, Haroun's father, interprets Mudra's language of gesture:

> 'Khattam-Shud [. . .] has plunged so deeply into the Dark Art of sorcery that he has become Shadowy himself – changeable, dark, more like a Shadow than a Person. And as he has come to be more Shadowy, so his Shadow has come to be more like a Person. And the point has come at which it's no longer possible to tell which is Khattam-Shud's Shadow and which his substantial Self – because he has done what no other Chupwala has ever dreamt of – that is, he has separated himself from his Shadow! He goes about in the darkness, entirely Shadowless, and his Shadow goes wherever it wishes. *The Cultmaster Khattam-Shud can be in two places at once!*' (*Haroun and the Sea of Stories*, p. 133; emphases Rushdie's)

[24]Salman Rushdie, *Haroun and the Sea of Stories* (London: Granta, 1990), p. 125. Further references in the text to this edition.

Here is the ultimate instance of paradox, in that Khattam-Shud's deceptive treachery, the only means available to him of holding on to the Power he needs to survive, has been achieved by an act of imaginative, creative assertion. He is Silence, the last word, but sustains himself through the means required to invent a Story. In contrast, we have Haroun's reflection on the climax to Mudra's dance:

> Mudra's Shadow [went] into a positive frenzy of changes, growing enormous, scratching itself all over, turning into the silhouette of a flame-breathing dragon, and then into other creatures: a gryphon, a basilisk, a manticore, a troll. And while the Shadow behaved in this agitated fashion, Mudra himself retreated a few steps, leant on a tree-stump and pretended to have grown very bored indeed, examining his fingernails, yawning, twiddling his thumbs. 'This Warrior and his Shadow are a fine team,' Haroun thought. 'They put on opposite acts, so nobody knows what they really feel; which may of course be a third thing completely.' (*Haroun and the Sea of Stories*, pp. 134–35)

Here, whatever it is that this 'third thing' is, remains obscure, inscrutable, genuinely shadowy: it is the 'privileged arena' of confrontation between the literal and its figure, the Warrior and his Shadow, an object and what it mirrors.

The Moor's Last Sigh is a huge, wheeling circular narrative that seemed to many of its readers to mark a return to the bravura of *Midnight's Children*. A family chronicle recounting the destiny of the da Gama-Zogoiby dynasty (covering the sweep of the entire twentieth century), which has made its fortune from spices, *The Moor's Last Sigh* begins and ends in the immediate future 'in the Andalusian mountain-village of Benengeli'.[25]

[25]Salman Rushdie, *The Moor's Last Sigh* (London: Cape, 1995), pp. 3, 419. Further references in the text to this edition.

The title is several things, ranging from a stolen picture painted by the narrator's dominating mother, Aurora da Gama – with whom the thief, Vasco Miranda, is obsessed – to what is now a desolate gas station, El Ultimo Súspiro – alleged to be the site at which the sultan Boabdil cast his final glance at the city of Granada, from which he was expelled in 1492 ('*Well may you weep like a woman for what you could not defend like a man*' – italics Rushdie's – is a recurring motif). In typically Rushdiean fashion, the colonial significance of 1492 is blended with the allusion to Vasco da Gama's slightly earlier voyages from Portugal to India, and the narrator Moraes Zogoiby is meshed, through the names of his family on the distaff side and of the man (the thieving colonizer?) obsessed by Moraes' mother (the most controversial of India's assassinated Prime Ministers?), into the entire history of the relatively independent state of Cochin in Portuguese India.

As a result, the emphasis of *The Moor's Last Sigh* shifts away from Islam (contrast *Shame* and *The Satanic Verses*) to a Bombay in which hybridity of religion (Judaism, Catholicism, Hinduism) and race (Portuguese, British, Indian) is celebrated with a vigour remarkable even by Rushdie's standards. The novel is as satirical as its predecessors yet more benign; the period encompassing the lives of Moraes ('Moor') and his three elder sisters, 'Ina' (Christina), 'Minnie' (Inamorata) and 'Mynah' (Philomena) – the entire family's nicknames making up a playground jingle passed down orally through generations of English-speaking children – is the post-Independence era from Jahawarlal Nehru through the Emergency to the deaths of Indira Ghandi and both her sons.

There is an extraordinary garrulousness about Moraes' narrative performance that is coupled with his living life in 'fast forward', at twice the normal biological rate, and disintegrating like a radioactive compound with a limited 'half-life'. This desperation leads to the need for total inclusiveness: all possible allusions – literary, filmic (both Hollywood and 'Bollywood') and historical – have to be got in. Among countless riches are references to *Othello*, *Alice in Wonderland*, *A Passage to India* (the names Malabar and Fielding recur), *The Wizard of Oz*, even *Midnight's Children* itself, when at one point Moraes' adoptive brother metamorphoses into the composite figure 'Aadam Sinai' (*Moor's Last Sigh*, p. 358).

In *The Moor's Last Sigh* Rushdie not only celebrates the qualities of hybridity and mongrelization that he claimed in defence of *The Satanic Verses*: like Dora Chance in Angela Carter's *Wise Children*, he performs as the 'high-born cross-breed' he claims to be (*Moor's Last Sigh*, p. 5). Just as Marina Warner's *Indigo* is fed by a taste for sugar, so spices and above all pepper, 'the Black Gold of Malabar' (*Moor's Last Sigh*, p. 375), are the traded condiments. Rushdie's post-colonial garrulousness actually gives off sexual heat. In an admission reminding us of the attractiveness of 'Oliver's riffs' in Julian Barnes's *Talking It Over*, Moraes confesses at one point that:

> . . . gabbiness [. . .] to this day retains, for me, a powerful erotic charge. When I chatter on, or am assailed by the garrulity of others, I find it – how-to-say? – arousing. Often, in the heat of *bavardage*, I must place my hands on my lap to conceal the movements there from the eyes of my companions, who would be puzzled by such arousal; or, more probably, amused. (*Moor's Last Sigh*, p. 191)

A constant chattering punning voice performatively lights up the places that traditional stories have allowed to remain hidden, and gives voices to those presences that have been silenced. In all its socially, genetically and geographically hybrid complexity, *The Moor's Last Sigh* is a novel for our times, a quintessential achievement as fiction in Britain approaches the new century and the new millennium.

It is not surprising, then, that *The Moor's Last Sigh* was the first ever odds-on favourite to win the Booker Prize. Yet it failed to do so. I want to use my conclusion to offer some thoughts on the general astonishment, and to suggest why the Booker Prize, like Rushdie's fiction as well as serious literary fiction in Britain generally, may be nevertheless considered in good health today.

Conclusion

Salman Rushdie's *The Moor's Last Sigh*, the clear favourite to win the 1995 Booker Prize, failed to do so. In failing to do so Rushdie also failed (as he had failed in 1983 and 1988) to win the Booker Prize twice. The feat remains unachieved, and as long as it does so, an important piece of Booker mythology will prevail.

Little attention was paid to Barry Unsworth's presence on the shortlist, presumably because although he had also won the Prize before, that was in 1992, the year of the shared award with Michael Ondaatje. Although ten previously shortlisted novelists have gone on to win the Booker Prize in its history since 1969,[1] it is rarer to find previous winners appearing on subsequent shortlists. Apart from Unsworth and Rushdie, only three other outright winners have managed this accomplishment. But there has never been such intense speculation that history might really be about to be made by Salman Rushdie in 1995.

The intensity of this speculation is indicative of the transformation the Booker has undergone since the Golding–Burgess two-horse race of 1980 and the Rushdie triumph over Thomas in 1981. Bernice Rubens had won the Prize in 1970 and was shortlisted again in 1978, before the Booker had captured the

[1] They are: Iris Murdoch (shortlisted in 1969, 1970, 1973 and winner in 1978); Thomas Keneally (1972, 1975, 1979 and winner in 1982); Kingsley Amis (1974, winner in 1986); Penelope Lively (1977, winner in 1987); Penelope Fitzgerald (1978, winner in 1979); Barry Unsworth (1980, joint winner in 1992); Peter Carey (1985, winner in 1988); Kazuo Ishiguro (1986, winner in 1989); Roddy Doyle (1991, winner in 1993); and James Kelman (1989, winner in 1994).

public imagination; the same can be said of V. S. Naipaul, who had won in 1971 and was shortlisted in 1979. Although the 1978 winner, Iris Murdoch, was shortlisted twice more, in 1985 and 1987, no one really thought it conceivable that she would win in either of those years; likewise the 1979 winner, Penelope Fitzgerald, who was also shortlisted twice more, in 1988 and 1990. But Rushdie, in 1983, 1988 and 1995, seems to have been a different case. Part of the explanation is attributable to generation: the average age of winners and indeed shortlisted writers has been dropping slightly but steadily since 1980. In addition, as we saw in the first section of this book, both winners and shortlisted writers have been drawn, increasingly, from a much more culturally plural fund. The nature of this fund raises fascinating implications about what it is to be a novelist in Britain in 1995, and I want to close with some reflections on this point.

We have discussed in the first section above the nature of Britain's postcolonial inheritance, and the ways in which the energy once perceived as emanating from the centre and being diffused outwards to what was once the Empire has now been reversed, and directed in from those various peripheries to a largely hollow centre. This paradigm needs a certain nuancing, however, and I'll take up two issues briefly here.

Firstly, it should not of course be assumed that all the culturally pluralist fiction in Britain today, some of which we have discussed above, is by definition 'postcolonial'. Kazuo Ishiguro, born in Nagasaki in 1954 of Japanese parentage, came to Britain at the age of six. His third novel, *The Remains of the Day*, won the 1989 Booker Prize. Tibor Fischer, who was shortlisted in 1993 with *Under the Frog* and in the same year included in *Granta*'s 'Best of Young British Novelists 2', was born in Stockport in 1959 to Hungarian parents who, as professional basketball players, had emigrated to England in 1956, the year of the Hungarian uprising. The mothers of Marina Warner (shortlisted in 1988 with *The Lost Father*) and Michèle Roberts (shortlisted in 1992 with *Daughters of the House*) are Italian and French respectively.

All these British novelists and many more partake (as their work reveals) in more than one culture: their 'non-Britishness' has nothing to do with the nation's collective imperial history[2] but arises instead from private decisions taken by their parents (sometimes out of political necessity, admittedly; perhaps more often from personal and/or professional motivation). Naturally, none of this is in itself new (we may think not only of Joseph Conrad [1857–1924] but of a rich diaspora resulting from more recent European upheavals, to say nothing of Anglo-American writers from Henry James [1843–1916] onwards), but the kinds of attention we pay to cultural interminglings that are other than postcolonial in nature do represent a change that parallels the other changes this book has attempted to document.

Secondly, it would be improper to suggest that the former imperial centre is 'hollow' without taking account of the many ways in which 'Englishness' in fiction has become more self-confidently regional during the 1980s and 1990s. My chapter on Scotland and my remarks on Ireland demonstrate that the term 'British' when used of the British Isles is a complex one. My chapter on London was intended to throw a shaft of light on metropolitan writing that I regard as uniquely characteristic of the 1980s and 1990s. In discussing A. S. Byatt, Graham Swift and Julian Barnes, I wanted to show something of the vigour of Englishness in fiction today.

The 1995 Booker winner, Pat Barker's *The Ghost Road*, offers us a vantage point from which to survey the immensely maturing distance English fiction – or, rather, the public perception of English fiction – has travelled during the 1980s and 1990s. The argument of this book leads inexorably to the suggestion that the entrepreneurial 1980s and 1990s have proved to be an era in which writers are aware of each other's work in ways that may well be without precedent in the history of fiction in Britain.

Perhaps it is fitting that Pat Barker's writing was honoured

[2]The rather exceptional case of Marina Warner, however, is discussed in Chapter 6 above.

in a year that saw yet another astonishing performance by Salman Rushdie. Barker began her career in the early 1980s as a skilful practitioner of a distinctly regional social realism. The area in which her earliest work is set is the North-East of England. During the later 1980s the social realism was enhanced by an extension into a twentieth century that was less contemporaneous, and by something that one might term a singularly English form of magical realism. Thus *The Man Who Wasn't There* (1988), set in the early 1940s, contrives to explore through the sharply streetwise consciousness of the twelve-year-old Colin Harper the areas in which fantasy and reality adjoin and interfold, as Colin begins an increasingly sinister search for his missing father, the man who wasn't there.

With *The Ghost Road* Barker completed a trilogy distanced still further from the present, and intermixed with yet another ingredient. The spatial setting of the trilogy is regionally more diffuse not only because of its setting in time (the closing years of the First World War), but because of its astonishingly daring play with a mixture of real (that is 'historically attested') and fictional characters and episodes. We, the posterity who read the trilogy, know what happened to the poets Siegfried Sassoon and Wilfred Owen, and to the equally historical army psychologist W. H. R. Rivers, who is treating cases of severe shell-shock. We do not know, until laying the book down, what will happen to the fictional Billy Prior. Barker's achievement is to weave the historically recorded, privileged, listened-to voices, and the fictional, marginalized, unheard voices into a seamless narrative. In it the terrifying variety of traumatic experience, and the astonishingly diverse range of behavioural dysfunction it induces, together contrive to suggest something of the dimensions an English 'magical realism' might achieve.

Of course it would be foolish to try to argue that Barker's work could not have been produced had not the 1980s and 1990s seen such a heterogeneity of fictional voices in Britain. But that heterogeneity can be seen as a part of the atmosphere created by the way in which the Booker Prize and its shortlist have captured the imagination of the consumer of serious literary fiction in Britain, and by the role other prizes have since come to play as a result of that development. That atmosphere has become enriched in turn by an admixture of a 'meet the author' culture that has benefited from redefinition of the roles, not just of author and publisher, but of so many other parties involved in the book trade: agents, publicists, booksellers, reviewers and even academics.

Insight into the richness and variety of serious literary fiction in the 1980s and the 1990s thus absolutely depends on our willingness to recognize the presence of the mechanisms by which – at so many different levels simultaneously – we now consume that fiction. Possessed of this willingness, we will be positioned to discern, and perhaps to marvel at, the extraordinary energy that has transformed serious literary fiction in Britain into a truly global literature since the Booker Prize first really attracted public attention back in the early 1980s.

Appendix A

Booker shortlists and winners 1980–95

The winner appears first in **bold**; the rest of the shortlist in alphabetical order by author. Six titles appear on the complete list in each year except 1995 (five), 1981 (seven) and 1980 (seven). There were two (joint) winners in 1992. Publishers are given in parentheses; the place of publication is London unless otherwise stated.

1995:   **Pat Barker, *The Ghost Road* (Viking)**
          Justin Cartwright, *In Every Face I Meet* (Sceptre)
          Salman Rushdie, *The Moor's Last Sigh* (Jonathan Cape)
          Barry Unsworth, *Morality Play* (Hamish Hamilton)
          Tim Winton, *The Riders* (Picador)
1994:   **James Kelman, *How Late It Was, How Late* (Secker & Warburg)**
          Romesh Gunesekera, *Reef* (Granta)
          Abdulrazak Gurnah, *Paradise* (Hamish Hamilton)
          Alan Hollinghurst, *The Folding Star* (Chatto & Windus)
          George Mackay Brown, *Beside the Ocean of Time* (John Murray)
          Jill Paton Walsh, *Knowledge of Angels* (Cambridge: Green Bay)
1993:   **Roddy Doyle, *Paddy Clarke Ha Ha Ha* (Secker & Warburg)**
          Tibor Fischer, *Under the Frog* (Polygon)
          Michael Ignatieff, *Scar Tissue* (Chatto & Windus)
          David Malouf, *Remembering Babylon* (Chatto & Windus)
          Caryl Phillips, *Crossing the River* (Bloomsbury)
          Carol Shields, *The Stone Diaries* (Fourth Estate)

1992:   Michael Ondaatje, *The English Patient* (Bloomsbury)
        Barry Unsworth, *Sacred Hunger* (Hamish Hamilton)
        Christopher Hope, *Serenity House* (Macmillan)
        Patrick McCabe, *The Butcher Boy* (Picador)
        Ian McEwan, *Black Dogs* (Jonathan Cape)
        Michèle Roberts, *Daughters of the House* (Virago)
1991:   **Ben Okri, *The Famished Road* (Jonathan Cape)**
        Martin Amis, *Time's Arrow* (Jonathan Cape)
        Roddy Doyle, *The Van* (Secker & Warburg)
        Rohinton Mistry, *Such a Long Journey* (Faber & Faber)
        Timothy Mo, *The Redundancy of Courage* (Chatto &
        Windus)
        William Trevor, *Reading Turgenev* (from *Two Lives*) (Viking)
1990:   **A. S. Byatt, *Possession* (Chatto & Windus)**
        Beryl Bainbridge, *An Awfully Big Adventure* (Duckworth)
        Penelope Fitzgerald, *The Gate of Angels* (Collins)
        John McGahern, *Amongst Women* (Faber & Faber)
        Brian Moore, *Lies of Silence* (Bloomsbury)
        Mordecai Richler, *Solomon Gursky Was Here* (Chatto &
        Windus)
1989:   **Kazuo Ishiguro, *The Remains of the Day* (Faber &
        Faber)**
        Margaret Atwood, *Cat's Eye* (Bloomsbury)
        John Banville, *The Book of Evidence* (Secker & Warburg)
        Sybille Bedford, *Jigsaw* (Hamish Hamilton)
        James Kelman, *A Disaffection* (Secker & Warburg)
        Rose Tremain, *Restoration* (Hamish Hamilton)
1988:   **Peter Carey, *Oscar and Lucinda* (Faber & Faber)**
        Bruce Chatwin, *Utz* (Jonathan Cape)
        Penelope Fitzgerald, *The Beginning of Spring* (Collins)
        David Lodge, *Nice Work* (Secker & Warburg)
        Salman Rushdie, *The Satanic Verses* (Viking)
        Marina Warner, *The Lost Father* (Chatto & Windus)
1987:   **Penelope Lively, *Moon Tiger* (André Deutsch)**
        Chinua Achebe, *Anthills of the Savannah* (William
        Heinemann)
        Peter Ackroyd, *Chatterton* (Hamish Hamilton)
        Nina Bawden, *Circles of Deceit* (Macmillan)
        Brian Moore, *The Colour of Blood* (Jonathan Cape)

Iris Murdoch, *The Book and the Brotherhood* (Chatto & Windus)

1986: **Kingsley Amis, *The Old Devils* (Hutchinson)**
Margaret Atwood, *The Handmaid's Tale* (Jonathan Cape)
Paul Bailey, *Gabriel's Lament* (Jonathan Cape)
Robertson Davies, *What's Bred in the Bone* (Viking)
Kazuo Ishiguro, *An Artist of the Floating World* (Faber & Faber)
Timothy Mo, *An Insular Possession* (Chatto & Windus)

1985: **Keri Hulme, *The Bone People* (Hodder & Stoughton)**
Peter Carey, *Illywhacker* (Faber & Faber)
J. L. Carr, *The Battle of Pollocks Crossing* (Viking)
Doris Lessing, *The Good Terrorist* (Jonathan Cape)
Jan Morris, *Last Letters from Hav* (Viking)
Iris Murdoch, *The Good Apprentice* (Chatto & Windus)

1984: **Anita Brookner, *Hotel du Lac* (Jonathan Cape)**
J. G. Ballard, *Empire of the Sun* (Victor Gollancz)
Julian Barnes, *Flaubert's Parrot* (Jonathan Cape)
Anita Desai, *In Custody* (William Heinemann)
Penelope Lively, *According to Mark* (William Heinemann)
David Lodge, *Small World* (Secker & Warburg)

1983: **J. M. Coetzee, *Life & Times of Michael K* (Secker & Warburg)**
Malcolm Bradbury, *Rates of Exchange* (Secker & Warburg)
John Fuller, *Flying to Nowhere* (Salamander)
Anita Mason, *The Illusionist* (Hamish Hamilton)
Salman Rushdie, *Shame* (Jonathan Cape)
Graham Swift, *Waterland* (William Heinemann)

1982: **Thomas Keneally, *Schindler's Ark* [US title: *Schindler's List*] (Hodder & Stoughton)**
John Arden, *Silence Among the Weapons* (Methuen)
William Boyd, *An Ice-Cream War* (Hamish Hamilton)
Lawrence Durrell, *Constance or Solitary Practices* (Faber & Faber)
Alice Thomas Ellis, *The 27th Kingdom* (Duckworth)
Timothy Mo, *Sour Sweet* (André Deutsch)

1981: **Salman Rushdie, *Midnight's Children* (Jonathan Cape)***
Molly Keane, *Good Behaviour* (André Deutsch)
Doris Lessing, *The Sirian Experiments* (Jonathan Cape)

Ian McEwan, *The Comfort of Strangers* (Jonathan Cape)
Ann Schlee, *Rhine Journey* (Macmillan)
Muriel Spark, *Loitering with Intent* (Bodley Head)
D. M. Thomas, *The White Hotel* (Victor Gollancz)

1980: **William Golding, *Rites of Passage* (Faber & Faber)**
Anthony Burgess, *Earthly Powers* (Hutchinson)
Anita Desai, *Clear Light of Day* (William Heinemann)
Alice Munro, *The Beggar Maid* (Allen Lane)
Julia O'Faolain, *No Country for Young Men* (Allen Lane)
Barry Unsworth, *Pascali's Island* (Michael Joseph)
J. L. Carr, *A Month in the Country* (Brighton: Harvester)

Source: Book Trust

---

* In 1993 *Midnight's Children* was chosen by three former Chairs – Malcolm Bradbury (1981), David Holloway (1970) and W. L. Webb (1969) – as the 'Booker of Bookers' (that is, the best of the previous winners going all the way back to 1969) to mark the twenty-fifth anniversary of the Booker Prize.

Appendix B

Literary novels appearing in Alex Hamilton's annual list of the top hundred paperback 'fastsellers' since 1982

These lists have been compiled annually by Alex Hamilton between 1979 and 1996. In 1982, for the first time, a paperback reprint of the previous year's Booker Prize winner, in this case Salman Rushdie's *Midnight's Children*, made it into Hamilton's top hundred, selling over 100,000 copies within one year.

The Booker winner achieved this feat in every year to 1994, with the exception of J. M. Coetzee's *Life & Times of Michael K* in 1984 and the 1992 joint winner Barry Unsworth's *Sacred Hunger* (although Unsworth's paperback sales apparently exceeded 80,000 in 1993; the title was also a Waterstone's Book of the Month). Similarly James Kelman's *How Late It Was, How Late* fell short in 1995. Titles are given in descending order of total sales volume (both home and export), followed in parentheses by the ordinal number on the list of 100 and total sales in the calendar year in question. Every author listed here is mentioned in the main part of this book.

It must be stressed that Hamilton does not include a title twice, so that total *aggregate* paperback sales can, as Hamilton has more than once shown, rise substantially over the following years. By the end of 1988, for instance, *Midnight's Children* had exceeded 400,000 (seven years after publication) and *The Empire of the Sun* 550,000 (four years after) (*Guardian*, 13 January 1989, p. 23).

These very succinct versions of Hamilton's listings show how subsequent titles by certain writers (Barnes, Boyd, Brookner) can capitalize on earlier Booker notice. Names also enter the list with titles that have been expected to be shortlisted but have failed to do so (Amis in 1990, McEwan in 1991). Murdoch's success with

Nuns and Soldiers in 1982 (the book was published in hardback in 1980) seems consistent with the longer shelf life of her paperback fiction during the 1970s. The reprint of the Booker-winning *The Sea, The Sea* does not appear to have exceeded 100,000 in the first year of paperback publication, nor did those of either of the novels with which she was actually shortlisted in 1985 and 1987. Graham Greene's continued commercial standing in the 1980s also gains context from these lists.

The only Booker winners to have exceeded 250,000 in the first year of paperback publication were Roddy Doyle in 1994, A. S. Byatt in 1991, and Thomas Keneally in 1983 (leaving aside the phenomenal success of the Keneally film tie-in in 1994). Since 1982 the only Booker-shortlisted authors to have exceeded 250,000 in the first year of paperback publication were David Lodge in 1989, J. G. Ballard in 1985, and D. M. Thomas in 1982.

The reader may also be able to trace the impact of the Waterstone's Book of the Month initiative in the 1990s. That phenomenon is discussed more fully in Chapter 3 above. In 1994 twice as many Books of the Month were novels than was the case in 1995. Moreover one of the fiction titles on the 1995 Book of the Month list (William Trevor's *Felicia's Journey*) appeared in both hardback and paperback in 1995, and another (Salman Rushdie's *The Moor's Last Sigh*) only in hardback. In paperback, both the Rushdie title and the 1995 Booker winner, Pat Barker's *The Ghost Road*, will certainly make it on to the 1996 fastseller list.

1995   Irvine Welsh, *Trainspotting* (72nd; 134,223)
1994   †Thomas Keneally, *Schindler's List* (2nd; 873,716)
       *§Roddy Doyle, *Paddy Clarke Ha Ha Ha* (20th; 354,017)
       §Vikram Seth, *A Suitable Boy* (22nd; 332,869)
       §Sebastian Faulks, *Birdsong* (47th; 175,961)
       §Iain Banks, *Complicity* (62nd; 139,165)
       §Elizabeth Jane Howard, *Confusion* (75th; 121,658)
       §William Boyd, *The Blue Afternoon* (92nd; 110,017)
1993   **§Michael Ondaatje, *The English Patient* (64th; 141, 672)
       Iain Banks, *The Crow Road* (89th; 110,779)
1992   *§Ben Okri, *The Famished Road* (37th, 187,416)

David Lodge, *Paradise News* (41st; 173,522)
§Julian Barnes, *Talking It Over* (71st; 117,212)
¶§Roddy Doyle, *The Van* (88th; 103,354)
§Angela Carter, *Wise Children* (94th; 100,966)

1991 *A. S. Byatt, *Possession* (26th; 253,921)
William Boyd, *Brazzaville Beach* (62nd; 138,931)
Ian McEwan, *The Innocent* (79th; 116,759)

1990 Julian Barnes, *A History of the World in 10½ Chapters* (36th; 231,710)
*Kazuo Ishiguro, *The Remains of the Day* (42nd; 205,804)
Martin Amis, *London Fields* (46th; 194,860)
‡Bruce Chatwin, *What Am I Doing Here?* (90th; 116,596)
Margaret Drabble, *A Natural Curiosity* (94th; 112,781)
Fay Weldon, *The Cloning of Joanna May* (100th; 105,950)

1989 ¶David Lodge, *Nice Work* (29th; 284,079)
*Peter Carey, *Oscar and Lucinda* (72nd; 143,344)
Anita Brookner, *Latecomers* (96th; 118,439)

1988 Margaret Drabble, *The Radiant Way* (53rd; 162,242)
*Penelope Lively, *Moon Tiger* (55th; 155,477)
Fay Weldon, *The Hearts and Lives of Men* (93rd; 111,832)

1987 *Kingsley Amis, *The Old Devils* (40th; 190,563)
Anita Brookner, *A Misalliance* (97th; 104,786)

1986 John Fowles, *A Maggot* (56th; 146,933)
Anita Brookner, *Family and Friends* (63rd; 129,880)
Graham Greene, *The Tenth Man* (68th; 126,000)
*Keri Hulme, *The Bone People* (79th; 116,674)

1985 ¶J. G. Ballard, *Empire of the Sun* (26th; 329,583)
*Anita Brookner, *Hotel du Lac* (43rd; 221,072)

1984 Graham Greene, *Monsigneur Quixote* (69th; 154,563)
*Salman Rushdie, *Shame* (82nd; 136,990)

1983 *Thomas Keneally, *Schindler's Ark* (27th; 307,911)
¶William Boyd, *An Ice-Cream War* (89th; 115,580)

1982 ¶D. M. Thomas, *The White Hotel* (29th; 263,220)
*Salman Rushdie, *Midnight's Children* (57th, 172,325)
Iris Murdoch, *Nuns and Soldiers* (93rd; 105,211)

Legend:
*Previous year's Booker winner (**joint winner)
¶Previous year's Booker shortlist
§Waterstone's Book of the Month
†Film tie-in of *Schindler's Ark*, the 1983 Booker winner
‡Posthumously collected memoir

Select Bibliography

This is in three parts: (a) novels discussed, however briefly: in each case, reference is to first (usually hardback) publication, and is not necessarily the imprint quoted from in this book; (b) substantial critical and/or analytical works; either books, or articles collected in book form; (c) uncollected articles and substantial reviews. Only works actually cited or drawn upon are included.

(a) Novels

Chinua Achebe (1930)
Anthills of the Savannah (London: William Heinemann, 1987)

Peter Ackroyd (1949)
The Great Fire of London (London: Hamish Hamilton, 1982)
Hawksmoor (London: Hamish Hamilton, 1985)
Chatterton (London: Hamish Hamilton, 1987)
First Light (London: Hamish Hamilton, 1989)
The House of Doctor Dee (London: Hamish Hamilton, 1993)
Dan Leno and the Limehouse Golem (London: Sinclair-Stevenson, 1994)

Fred D'Aguiar (1957)
The Longest Memory (London: Chatto & Windus, 1994)

Kingsley Amis (1922–95)
The Alteration (London: Jonathan Cape, 1976)
The Old Devils (London: Jonathan Cape, 1986)

Martin Amis (1949)
The Rachel Papers (London: Jonathan Cape, 1973)
Other People: A Mystery Story (London: Jonathan Cape, 1981)
Money: A Suicide Note (London: Jonathan Cape, 1984)
London Fields (London: Jonathan Cape, 1989)
Time's Arrow (London: Jonathan Cape, 1991)
The Information (London: HarperCollins, 1995)

Margaret Atwood (1939)
The Handmaid's Tale (London: Jonathan Cape, 1986)
Cat's Eye (London: Bloomsbury, 1989)

Paul Bailey (1937)
Gabriel's Lament (London: Jonathan Cape, 1986)

J. G. Ballard (1930)
The Empire of the Sun (London: Gollancz, 1984)

Iain Banks (1954)
The Wasp Factory (London: Macmillan, 1984)
The Bridge (London: Macmillan, 1986)
The Crow Road (London: Scribner's, 1992)
Complicity (London: Little, Brown, 1993)

John Banville (1945)
The Book of Evidence (London: Secker 1989)

Pat Barker (1943)
The Man Who Wasn't There (London: Virago, 1989)
Regeneration (London: Viking, 1991)
The Eye in the Door (London: Viking, 1993)
The Ghost Road (London: Viking, 1995)

**Julian Barnes (1946) [also, between 1980 and 1987, published
    detective fiction under the pseudonym Dan Kavanagh]**
Metroland (London: Jonathan Cape, 1980)
Before She Met Me (London: Jonathan Cape, 1982)
Flaubert's Parrot (London: Jonathan Cape, 1984)
Staring at the Sun (London: Jonathan Cape, 1986)
A History of the World in 10½ Chapters (London: Jonathan
    Cape, 1989)
Talking It Over (London: Jonathan Cape, 1991)

The Porcupine (London: Jonathan Cape, 1992)
See also Dan Kavanagh, *The Duffy Omnibus* (London: Penguin, 1991), comprising *Duffy* (1980), *Fiddle City* (1981), *Putting the Boot In* (1985) and *Going to the Dogs* (1987) [these four novels originally published by Jonathan Cape]

William Boyd (1952)
An Ice-Cream War (London: Hamish Hamilton, 1982)
The New Confessions (London: Hamish Hamilton, 1987)
Brazzaville Beach (London: Sinclair-Stevenson, 1990)
The Blue Afternoon (London: Sinclair-Stevenson, 1993)

Anita Brookner (1928)
Hotel du Lac (London: Jonathan Cape, 1984)
Family and Friends (London: Jonathan Cape, 1985)
A Misalliance (London: Jonathan Cape, 1986)

Anthony Burgess (1917–93)
Earthly Powers (London: Hutchinson, 1980)

A. S. Byatt (1936)
Shadow of a Sun (London: Chatto & Windus, 1964)
The Game (London: Chatto & Windus, 1967)
The Virgin in the Garden (London: Chatto & Windus, 1978)
Still Life (London: Chatto & Windus, 1985)
Possession: A Romance (London: Chatto & Windus, 1990)
Angels and Insects (London: Chatto & Windus, 1992)
The Matisse Stories (London: Chatto & Windus, 1993)
The Djinn in the Nightingale's Eye (London: Chatto & Windus, 1994)

Peter Carey (1943)
Bliss (London: Faber, 1981)
Illywhacker (London: Faber & Faber, 1985)
Oscar and Lucinda (London: Faber & Faber, 1988)
The Unusual Life of Tristan Smith (London: Faber & Faber, 1994)

Angela Carter (1940–92)
Nights at the Circus (London: Chatto & Windus, 1984)
Wise Children (London: Chatto & Windus, 1991)

Bruce Chatwin (1946–89)
The Songlines (London: Jonathan Cape, 1987)
Utz (London: Jonathan Cape, 1988)

Amit Chaudhuri (1962)
A Strange and Sublime Address (London: Heinemann, 1991)

J. M. Coetzee (1940)
Life & Times of Michael K (London: Secker & Warburg, 1983)
Foe (London: Secker & Warburg, 1986)

Robertson Davies (1913–95)
Murther & Walking Spirits (London: Viking, 1991)

Michael Dibdin (1947)
The Last Sherlock Holmes Story (London: Jonathan Cape, 1978)

Roddy Doyle (1958)
The Van (London: Secker & Warburg, 1991)
This was reissued, along with *The Commitments* (1987) and *The
    Snapper* (1990), as *The Barrytown Trilogy* (London: Secker &
    Warburg, 1992)
Paddy Clarke Ha Ha Ha (London: Secker & Warburg, 1993)

Margaret Drabble (1939)
The Radiant Way (London: Weidenfeld & Nicolson, 1987)
A Natural Curiosity (London: Viking, 1989)

Helen Dunmore (1952)
A Spell of Winter (London: Viking, 1996)

J. G. Farrell (1935–79)
The Siege of Krishnapur (London: Jonathan Cape, 1973)
The Singapore Grip (London: Jonathan Cape, 1978)

Sebastian Faulks (1953)
Birdsong (London: Hutchinson, 1993)

Tibor Fischer (1956)
Under the Frog (London: Polygon, 1992)

John Fowles (1926)
The Magus (London: Jonathan Cape, 1966, 1977)
The French Lieutenant's Woman (London: Jonathan Cape, 1969)
Daniel Martin (London: Jonathan Cape, 1977)

Stephen Fry (1957)
The Liar (London: Heinemann, 1991)

William Golding (1911–93)
Lord of the Flies (London: Faber & Faber, 1954)
Rites of Passage (London: Faber & Faber, 1980)
Close Quarters (London: Faber & Faber, 1987)
Fire Down Below (London: Faber & Faber, 1989)
All three published as *To the Ends of the Earth: A Sea Trilogy*
  (London: Faber & Faber, 1991)

Alasdair Gray (1934)
Lanark: A Life in Four Books (Edinburgh: Canongate, 1981)
1982, Janine (Edinburgh: Canongate, 1984)
The Fall of Kelvin Walker (Edinburgh: Canongate, 1985)
Something Leather (London: Jonathan Cape, 1990)
Poor Things (London: Bloomsbury, 1992)

Dermot Healy (1947)
A Goat's Song (London: Harvill, 1994)

Alan Hollinghurst (1954)
The Swimming-pool Library (London: Chatto & Windus, 1988)
The Folding Star (London: Chatto & Windus, 1994)

Elizabeth Jane Howard (1923)
Confusion (London: Macmillan, 1993)

Keri Hulme (1947)
The Bone People (London: Hodder & Stoughton, 1985)

Kazuo Ishiguro (1954)
The Remains of the Day (London: Faber & Faber, 1989)
The Unconsoled (London: Faber & Faber, 1995)

Ruth Prawer Jhabvala (1927)
Heat and Dust (London: John Murray, 1975)

James Kelman (1946)
A Disaffection (London: Secker & Warburg, 1989)
How Late It Was, How Late (London: Secker & Warburg,
  1994)

Thomas Keneally (1935)
Schindler's Ark (London: Hodder & Stoughton) (subsequently reprinted, and better known, as *Schindler's List*)

A. L. Kennedy (1965)
Looking for the Possible Dance (London: Secker & Warburg, 1993)
So I Am Glad (London: Jonathan Cape, 1995)

Hanif Kureishi (1954)
The Buddha of Suburbia (London: Faber & Faber, 1990)
Black Album (London: Faber & Faber, 1995)

Doris Lessing (1919)
The Good Terrorist (London: Jonathan Cape, 1985)

David Lodge (1935)
Nice Work (London: Secker & Warburg, 1988)
Paradise News (London: Secker & Warburg, 1991)

Penelope Lively (1933)
Moon Tiger (London: André Deutsch, 1987)

Ian McEwan (1948)
The Child in Time (London: Jonathan Cape, 1987)
The Innocent (London: Jonathan Cape, 1990)
Black Dogs (London: Jonathan Cape, 1992)

John McGahern (1934)
Amongst Women (London: Faber & Faber, 1990)

Candia McWilliam (1955)
A Case of Knives (London: Bloomsbury, 1987)
A Little Stranger (London: Bloomsbury, 1989)
Debatable Land (London: Bloomsbury, 1994)

David Malouf (1934)
Remembering Babylon (London: Chatto & Windus, 1993)

Allan Massie (1938)
The Sins of the Father (London: Hodder & Stoughton, 1991)

Timothy Mo (1950)
The Monkey King (London: André Deutsch, 1978)
Sour Sweet (London: André Deutsch, 1982)

An Insular Possession (London: Chatto & Windus, 1987)
The Redundancy of Courage (London, Chatto & Windus, 1991)
Brownout on Breadfruit Boulevard (London: Paddleless, 1995)

Brian Moore (1921)
The Colour of Blood (London: Jonathan Cape, 1987)
Lies of Silence (London: Bloomsbury, 1990)

Nicholas Mosley (1923)
Hopeful Monsters (London: Secker & Warburg, 1990)

Iris Murdoch (1919)
The Black Prince (London: Chatto & Windus, 1973)
The Sea, The Sea (London: Chatto & Windus, 1978)
The Good Apprentice (London: Chatto & Windus, 1985)
The Book and the Brotherhood (London: Chatto & Windus, 1987)
The Green Knight (London: Chatto & Windus, 1993)

V. S. Naipaul (1932)
In a Free State (London: André Deutsch, 1971)
A Bend in the River (London: André Deutsch, 1979)

Lawrence Norfolk (1963)
Lemprière's Dictionary (London: Sinclair-Stevenson, 1991)

Ben Okri (1959)
The Famished Road (London: Jonathan Cape, 1991)
Songs of Enchantment (London: Jonathan Cape, 1993)

Michael Ondaatje (1943)
The English Patient (London: Bloomsbury, 1992)

Charles Palliser (1947)
The Quincunx (Edinburgh: Canongate, 1989)

Caryl Phillips (1958)
The Final Passage (London: Faber & Faber, 1985)
Higher Ground (London: Viking, 1989)
Cambridge (London: Bloomsbury, 1991)
Crossing the River (London: Bloomsbury, 1993)

Mordecai Richler (1931)
St Urbain's Horseman (London: Weidenfeld & Nicolson, 1971)
Solomon Gursky Was Here (London: Chatto & Windus, 1990)

Michèle Roberts (1949)
Daughters of the House (London: Virago, 1992)

Salman Rushdie (1947)
Grimus (London: Victor Gollancz, 1975)
Midnight's Children (London: Jonathan Cape, 1981)
Shame (London: Jonathan Cape, 1983)
The Satanic Verses (London: Viking, 1988)
Haroun and the Sea of Stories (London: Granta, 1990)
The Moor's Last Sigh (London: Jonathan Cape, 1995)

Paul Scott (1920–78)
Staying On (William Heinemann, 1977)

Vikram Seth (1952)
A Suitable Boy (London: Phoenix House, 1993)

Nicholas Shakespeare (1957)
The Vision of Eleanor Silves (London: Collins, 1989)

Iain Sinclair (1943)
White Chappell, Scarlet Tracings (London: Goldmark, 1987)
Downriver (Or, The Vessels of Wrath): A Narrative in Seven Tales (London: Jonathan Cape, 1992)
The Radon Daughters (London: Jonathan Cape, 1994)

Muriel Spark (1918)
The Only Problem (London: The Bodley Head, 1984)

David Storey (1933)
Saville (London: Jonathan Cape, 1976)

Graham Swift (1949)
Waterland (London: William Heinemann, 1983)
Out Of This World (London: Viking, 1988)
Ever After (London: Viking, 1992)

Emma Tennant (1937)
The Bad Sister (London: Gollancz, 1978)

D. M. Thomas (1935)
The White Hotel (London: Gollancz, 1981)

Jeff Torrington (1935)
Swing Hammer Swing! (London: Secker & Warburg, 1992)

Rose Tremain (1943)
Restoration (London: Hamish Hamilton, 1989)
Sacred Country (London: Sinclair-Stevenson, 1992)

William Trevor (1928)
Two Lives (London: Viking, 1991) (*Reading Turgenev* and *My House in Umbria*)
Felicia's Journey (London: Viking, 1994)

Barry Unsworth (1930)
Pascali's Island (London: Michael Joseph, 1980)
Sugar and Rum (London: Hamish Hamilton, 1988)
Sacred Hunger (London: Hamish Hamilton, 1992)
Morality Play (London: Hamish Hamilton, 1995)

Marina Warner (1946)
The Lost Father (London: Chatto & Windus, 1988)
Indigo, or Mapping the Waters (London: Chatto & Windus, 1992)

Fay Weldon (1931)
The Hearts and Lives of Men (London: Viking, 1987)
The Cloning of Joanna May (London: Collins, 1989)

Irvine Welsh (1958)
Trainspotting (London: Secker & Warburg, 1993)

Jeanette Winterson (1959)
Written on the Body (London: Jonathan Cape, 1992)

(b) Substantial critical and/ or analytical works; either books, or articles collected in book form

Appignanesi, Lisa, and Sara Maitland, eds., *The Rushdie File* (London: ICA/Fourth Estate, 1989)
Bergonzi, Bernard, *The Situation of the Novel* (1970; revised edn. London: Macmillan, 1979)

Bhabha, Homi K., *The Location of Culture* (London & New York: Routledge, 1993)

Bloom, Harold, *The Western Canon: The Books and School of the Ages* (New York: Harcourt Brace, 1994. London: Macmillan, 1995)

Boehmer, Elleke, *Colonial and Postcolonial Literature* (Oxford: OUP, 1995)

Boylan, Clare, ed., *The Agony and the Ego: The Art and Strategy of Fiction Writing Explored* (Harmondsworth: Penguin, 1993) [Contains Marina Warner's essay 'Rich Pickings']

Bradbury, Malcolm, and David Palmer, eds., *The Contemporary English Novel* (London: Arnold, 1979)

Bradbury, Malcolm, *The Modern British Novel* (1993; London: Penguin, 1994)

Brewer, John and Roy Porter, eds., *Consumption and the World of Goods* (London & New York: Routledge, 1993)

Burgess, Anthony, *99 Novels: The Best in English Since 1939* (London: Allison & Busby, 1984)

Byatt, A. S., *Passions of the Mind: Selected Writings* (London: Chatto & Windus, 1991)

Calder, Angus, *Revolving Cultures: Notes from the Scottish Republic* (London & New York: I. B. Tauris, 1994)

Colley, Linda, *Britons: Forging the Nation, 1707–1837* (1992; London: Pimlico, 1994)

Connor, Steven, 'Rewriting Wrong: On the Ethics of Literary Reversion'. In Theo D'haen & Hans Bertens, eds., *Liminal Postmodernisms: The Postmodern, the (Post-)Colonial and the (Post-)Feminist* (Amsterdam & Atlanta, GA: Rodopi, 1994, pp. 79–97)

Dipple, Elizabeth, *Iris Murdoch: Work for the Spirit* (London: Methuen, 1982)

Dipple, Elizabeth, *The Unresolvable Plot: Reading Contemporary Fiction* (New York & London: Routledge, 1988)

Elias, Amy J., 'Meta-*mimesis*? The Problem of British Postmodern Realism'. In Theo D'haen and Hans Bertens, eds., *British Postmodern Fiction* (Amsterdam & Atlanta, GA: Rodopi, 1993), pp. 9–31

Gindin, James, *Postwar British Fiction: New Accents and Attitudes* (Berkeley: University of California Press, 1962)

Goff, Martyn, ed., *Prize Writing* (London: Hodder & Stoughton/ Sceptre, 1989)

Gorra, Michael, *The English Novel at Mid-Century* (London: Macmillan, 1990)

Haffenden, John, *Novelists in Interview* (London: Methuen, 1985)

Hutchinson, Linda, *A Poetics of Postmodernism: History, Theory, Fiction* (New York & London: Routledge, 1988)

Karl, Frederick R., *A Reader's Guide to the Contemporary English Novel* (1959; revised edn. London: Thames & Hudson, 1963)

Kermode, Frank, *The Art of Telling: Essays on Fiction* (Cambridge MA: Harvard UP, 1983)

Kermode, Frank, *The Uses of Error* (Cambridge, MA: Harvard UP, 1991) [Contains 'Obsessed with Obsession: Julian Barnes' (pp. 362–68) and 'Losers: Anita Brookner' (pp. 369–74)]

Lee, Alison, *Realism and Power: Postmodern British Fiction* (London & New York: Routledge, 1990)

Lodge, David, 'The Novelist Today: Still at the Crossroads?'. In Malcolm Bradbury and Judy Cooke, eds., *New Writing Today* (London: Minerva in association with the British Council, 1992), pp. 203–15.

McHale, Brian, *Postmodernist Fiction* (London & New York: Methuen, 1987)

Maher, Terry, *Against My Better Judgement: Adventures in the City and in the Book Trade* (London: Sinclair-Stevenson, 1994)

Mason, Michael, *The Making of Victorian Sexuality* (Oxford: Clarendon, 1994)

Mason, Michael, *The Making of Victorian Sexual Attitudes* (Oxford: Clarendon, 1994)

Miller, Karl, *Doubles: Studies in Literary History* (London: OUP, 1985)

Murray, Isobel, and Bob Tait, eds., *Ten Modern Scottish Novels* (Aberdeen: Aberdeen UP, 1984)

Nairn, Tom, *The Break-Up of Britain: Crisis and Representation* (1977; 2nd, expanded, edn. London: New Left Books, 1981)

O'Connor, William Van, *The New University Wits and the End of Modernism* (Carbondale, IL: Southern Illinois UP, 1963)

Porter, Roy, *London: A Social History* (London: Hamish Hamilton, 1994)

Rabinovitz, Rubin, *The Reaction Against Experiment in the English Novel: 1950–1960* (New York: Columbia UP, 1967)

Rushdie, Salman, *Imaginary Homelands: Essays and Criticism 1981–1991* (London: Granta, 1991)

Ruthven, Malise, *A Satanic Affair: Salman Rushdie and the Wrath of Islam* (1990; London: The Hogarth Press, 1991)

Sage, Lorna, *Angela Carter. Writers and their Work* (Plymouth: Northcote House in association with the British Council, 1994)

Sage, Lorna, ed., *Flesh and the Mirror: Essays on the Art of Angela Carter* (London: Virago, 1994)

Said, Edward, *Orientalism* (1978; London: Penguin, 1985. Revised 1995)

Sutherland, John, *Bestsellers* (London: Routledge & Kegan Paul, 1981)

Sutherland, John, *Fiction and the Fiction Industry* (London: Athlone Press, 1978)

Taylor, D. J., *After the War: The Novel and England since 1945* (London: Chatto & Windus, 1993)

Thieme, John, 'Passages to England'. In Theo D'haen & Hans Bertens, eds., *Liminal Postmodernisms: The Postmodern, the (Post-)Colonial and the (Post-)Feminist* (Amsterdam & Atlanta, GA: Rodopi, 1994), pp. 55–78.

Tredell, Nicolas, *Conversations with Critics* (Manchester: Carcanet, 1994)

Turner, Barry, 'Free to Trade: The Decline and Fall of the Net Book Agreement'. In Barry Turner, ed., *The Writers' Handbook 1995* (London: Macmillan, 1994), pp. 150–51.

Wallace, Gavin, and Randall Stevenson, eds., *The Scottish Novel since the Seventies* (Edinburgh: Edinburgh UP, 1993)

Warner, Marina, *From the Beast to the Blonde: On Fairytales and their Tellers* (London: Chatto & Windus, 1994)

Warner, Marina, *Managing Monsters: Sixth Myths of Our Time* [The 1994 Reith Lectures.] (London: Vintage, 1994)

Waugh, Patricia, *Harvest of the Sixties: English Literature and Its Background, 1960 to 1990* (London: OUP, 1995)

Wright, Patrick, *A Journey through Ruins* (1992; London: Flamingo, 1993)

Young, Robert, 'Colonialism and the Desiring-Machine'. In

Theo D'haen & Hans Bertens, eds., *Liminal Postmodernisms: The Postmodern, the (Post-)Colonial and the (Post-)Feminist* (Amsterdam & Atlanta, GA: Rodopi, 1994), pp. 11–34.

Zamora, Lois Parkinson and Wendy B. Faris, eds., *Magical Realism: Theory, History, Community* (Durham & London: Duke UP, 1995)

(c) Uncollected articles and substantial reviews

Ackroyd, Peter, 'Cockney Visionaries', *Independent*, 18 December 1993, p. 27.

Annan, Gabriele, 'On the High Wire', *New York Review of Books*, 7 December 1989, pp. 3–4 [On Kazuo Ishiguro].

Bailey, Paul, 'Settling for Suburbia', *Times Literary Supplement*, 28 March 1980, p. 345 [Review of Julian Barnes's *Metroland*].

Baker, Nicholson, 'Lost Youth', *London Review of Books*, 9 June 1994, p. 6 [Review of Alan Hollinghurst's *The Folding Star*].

Calder, Liz, 'Bandwagon Blues', *Bookseller*, 20 February 1982, pp. 640–43 [On the success of Salman Rushdie's *Midnight's Children*].

Clapp, Susannah, 'Diary', *London Review of Books*, 12 March 1992, p. 25 [Obituary of Angela Carter].

Driver, Christopher, 'Floating', *London Review of Books*, 6–19 October 1983, p. 20. [Review of Graham Swift's *Waterland*].

Figes, Kate, 'Those Crucial Six Weeks', The Sunday Review, *Independent on Sunday*, 12 November 1995; pp. 32–33 [On promoting lead fiction titles].

Hamilton, Ian, 'Real Questions', *London Review of Books*, 6 September 1986, p. 7 [Review of Julian Barnes's *Staring at the Sun*].

Harris, Wendell V., 'Canonicity', *Publications of the Modern Language Association of America* 106/1 (January 1991), pp. 110–21.

Herman, Luc, 'Peter Ackroyd'. In *Postwar Literatures in English: A Lexicon of Contemporary Authors* 7 (March 1990).

Herman, Luc, 'Peter Carey'. In *Postwar Literatures in English: A Lexicon of Contemporary Authors* 14 (December 1991).

Hollinghurst, Alan, 'Of time and the river', *Times Literary Supplement*, 7 October 1983, p. 1073 [Review of Graham Swift's *Waterland*].

Imlah, Mick, 'Giving the Authorized Version', *Times Literary Supplement*, 12 July 1991, p. 19 [Review of Julian Barnes's *Talking It Over*].

Jones, Hugh, 'Life Plus Seventy', *Bookseller*, 1 April 1994, pp. 20–21 [On European copyright law].

Kakutani, Michiko, 'British Writers Embrace the Offbeat', *New York Times Magazine*, 5 July 1990, pp. C11, C15.

Kermode, Frank, 'Stowaway Worm', *London Review of Books*, 22 June 1989, p. 20 [Review of Julian Barnes's *A History of the World in 10½ Chapters*].

Kermode, Frank, 'Wannabee', *London Review of Books*, 8 October 1992, p. 14 [Review of Rose Tremain's *Sacred Country*].

Ledent, Bénédicte, 'Caryl Phillips'. In *Postwar Literatures in English: A Lexicon of Contemporary Authors* 19 (March 1993).

Lehmann-Haupt, Christopher, 'When There Was Such a Thing as Romantic Love', *New York Times*, 25 October 1990, p. C24. [Review of A. S. Byatt's *Possession*].

Lyall, Roderick J., 'Postmodernist otherworld, postcalvinist purgatory: An approach to [Iain Banks's] *Lanark* and *The Bridge*', *Etudes écossaises* 2 (1993), pp. 41–52.

McCrum, Robert, 'Lunatics and suits', *Guardian Weekend*, 4 March 1995, p. 24. [On the Martin Amis advance controversy].

Mars-Jones, Adam, 'Looking on the blight side', *Times Literary Supplement*, 24 March 1995, pp. 19–20. [Review of Martin Amis's *The Information*].

Parini, Jay, 'Unearthing the Secret Lover', *New York Times Book Review*, 21 October 1990, §7; pp. 9, 11. [Review of A. S. Byatt's *Possession*].

Parrinder, Patrick, 'Let's get the hell out of here', *London Review of Books*, 29 September 1988, pp. 11–13 [Includes review of Salman Rushdie's *The Satanic Verses*].

Parrinder, Patrick, 'Sea Changes', *London Review of Books*, 27 February 1992, p. 12 [Review of Marina Warner's *Indigo*].

Rothstein, Mervyn, 'Best Seller Breaks Rule on Crossing the

Atlantic', *New York Times*, 31 January 1991, p. C17, C22 [On A. S. Byatt's *Possession*].

Sinclair, Iain, 'The Cadaver Club', *London Review of Books*, 22 December 1994, p. 21. [Review of Peter Ackroyd's *Dan Leno and the Limehouse Golem*].

Slagter, Nicole, diss., 'Worlds made of words: a response to Brian McHale's postmodernist fiction', Amsterdam, Vrije Universiteit, September 1989.

Spice, Nicholas, 'Phattbookia Stupenda', *London Review of Books*, 18 April 1985, p. 20. [Review of Peter Carey's *Illywhacker*].

Stout, Mira, 'What Possessed A. S. Byatt?', *New York Times Magazine* 26 May 1991, pp. 13–15, 24–25.

Sutherland, John, 'Binarisms', *London Review of Books*, 18 November 1993, pp. 24–25. [On Iain Banks and Iain M. Banks].

Sutherland, John, 'Pseud's Corner', *London Review of Books*, 17 July–6 August 1980, pp. 14–16. [On Dan Kavanagh's *Duffy*].

Symons, Julian, 'Darts for art's sake', *London Review of Books*, 28 September 1989, pp. 7–8. [Review of Martin Amis's *London Fields*].

Taubman, Robert, 'Experiments with truth', *London Review of Books*, 7–20 May 1981, pp. 3, 5–6. [Review of Salman Rushdie's *Midnight Children*].

Trewin, Ion, 'Handling a High-Flying Winner', *Bookseller*, 5 March 1983, p. 816. [On the success of Thomas Keneally's *Schindler's Ark*].

Warner, Marina, '*Indigo*: Mapping the Waters', *Etudes britanniques contemporaines* 5 (December 1994), pp. 1–11.

Wilson, Keith, '*Midnight's Children* and Reader Responsibility', *Critical Quarterly* 26/3 (1984), pp. 23–37.

Index